TEXTUAL PERFORMANCES

This important collection brings together leading scholars to examine crucial questions regarding the theory and practice of editing Shakespeare's plays. In particular the essays look at how best to engage editorially with evidence provided by historical research into the playhouse, author's study, and printing house. How are editors of playscripts to mediate history, in its many forms, for modern users? Considering our knowledge of the past is partial (in the senses both of incomplete and ideological), where are we to draw the line between legitimate editorial assistance and unwarranted interference? In what innovative ways might current controversies surrounding the mediation of Shakespeare's drama shape future editorial practice? Focusing on the key points of debate and controversy of the present moment, this collection makes a vital contribution to a better understanding of how editorial practice (on the page and in cyberspace) might develop in the twenty-first century.

LUKAS ERNE, Professor of English Literature at the University of Neuchâtel, Switzerland, is the author of *Shakespeare as Literary Dramatist* (Cambridge, 2003) and *Beyond 'The Spanish Tragedy': A Study of the Works of Thomas Kyd* (2001).

MARGARET JANE KIDNIE is Associate Professor of English at the University of Western Ontario, Canada. She is the editor of *Ben Jonson: 'The Devil is an Ass' and Other Plays* (2000), and *Philip Stubbes, 'The Anatomie of Abuses'* (2002).

TEXTUAL PERFORMANCES
The Modern Reproduction of Shakespeare's Drama

EDITED BY
LUKAS ERNE AND MARGARET JANE KIDNIE

PUBLISHED BY THE PRESS SYNDICATE OF THE UNIVERSITY OF CAMBRIDGE
The Pitt Building, Trumpington Street, Cambridge, United Kingdom

CAMBRIDGE UNIVERSITY PRESS
The Edinburgh Building, Cambridge CB2 2RU, UK
40 West 20th Street, New York, NY 10011-4211, USA
477 Williamstown Road, Port Melbourne, VIC 3207, Australia
Ruiz de Alarcón 13, 28014 Madrid, Spain
Dock House, The Waterfront, Cape Town 8001, South Africa

http://www.cambridge.org

© Cambridge University Press 2004

This book is in copyright. Subject to statutory exception
and to the provisions of relevant collective licensing agreements,
no reproduction of any part may take place without
the written permission of Cambridge University Press.

First published 2004

Printed in the United Kingdom at the University Press, Cambridge

Typeface Adobe Garamond 11/12.5 pt   *System* LATEX 2_ε [TB]

A catalogue record for this book is available from the British Library

ISBN 0 521 83095 8 hardback

The publisher has used its best endeavours to ensure that the URLs for external websites referred to in
this book are correct and active at the time of going to press. However, the publisher has no
responsibility for the websites and can make no guarantee that a site will remain live or that the
content is or will remain appropriate.

For Jeremy

Contents

List of illustrations	*page* ix
Preface	xi
List of contributors	xii
Introduction *Lukas Erne and Margaret Jane Kidnie*	1

PART I: ESTABLISHING THE TEXT

1. The two texts of *Othello* and early modern constructions of race — 21
   Leah S. Marcus

2. 'Work of permanent utility': editors and texts, authorities and originals — 37
   H. R. Woudhuysen

3. Housmania: episodes in twentieth-century 'critical' editing of Shakespeare — 49
   Paul Werstine

4. Addressing adaptation: *Measure for Measure* and *Sir Thomas More* — 63
   John Jowett

5. The New Bibliography and its critics — 77
   Ernst Honigmann

6. Scholarly editing and the shift from print to electronic cultures — 94
   Sonia Massai

PART II: PRESENTING THE PLAY

7. 'Your sum of parts': doubling in *Hamlet*   111
   Ann Thompson and Neil Taylor

8. The perception of error: the editing and the performance of the opening of *Coriolanus*   127
   Michael Warren

9. Modern spelling: the hard choices   143
   David Bevington

10. The staging of Shakespeare's drama in print editions   158
    Margaret Jane Kidnie

11. Open stage, open page? Editing stage directions in early dramatic texts   178
    John D. Cox

12. Two varieties of digital commentary   194
    John Lavagnino

13. New collaborations with old plays: the (textual) politics of performance commentary   210
    Barbara Hodgdon

Index   224

Illustrations

PLATES

1 *Measure for Measure* 1.2.71–104, as it will appear in the Oxford edition of Thomas Middleton's *Collected Works*. With permission of the general editors, Gary Taylor and John Lavagnino. *page* 70
2 *The Second Maiden's Tragedy*, MS. Lansdowne 807, f. 55b. Published with permission of the British Library. 166
3 *The Book of Sir Thomas Moore*, MS. Harley 7368, f. 7b. Published with permission of the British Library. 167
4 The second quarto of *Hamlet* (1604), sig. B3r. Published with permission of the Folger Shakespeare Library. 168
5 *Troilus and Cressida*, Through Line Number 2549–626 (Act 4.6), layout design prepared by Margaret Jane Kidnie. 170
6 *Romeo and Juliet*, Through Line Number 666–94 (Act 1.5), layout design prepared by Margaret Jane Kidnie. 174
7 William Shakespeare, *3 Henry VI*, from the First Folio (1623), sig. Pp4 (Through Line Number 1568–91, Act 3.2). 189

TABLES

7.1 Casting chart for Q1 *Hamlet* from Arden3, ed. Thompson and Taylor 116
7.2 Casting chart for Q2 *Hamlet* from Arden3, ed. Thompson and Taylor 118
7.3 Casting chart for F *Hamlet* from Arden3, ed. Thompson and Taylor 120

Preface

Textual Performances grows out of a prolonged electronic correspondence between the volume's editors in the second half of 2001 which allowed us to identify and discuss what we thought of as vital questions about the modern reproduction of Shakespeare's drama. As the collection that proposes to explore these questions took shape, we received precious help from a number of friends and colleagues, especially Jeremy Ehrlich, James Purkis, and Stanley Wells. At Cambridge University Press, we wish to thank Sarah Stanton for her generous support, Emma Baxter, Margaret Berrill, Laura Hemming, and Jackie Warren for all their work on this book, and the Press's anonymous readers for their incisive comments.

Unless otherwise indicated, all quotations from and references to Shakespeare's plays and poems are keyed to the New Cambridge Shakespeare single-volume editions. Quotations from the First Folio are cited by Through Line Number (TLN) from Charlton Hinman's *The Norton Facsimile: The First Folio of Shakespeare*, 2nd edn, with an introduction by Peter W. M. Blayney (New York: Norton, 1996). *OED* refers to the second edition of the *Oxford English Dictionary* of 1989, while *STC* refers to *A Short-Title Catalogue of Books Printed in England, Scotland, and Ireland and of English Books Printed Abroad, 1475–1640*, by Alfred W. Pollard, G. R. Redgrave, W. A. Jackson, F. S. Ferguson, and Katharine F. Pantzer, 2nd edn, 3 vols. (London: The Bibliographical Society, 1976–91).

Contributors

DAVID BEVINGTON is the Phyllis Fay Horton Distinguished Service Professor in the Humanities at the University of Chicago, where he has taught since 1967. His studies include *From 'Mankind' to Marlowe*, 1962, *Tudor Drama and Politics*, 1968, and *Action Is Eloquence: Shakespeare's Language of Gesture*, 1985. He is also the editor of *Medieval Drama*, Houghton Mifflin, 1975; *The Bantam Shakespeare*, in 29 paperback volumes, 1988; and *The Complete Works of Shakespeare*, HarperCollins, 1992 (updated, Longman, 1997), as well as the Oxford *1 Henry IV* (1987), the New Cambridge *Antony and Cleopatra* (1990), and the Arden3 *Troilus and Cressida* (1998). He is the senior editor of the Revels Student Editions, and is a senior editor of the Revels Plays and of the forthcoming Cambridge edition of the works of Ben Jonson. He is senior editor of the recently published *Norton Anthology of Renaissance Drama* (2002). With Peter Holbrook he has edited a collection of essays on *The Politics of the Stuart Court Masque* (Cambridge University Press, 1998). His latest book, intended for general readers, is called simply *Shakespeare* (2002).

JOHN D. COX is the DuMez Professor of English at Hope College. He is the author most recently of *The Devil and the Sacred in English Drama, 1350 to 1642* and co-editor with Eric Rasmussen of the Arden3 *Henry VI*.

LUKAS ERNE, Professor of English Literature at the University of Neuchâtel, Switzerland, is the author of *Beyond 'The Spanish Tragedy': A Study of the Works of Thomas Kyd* (Manchester University Press, 2001) and of *Shakespeare as Literary Dramatist* (Cambridge University Press, 2003). He is editing *The First Quarto of Romeo and Juliet* for the New Cambridge Shakespeare series.

BARBARA HODGDON is Adjunct Professor at the University of Michigan, Ann Arbor. She is the author of *The Shakespeare Trade: Performances and*

Appropriations (University of Pennsylvania, 1998), *The End Crowns All: Closure and Contradiction in Shakespeare's History* (Princeton University Press, 1991), *Henry IV, Part 2* in the Shakespeare in Performance series (Manchester University Press, 1996), and *The First Part of King Henry the Fourth: Texts and Contexts* (Bedford–St Martin's, 1997). She is presently editing the Arden3 *Taming of the Shrew*.

E. A. J. HONIGMANN is Professor Emeritus at the University of Newcastle-upon-Tyne and the author of more than a dozen books on Shakespeare and his contemporaries, including *Shakespeare, Seven Tragedies: The Dramatist's Manipulation of Response*, *Myriad-Minded Shakespeare*, and *The Texts of 'Othello' and Shakespearian Revision*. Among the plays he has edited is the Arden3 *Othello*.

JOHN JOWETT is Reader in Shakespeare Studies at the Shakespeare Institute, University of Birmingham. He edited plays for the Oxford Shakespeare *Complete Works* (1986). He is currently an associate general editor of the forthcoming Oxford edition of Thomas Middleton's *Collected Works* and a member of the general editorial board of Arden Early Modern Drama. Publications include *Shakespeare Reshaped 1606–1623* (1993) with Gary Taylor, and the Oxford edition of *Richard III* (2000).

MARGARET JANE KIDNIE is Associate Professor of English at the University of Western Ontario. She has edited *Ben Jonson: 'The Devil is an Ass' and Other Plays* (Oxford University Press, 2000), and an old-spelling edition of *Philip Stubbes, The Anatomie of Abuses* for the Renaissance English Text Society (Arizona State University Press, 2002). She has published articles on bibliography, textual theory, and performance.

JOHN LAVAGNINO is Lecturer in Humanities Computing at King's College, London. His current topics of research include scholarly editing, early modern drama, and the use of computers in humanities research; he is one of the general editors of *The Collected Works of Thomas Middleton*, forthcoming from Oxford University Press.

LEAH S. MARCUS is Edwin Mims Professor of English at Vanderbilt University. Her books include *Childhood and Cultural Despair* (1978), *The Politics of Mirth* (1986), *Puzzling Shakespeare* (1988), and *Unediting the Renaissance* (1996). Most recently, with Janel Mueller and Mary Beth Rose, she has edited *Elizabeth I: Collected Works* (2000), of which

xiv   *List of contributors*

the paperback edition will appear in 2002 and the second volume in 2003.

SONIA MASSAI is a Lecturer in English Studies at King's College, London. Her editorial work includes *Titus Andronicus* (Penguin), *The Wise Woman of Hoxton* (Globe Quartos), *Edward III* (Internet Shakespeare Editions, in progress) and *'Tis Pity She's a Whore* (Arden Early Modern Drama, in progress). She has published articles in *Shakespeare Survey*, *New Theatre Quarterly*, and *Studies in English Literature*, and contributed to *The Oxford Companion to Shakespeare*, edited by Michael Dobson and Stanley Wells in 2001. She is currently editing a new collection of essays on *World-Wide Shakespeares* and writing a book on Shakespeare and the rise of editorial tradition in the sixteenth and seventeenth centuries.

NEIL TAYLOR is Director of Research at the University of Surrey, Roehampton. He has edited *Henry IV Part 2* (Ginn, 1972), co-edited with Bryan Loughrey *Thomas Middleton: Five Plays* (Penguin, 1988), and written a number of articles on editing Shakespeare, Shakespeare on film, and other aspects of Renaissance and modern drama.

ANN THOMPSON is Professor of English at King's College, London. She is a general editor of the Arden Shakespeare third series and she is co-editing the Arden3 *Hamlet* with Neil Taylor. She edited *The Taming of the Shrew* for the New Cambridge Shakespeare series (1984) and her other publications include *Shakespeare, Meaning and Metaphor* (with John Thompson, 1987), *Which Shakespeare?: A User's Guide to Editions* (1992) and *Women Reading Shakespeare, 1660–1900* (co-edited with Sasha Roberts, 1997).

MICHAEL WARREN is Professor Emeritus of English Literature at the University of California, Santa Cruz. With Gary Taylor he co-edited *The Division of the Kingdoms: Shakespeare's Two Versions of 'King Lear'*. He has also published *The Complete 'King Lear' 1608–1623*, of which the first part appeared separately as *The Parallel 'King Lear' 1608–1623*, and articles on the texts of English drama. He has recently completed *Shakespeare: Life, Language and Linguistics, Text, and the Canon: An Annotated Bibliography of Shakespeare Studies 1564–2000*, which is to appear in the Pegasus Shakespeare Bibliographies series.

PAUL WERSTINE teaches English at King's College and University of Western Ontario, London, Canada. He is general editor (with Richard Knowles) of the New Variorum edition of Shakespeare published by the

Modern Language Association, and co-editor (with Barbara A. Mowat) of the New Folger Library Shakespeare edition.

H. R. WOUDHUYSEN is Professor of English at University College, London. He has edited *Love's Labour's Lost* for Arden3 and is on the editorial committee of the Malone Society.

Introduction

Lukas Erne and Margaret Jane Kidnie

The century in which Shakespeare was born saw unprecedented awareness of the importance of informed textual reproduction. In the second and third decades of the sixteenth century, Reformers both within and outside the Catholic Church produced new editions of the Bible that challenged what had been the official Catholic version for more than a thousand years, Jerome's fourth-century Latin Vulgate. Erasmus's textual scholarship made clear that it was misleading in important points of theology, yet the Vulgate was powerfully defended, and many continued to base their interpretation of Scripture on it. In literary studies today, the conflict between those who advocate renewed attention to textual reproduction and those who resist such investigation is in a sense being re-enacted. For a long time, most critics felt free to base their analyses of texts by Shakespeare and others on just any edition at hand, giving no thought to the text's credentials and the editorial policy informing it. Now that editing and textual studies have become hot topics that attract ever-increasing attention – even in *The New Yorker* – this may have started to change.[1] Yet those whose criticism shows little or no awareness of the importance of the nature of modern textual reproduction remain numerous. As an influential textual scholar puts it, 'many a literary critic has investigated the past ownership and mechanical condition of his second-hand automobile... more thoroughly than he has looked into the qualifications of the text on which his critical theories rest'.[2] No one will deny that the consequences of a car accident can be rather more severe than those of uninformed criticism, but it is true that all those who remain unconcerned by editorial practices and policy run the risk, as many did in the sixteenth century, of having their interpretations marred by unexamined textual assumptions.

So why does attention to textual reproduction matter? How will our critical response to a Shakespeare play be shaped by an increased awareness of the choices informing modern editorial mediation? Let us start at the end;

Hamlet's end. For that, as we all know, is silence. Or so it was until the editors of the ground-breaking Oxford *Complete Works* came around in 1986 and told us that it wasn't silence after all.[3] Basing their edition on the 1623 Folio rather than the second quarto of 1604/5, they straightforwardly followed their copy-text which reads: 'The rest is silence. O, o, o, o.' The four letters can of course be construed in a variety of ways, from a discontinued last sigh to loud groans in tortured agony. Those who remember the importance of 'making a good end' in early modern England – as instanced by the carefully prepared performance into which John Donne turned his own death – do not need to be reminded of the importance of these final moments for the interpretation of a whole life. Whatever one's interpretation of the four letters is, a decision which any modern textual reproduction entails is their inclusion or their non-inclusion. Whether the arguably most famous fictional character in Western literature may end his life by contradicting, as it were, the last words he has just uttered seems a matter of sufficient critical interest to warrant attention to the relevant textual and editorial questions.[4]

A less familiar example is the male protagonist's attempted suicide in *Romeo and Juliet* (3.3). When Romeo has been informed by Friar Laurence of his banishment, the Nurse enters to them with news about Juliet's grief. As Romeo tries to stab himself, the Friar – in the second quarto of 1599 on which modern editions are usually based – shouts 'Hold thy desperate hand', but no stage direction explains what action accompanies his words. Most modern performances and films, including Zeffirelli's and Luhrmann's, have the Nurse shrink back in horror while the Friar bravely intervenes. Yet in the first edition of 1597, to which the unfortunate label 'bad quarto' is sometimes attached, we are told that when Romeo 'offers to stab himselfe', the 'Nurse snatches the dagger away'. G. Blakemore Evans, in the New Cambridge edition, integrates this stage direction into his edition.[5] Brian Gibbons's Arden2 edition, by contrast, provides no stage direction and explains in a footnote that 'There is nothing in the dialogue (or the characterization of the Nurse generally) to prepare for or to support this intervention by the Nurse.'[6] Jill L. Levenson, in the Oxford edition, inserts a stage direction reading 'Romeo offers to stab himself' and explains in a note how editors and directors have dealt with this passage.[7] Whatever decision we prefer, these forms of editorial intervention have an impact on the way we see the play dramatize gender distinctions. In a play which interrogates masculinity so incisively, which has the male protagonist end with the traditionally feminine suicide (poison) and Juliet with the masculine (she resolutely stabs herself), awareness of what informs editorial textual reproduction in the case of Romeo's attempted suicide seems of considerable importance.

Or take the ending of *A Midsummer Night's Dream*: Egeus, Hermia's father, wants to prevent his daughter's marriage to Lysander, preferring a match with Demetrius instead. Yet Theseus overrules him at 4.1, in effect destroying the patriarchal authority so central to Egeus's character. Egeus remains silent for the rest of the scene, allowing for considerable scope in the interpretation of the character on stage. Thereafter, in the version of the play best known to modern readers and theatregoers, the first quarto of 1600, he disappears entirely from the play. Yet in the Folio, he reappears in the last scene speaking most of the lines given in Q1 to Philostrate, the Master of the Revels, thus joining the lovers in the festivities. With Q1 excluding, but the Folio reintroducing, Egeus in the comic conclusion, the two texts seem to constitute comedies of a rather different type. As Northrop Frye wrote in his highly influential *Anatomy of Criticism*,

Comedy often includes a scapegoat ritual of expulsion which gets rid of some irreconcilable character, but exposure and disgrace make for pathos, or even tragedy. *The Merchant of Venice* seems almost an experiment in coming as close as possible to upsetting the comic balance. If the dramatic role of Shylock is ever so slightly exaggerated, as it generally is when the leading actor of the company takes the part, it is upset, and the play becomes the tragedy of the Jew of Venice with a comic epilogue.[8]

Does *A Midsummer Night's Dream* – like *The Merchant of Venice* – contain 'a scapegoat ritual of expulsion' which, as Frye shows, is central to one form of comedy? Or is it a more inclusive kind of comedy? Just what kind of comedy we think *A Midsummer Night's Dream* is has much to do with whether we read (an edition based on) the first quarto or the Folio edition.[9] Here and elsewhere, an awareness of the choices involved in the modern textual reproduction of Shakespeare's drama, and of the rationale informing them, seems essential for an informed critical response.

Textual Performances: The Modern Reproduction of Shakespeare's Drama aims at increasing this awareness. What motivates an editor to reproduce *this* reading, and not *that* reading? What larger issues of, for instance, evidence or authenticity or market does editorial choice raise, and how might such issues impact in turn on decisions concerning conventions of presentation? 1983 saw the publication of *The Division of the Kingdoms*, the ground-breaking collection on the texts of *King Lear*, edited by Gary Taylor and Michael Warren.[10] That volume, followed three years later by the publication of the Oxford *Complete Works*, revolutionized our thinking about the texts of Shakespeare's drama. Scholars, and readers of the plays more generally, became freshly aware of differences between the earliest surviving editions, not least as a result of the decision taken by the Oxford editors 'to prefer – where there is a choice – the text closer to the prompt-book of Shakespeare's company [over the authorial papers]'.[11] Accordingly, they relegated to appendices called 'Additional Passages' sometimes even quite famous speeches that nonetheless fail to appear in the more 'socialized' copy. They further made strikingly visible the existence of multiple textual witnesses by presenting two texts of *King Lear*.

Since then, New Cambridge have launched their 'Early Quartos' series, Arden3 and the Oxford single-volume editions sometimes include as part of their editorial material photofacsimiles of early quartos, Michael Warren has prepared the *Complete King Lear*, Jesús Pérez Tronch *A Synoptic Hamlet*, Paul Bertram and Bernice W. Kliman *The Three-Text Hamlet*, and Early English Books Online, an electronic photofacsimile resource, has become more widely and easily accessible.[12] Leah Marcus, Randall McLeod, and Michael Warren have all written persuasively about the interpretative importance of the sorts of textual details that are inevitably effaced through editorial mediation.[13] The arguments for 'unediting' the Renaissance, and access to the materials with which one might begin to do it, would seem to have arrived. And yet we continue to edit.

The impetus behind *Textual Performances* is not primarily to introduce readers to the idea of textual instability or to foreground textual cruxes – that level of consciousness raising, to a large extent, has already been accomplished. Instead, this collection seeks to gather together the points of key debate and controversy of the present moment to begin to understand the range of pragmatic editorial methodologies that are emerging from the fray, how they respond to the surviving documentary evidence, and how they might speak (or fail to speak) one to another. Robert Weimann – not explicitly or primarily a textual scholar – has recently insisted on the urgency of such investigations, arguing that while it is one thing to identify the limitations of earlier bibliographical standards, 'It is quite another question to define and clarify the new premises.'[14] Weimann's sense that clarification is required is perhaps indicative of the present state of textual and editorial studies, a feature of the paradigm shift in which Barbara Mowat argues we now find ourselves.[15]

Each of the essays in this volume asks very specific questions about, or focuses on a particular aspect of, the modern editions we study in the classroom or rehearsal room, or read for private enjoyment. In what ways might the imaginations of readers be engaged by performance, past and present? How might the evidence of extant early modern manuscript plays shape an editorial treatment of Shakespeare's (print) drama? What opportunities for editorial mediation are offered by electronic media? Should there be more consistency in the ways editors modernize spelling, and what can we do about the interpretative challenges that result from this now commonplace editorial practice? Do users want to read 'texts' or 'works' of Shakespeare's plays?

These questions speak to a shared concern about how best to engage editorially with evidence provided by historical research into the playhouse, author's study, and printing house, and into the complex relations among these spaces of early modern production. Contributors take as a starting-point the following theoretical considerations. First, our knowledge of events and practices of the past can never be anything but partial (in the senses both of incomplete and ideological). Secondly, the activity of textual reproduction can never be entirely disinterested or 'neutral', as historicist research into the editorial tradition by Margreta de Grazia and Laurie Maguire, among others, suggests.[16] How, then, are editors of playscripts to mediate history, in its many forms, for modern users? Should they have to? Where, considering our knowledge of the past is partial, are we to draw the line between legitimate editorial assistance and unwarranted interference? In what innovative way(s) might current controversies surrounding the mediation of Shakespeare's drama shape editorial practice?

The central issues around which this volume has been organized can thus be distilled into a couple of related questions. How can, or need, what we think we know (or are able to infer) about historical events and practices inform what we do as editors of Shakespeare's drama? And how is editorial intervention, or lack thereof, to be related to the perceived needs of users? These are debated areas that permit, at this moment at least, of no ready answers. *Textual Performances* does not advocate a party line, but instead brings into dialogue competing approaches in order to allow readers to assess for themselves how successfully each responds to the major questions of theory, history, and practice that have arisen since the 1980s. While it is not in the nature of paradigm shifts to allow for a clear awareness of what is to follow, this collection pursues the question of what directions editorial practice might take in the twenty-first century.

Part I, Establishing the Text, includes six essays that offer very different methodological and interpretative responses to the problem of uncertain textual provenance, and engage in a variety of ways the author and editor functions in contemporary editorial theory and practice. We do not here attempt to introduce the essays one by one in the received manner, but endeavour instead briefly to present the on-going scholarly debate in which the contributors are engaged. Each of the following essays stands on its own, but readers will particularly benefit, we believe, from observing how, and perhaps analysing why, many contributors in this collection address the same questions but arrive at different answers.

If we want to understand modern thinking on the question of textual provenance, we will do well, as Ernst Honigmann, Paul Werstine, and Henry Woudhuysen do, to return to a group of twentieth-century scholars led by A. W. Pollard, W. W. Greg, and R. B. McKerrow, now often subsumed under the label 'The New Bibliography'. Aiming at 'penetrating the veil of print',[17] the New Bibliographers classified Shakespeare's (now lost) manuscript playbooks into such groups as 'foul papers', 'promptbooks', and 'private transcripts' in an effort to discern the copy from which they believed the surviving printed texts had been set up.[18] Greg advocated that editions be based, when more than one substantive text has come down to us, on that which is closest to the state in which the dramatic text left the author's hands.[19] Few assumptions of the New Bibliography have gone unchallenged, and the turn from authorial to performance texts ushered in by the Oxford *Complete Works* of 1986 is reflected by several essays in this collection. The extent to which the above classifications accurately characterize the manuscript copy actually used in early modern printing houses is another particularly contentious issue. Woudhuysen and Honigmann acknowledge that editing techniques deriving from the New Bibliography are necessarily pragmatic and compromised, yet they take issue, in different ways, with emerging trends in textual studies: Woudhuysen offers a sustained analysis of the claims of the so-called 'uneditors', while Honigmann challenges the insights offered by the most recent generation of textual scholars as overly pessimistic. Werstine counters that editorial practice is best not based on either optimism or pessimism but on evidence from extant material witnesses, and presents such evidence to illustrate that our assumptions about so-called 'foul papers' are mistaken.[20]

These contributors agree, however, that the New Bibliography, despite what the label might suggest, was a group of scholars with rather more diverse opinions than some recent discussions suggest and that it in fact anticipated several of the current debates. As Honigmann shows, not only recent scholars but also Greg warned 'against hard-and-fast criteria for distinguishing foul papers from promptbooks' (p. 79); and, as Werstine reminds us, not only recent scholars but also McKerrow departed from the

Introduction 7

belief that an edition should necessarily try to recover a play as nearly as possible as it left the author's hands (pp. 51–2).

Just what an editor should strive to edit remains thus a difficult question, and the answers to it differ accordingly. A first important distinction several contributors establish is that between the document, the text, and the work. The precise definitions which attach to each of these terms are contested, as are the interrelationships between the categories, not least because such an exercise implies competing ideological attitudes towards evidence and authority. Woudhuysen maintains that a facsimile edition preserves many (though not all) material features of a dramatic document and is the most 'socialized' text of the kind Jerome J. McGann and D. F. McKenzie have advocated.[21] However, it does not cater to the needs of all readers. Another problem, as John Jowett shows, is that a material document can conceal central aspects of a text – in the specific cases he discusses, distinct layers of adaptation – which sophisticated textual studies, and an edition informed by them, can make visible to a reader. In such a situation, privileging the document over the text is invoked at the cost of invalidating other kinds of editorial intervention (p. 64). Sonia Massai argues, by contrast, that it is important for editors to make the textual users aware of the original dramatic documents and, specifically, of the 'presentational options native to the medium of print' (p. 102). Rather than reducing the medium through which the documents were produced to a corrupting agent interfering with authorial intentions, we need to understand it as a set of ideological as well as technological developments which partly constitute the text. She proposes that release of editorial control, as practised in her Internet Shakespeare edition of *Edward III*, does better justice both to the reader (or user), who is empowered, and to the original documents. As her essay shows, it is precisely the 'radical technological break from print culture' (p. 106) constituted by medium that allows editors to mediate important insights into early modern print culture.

If the distinction between text and document serves to highlight one area of disagreement, that between text and work pinpoints another. 'Work', in this context, tends to refer to the play as one might assume the author, in an ideal world, would have wished to see it presented. The editorial situation that best brings this distinction into focus is that of plays, such as *Othello* and *Romeo and Juliet*, of which more than one version has survived. If two, or even three, substantive editions of a play survive, should editors strive to recover, or construct, the play as Shakespeare conceived it, interpreting the extant versions as reflections, of different provenance and authority, of that same lost work? Or is that work simply unavailable, a Platonic idea fabricated by editorial narratives and unverifiable speculation? Werstine argues for the latter position, advocating 'the humanly possible goal of editing one or more of the early printed texts, without claiming to locate either author or work in relation to these printed versions' (p. 59). Woudhuysen, by contrast, states that 'most people understand that reading an edition of *Hamlet* is different from reading an edition of the second quarto of the play' (p. 40) and, drawing on the work of T. H. Howard-Hill, holds that the great majority of readers, including university teachers and students, want to read works, not texts. Honigmann emphasizes that editing separate versions fails to take account of the plays' normal evolution in Shakespeare's theatre and that 'the notion of the "single play" had at this time to be elastic' (p. 86). Yet Leah Marcus's advocacy of 'unediting' emphasizes what can be lost when versions of a play are conflated instead of studied separately: if the first quarto and Folio editions of *Othello* can be distinguished in their treatment of race, then an edition that presents these versions of *Othello* as a unified work may conceal something essential about the changes the play underwent in Shakespeare's time.[22]

A different way of framing the distinction between text and work is to ask whether, and if so in what way, editorial practice should continue to be 'critical' (or 'eclectic'). Editing works implies eclecticism (and at least local conflation) insofar as more than one version will be drawn upon for the edition. Woudhuysen maintains that there is still space enough 'for the critical editing of works' (p. 47), but Werstine insists that '"critical" editing of Shakespeare has had its day' (p. 58). A question this debate raises is how to deal with errors in the copy-text if editors are bent on avoiding eclecticism. McKerrow, as Werstine reminds us, advocated sticking to copy unless its readings appear to be certainly corrupt, but Woudhuysen and Honigmann believe that such a position is fraught with problems: 'if errors are to be corrected, where should the editor stop and how confident can we be that *this* is an error but *that* is not?' (Woudhuysen, p. 44). Similarly, Honigmann believes 'editors committed to an anti-conflation policy still persist in conflating' (p. 87). While Werstine seems less sure than Woudhuysen and Honigmann that the New Bibliography has equipped us with adequate tools to identify 'foul papers',[23] Woudhuysen and Honigmann seem less sure than Werstine that editors can know what is and what is not textual error and that conflation and critical (or eclectic) editing can be entirely resisted.

The growing awareness since the 1970s that Shakespeare may have revised some of his plays further complicates the question of whether to edit texts or works.[24] Is it legitimate to try to recover the work of *King Lear* (Honigmann, pp. 86–7), or is it not because it never was a single work in the first place (Woudhuysen, p. 43)? Honigmann warns us that the signs of revision and those of corruption may be difficult to keep apart, yet Marcus believes that, in the case of *Othello*, the different treatment of race in quarto and Folio does argue for (quite possibly authorial) revision. A 'two-text model' is also pursued by Jowett in his work on *Sir Thomas More* and *Measure for Measure* as texts which survive in their adapted forms. Editing these plays for the Arden Shakespeare and the Middleton *Collected Works* respectively, he points out that readers will have to know why *Measure for Measure* and *Sir Thomas More* qualify for inclusion in these editorial projects in the first place. His editorial recovery of adaptation points back to authors at the same time as these authors are seen as functioning within a theatrical enterprise in which solitary authorship did not reign supreme, in which theatrical texts were adapted by a writer who had no hand in the original composition.

As all of these approaches and debates imply, editorial practices in the twenty-first century are bound up with the question of how far the extant dramatic documents allow us to get back to the author. No one doubts that Shakespeare and others wrote plays, but how far can the author(s) of a dramatic work be recovered through the socialized texts that may have been mediated by actors, scribes, compositors, and proof-readers? Werstine believes that the quest for the author should be abandoned, while Honigmann argues that, the necessary caution granted, the good quartos may well give us limited access to Shakespeare. This opposition may seem to re-enact the controversy over whether to edit texts or works, but Marcus's essay bears out that, paradoxically, it is by making available the versions rather than the work of *Othello* that readers are led back to Shakespeare, a revising Shakespeare who does not resemble 'the "gentle Shakespeare" we have been taught to know and love' (p. 33). Massai adds that the notion of the author is 'medium-specific' (p. 105), significant in early modern print culture but obsolete in modern-day electronic culture. She sees the electronic medium as offering new editorial opportunities precisely because it can foreground evidence of textual instability that might allow readers to discern how non-authorial agents 'construct[ed] the printed texts from which "Shakespeare" emerged as an early modern dramatic author' (p. 96). The sum of these essays suggests that whether, and if so how, we have access to authors (rather than just manuscripts and printed texts) is a question that remains wide open.

What precedes makes abundantly clear that current thinking on textual provenance and on how to theorize the role of the editor, the text, the work, and the author in relation to editorial practice is sharply divided. While *The Division of the Kingdoms* in 1983 assembled a group of contributors most of whom were united in advancing the case for Shakespeare's revision of *King Lear*, *Textual Performances* stages the current division among Shakespearean textualists. It does so in the hope of sharpening our readers' awareness of the key issues in today's debates as well as of providing guidance to students and practitioners of the modern reproduction of Shakespeare's drama.

The seven essays included in Part II, Presenting the Play, continue this analysis of evidence and authority. Here the debate is framed in terms of what might be described as an editorial overlay – decisions concerning spelling, annotation, page layout, and appendices which are often invisible, taken for granted, or even determined in advance by publishing houses. These essays offer a sustained examination of the relation between interpretation and presentation, and explore how, and to what effect, a reader's experience of Shakespeare's drama is inflected – and might be inflected differently – by the way the text is shaped.

The vast majority of modern editions of Shakespeare are prepared with the student reader in mind. In an effort to make the drama more accessible, editors attempt to smooth over passages perceived as difficult through a combination of modernization and emendation. Some of these tactics, however, as David Bevington and Michael Warren emphasize, come at a price. There are probably now few people who would agree with Fredson Bowers that 'the preservation in any serious edition of the old-spelling characteristics of a text . . . scarcely needs defence'.[25] 'Serious' modern-spelling editions of Shakespeare come as standard these days. The pragmatic problem, however, as Bevington demonstrates, is that there is as yet little consistency in the way editors approach the task of modernization. As a result, 'misinformation that is culturally and linguistically revealing' (p. 146) (false etymologies, for instance) is preserved erratically in modern editions, or erased without comment. The more an editor intrudes to dress a play in a twenty-first-century guise, the more fully the play is subjected to his or her critical understanding of language and action. Michael Warren places a slightly different emphasis on the dangers of intervention by examining how the speech prefixes of the First and Second Citizens in the opening lines of *Coriolanus* are typically, and unnecessarily, altered to conform to editors' notions of 'playability' and psychological realism. What constitutes error – and our willingness to find it – is thus brought into question: 'Error is a risky concept; the idea of others' error is a temptation' (p. 138).

Warren and Bevington draw to our attention some of the costs of an editorial overlay that seeks to mediate early modern scripts for twenty-first-century readers. It would seem that modernization and emendation must distance readers from the surviving documentary witnesses: nuances of meaning are flattened out, interpretative flexibility is constricted, the text becomes vulnerable to an editor's, and the editorial tradition's, contingent sense of 'correctness'. The view, though, that something is 'lost' through editorial mediation begs the question of what exactly one might by other means attempt to preserve. Part II and, indeed, the volume as a whole, struggles in different ways with the awareness that our knowledge of events and practices of the past can never be anything but partial. Cultural mindsets, linguistic usages, theatrical conventions, printing house procedures can now, at best, be only partly recovered, and the evidence bearing on such areas of inquiry is subject to shifting modes and structures of interpretation.

So how might one respond to this problem of history? The essays offered here provide at least two possible editorial attitudes to the authority of origins, the one seeking to recover the past, the other working with the realization that history is an on-going process. The first orientation attempts to find means to reinterpret the available evidence about the working conditions within which these plays first found an existence in print and performance, and to make the past accessible, as far as possible, to readers who might otherwise be oblivious to the historical otherness of Shakespeare's drama. Some essays propose meeting this challenge through innovative forms of editorial presentation; others through annotation. We know, for instance, that doubling was a routine practice on the Elizabethan and Jacobean stage, and 'that for most of his career [Shakespeare] was writing for a stable company of around ten men and three or four boys' (p. 112). Ann Thompson and Neil Taylor make this theatrical convention visible to modern readers of *Hamlet* through the construction of casting charts for each of the play's three versions. What casting charts cannot tell us, of course, is how *Hamlet* was *actually* doubled in performance (not least because particular doubling strategies may well have altered from one performance to another). Instead, this method of presentation engages editors and readers in what was once, but is no longer, a customary practice, and encourages us to consider the possible physical demands placed by different plays on theatrical companies.

Two essays included in Part I similarly investigate means of presentation able to make now unfamiliar, or even obsolete, historical processes visible to modern readers. Massai and Jowett address from different perspectives issues of textual instability, devising forms of presentation able to highlight to a reader, in the first case, evidence of extra-authorial agency in the printing house, and in the second case, evidence of adaptation. Massai turns to a mode of electronic presentation that 'can overcome the limits of the codex form' (p. 96) through its ability to present to the reader's eye variant readings both within and between editions. Rather than bury textual variants in the apparatus, Massai uses dancing type and full-text electronic editions of the two early quartos of *Edward the Third* to argue, in part, that the printer's copy behind the second quarto was prepared with care by an early modern editor. Jowett, by contrast, tailors forms of editorial display in the print medium to the surviving print and manuscript characteristics of *Measure for Measure* and *Sir Thomas More*. In each instance, the format deliberately disrupts the reader's linear experience of the play in order to mark multiple textual strata and so the effects of adaptation. Jowett's innovative methods of presentation serve to make visible a process of revision whereby an original layer by one author becomes distinguishable from a revised layer by another author, or other authors. He thus acts on what we think we can know about a past, and now lost, moment (or set of moments) of creative production in order to develop document-specific editorial models able to convey to a reader diachronic process, rather than synchronic product. Although the degree of editorial intervention such models occasion, as Jowett notes, might be regarded by some as 'polemical' (p. 72), his effort to recover history and to make it readily available to a reader is not categorically different from the sorts of strategies proposed by either Massai or Thompson and Taylor.

One of the most pressing points of disagreement that emerges from Part II is the extent to which editors shape the text in response to theories about some aspect of the original creative, theatrical, manuscript, or print production of early modern drama. John D. Cox puts the case strongly in relation to editorially inserted stage directions designed to help the reader visualize the action. Along with Warren, he explores some of the pitfalls that attend interventionist strategies as they are commonly applied to issues of staging. Keenly aware that the question of what actually happened in Shakespeare's theatres remains a serious problem of knowledge, and arguing that the 'choice to offer readers closure ... may well take them further from early stage practice, not closer to it' (p. 180), Cox suggests that an editor's safest course of action is to discuss possible stagings in the commentary, leaving the scripts themselves open to readerly interpretation. Commentary, in this answer to the problem of historical recovery, emerges as the editor's primary, even exclusive, means of communication with a reader; rather than embed one's position in the text, one adopts the less textually intrusive option of providing a discursive explanation at the foot of the page or back of the book. A compromise position, of course, and one advocated by Bevington in relation to modernized spelling, would be to use commentary to remedy what is lost through editorial intervention.

This turn to commentary raises very practical considerations about the length of editions, and about how much information readers can reasonably be expected to absorb while simultaneously working their way through a play. 'Cf. Holinshed, 858', 'Tilley L452, W62', 'See 26 n. above', 'Abbott §1' – these and similar sorts of cryptic symbols and phrasings have been developed precisely in order to prevent commentary from visually overwhelming the edited page. Are there ways to use the commentary for more extensive, even exploratory, critical discussion, without unduly tipping the balance between text and annotation? The infinite space provided by electronic commentary seems to provide options not available to editors working in a print medium. Archives offering searchable full-text secondary materials – albeit, as Woudhuysen argues, 'too obviously manipulated to convince most people that they are "unedited"' (p. 43) – can nonetheless be browsed by readers in unpredictable ways, 'transform[ing] the *reader*', as Massai puts it, 'into a *user*, or what can be described as a "Barthesian" reader' (p. 103). This particular approach to textual annotation, perhaps better characterized as a digital library than a commentary, avoids what John Lavagnino describes as the 'violence' (p. 202) done to scholarly literature through fragmented citation, but may not be ideal for every type of reader. Lavagnino argues that modern commentary is in large part driven by the market, and that the market is currently meeting two distinct readerly needs: either commentary is designed to accompany the reading of a play in its entirety and so has to lend itself to quick glances at the bottom of the page, or it is copious and therefore only consulted for specific insights into local passages. The advent of electronic editing does not impact on these two basic functions of commentary, and as a result, editors should not expect that digital publication can provide significant innovations of form: where 'it's the reading experience above all that matters... the highly-developed technology of the book is not easy to improve upon' (p. 203).

These interrelated questions of history, interpretation, and presentation seem not to permit of easy or obvious answers. There remains an on-going debate about how best to find a balance between, on the one hand, sharing with a reader one's editorial and historical expertise, and, on the other, closing down interpretative options by reconfiguring the script according to one's partial knowledge of the past. A very different response to the demands of history, as mentioned earlier, is to resist the siren song of origins, recognizing that history does not end with the early modern period. The impulse here is to present the scripts less in terms of what *was*, than what *might be*. Margaret Jane Kidnie draws on the possibilities implicit in the marginal stage direction, a characteristic feature of early modern manuscript plays and playbooks, to explore a page layout 'with which we might guide users... to an awareness of choice and an imaginative interaction with the drama' (pp. 164–5). She is working with an interventionist model, but one that prompts a different sort of (non-linear) reading strategy, one which is directed towards not a lost moment, but an as-yet-unimagined moment.

This desire to build indeterminacy into the reading experience, to transform readers from passive witnesses to the (editor's) textual performance into players on whose imaginative input the script regularly draws is of a piece with objections to prescriptive editorial miscontrol of the plays' staging mounted by Cox, Warren, and Barbara Hodgdon. There is little certainty about how and at which points an editor should flesh out the stage directions of early modern drama. '[T]he theatre historian's dirty little secret', as Alan Dessen confides elsewhere, is 'how little we actually know about how these plays were first conceived and performed'.[26] Faced with such a situation, editors are forced to speculate about the conventions of the early modern stage, often drawing heavily on their own sense of theatrical and performative propriety. But even if we were able to find that elusive videotape of a seventeenth-century Globe performance, should the insights it might provide into the open platform stage necessarily or in every instance determine an editor's treatment of staging? This returns us to the issue of one's orientation towards history. Hodgdon suggests that existing editorial protocols are anti-theatrical in the way they tacitly attach less 'use-value' to modern performance choices than to those of the absent (and largely irrecoverable) 'original' production, and she argues that 'relinquishing this Globe-al space would be an initial step towards creating a less restrictive commentary, one attuned to changing spaces and to fluid potentialities of how bodies and texts take on meanings in such spaces' (pp. 216–17). Hodgdon's idea is to develop a form of editorial commentary able to embrace a more wide-ranging account of a play's performative potential and theatre history, an initiative that will require a change in the codes and languages through which a reader's engagement with drama-as-theatre is currently shaped.

We thus come around, once again, to the identification of annotation as a key site for debate and exploration. Issues of design have become scholarly matters; editorial conventions, often unspoken, are being subjected to new interrogation; and as a consequence, the recognition is growing that the presentation of the drama – all the various elements that constitute the editorial overlay – should neither be conceded to the enervating force of the editorial tradition, nor considered the exclusive domain of modern publishing houses. While the answers these essays provide to the problems posed by history and interpretation are not always compatible, many of them encourage an increased attention to the precise ways in which the plays are, and might be in the future, mediated for the reader.

NOTES

1. See Ron Rosenbaum, 'Shakespeare in Rewrite', *The New Yorker* (13 May 2002), 68–77.
2. Fredson Bowers, *Textual and Literary Criticism*, the Sanders Lectures in Bibliography, 1957–8 (Cambridge University Press, 1959), p. 5.
3. Stanley Wells and Gary Taylor, with John Jowett and William Montgomery (eds.), *William Shakespeare: The Complete Works* (Oxford: Clarendon Press, 1986).
4. See Terence Hawkes, *That Shakespeherian Rag: Essays on a Critical Process* (London: Methuen, 1986), pp. 73–91, and essays by John Russell Brown, Maurice Charney, and Dieter Mehl in *Connotations* 2 (1992) for discussions of the textual problem of Hamlet's last moments.
5. G. Blakemore Evans (ed.), *Romeo and Juliet* (Cambridge University Press, 1984), 3.3.108.1.
6. Brian Gibbons (ed.), *Romeo and Juliet* (London: Methuen, 1980), p. 180n.
7. Jill L. Levenson (ed.), *Romeo and Juliet* (Oxford University Press, 2000), p. 279n.
8. Northrop Frye, *Anatomy of Criticism: Four Essays* (Princeton University Press, 1957), p. 165.
9. Barbara Hodgdon discusses the textual and theatrical implications of Q1 and F *Dream* in '"Gaining a Father": the Role of Egeus in the Quarto and the Folio', *Review of English Studies* n.s., 37 (1986), 534–42. See also Peter Holland's appendix ('Shakespeare's Revisions of Act 5') to his edition of *A Midsummer Night's Dream* in the Oxford Shakespeare series (Oxford: Clarendon Press, 1994), pp. 257–68.
10. Gary Taylor and Michael Warren (eds.), *The Division of the Kingdoms* (Oxford: Clarendon Press, 1983).
11. Stanley Wells and Gary Taylor, with John Jowett and William Montgomery, *William Shakespeare: A Textual Companion* (Oxford: Clarendon Press, 1987), p. 15.
12. Michael Warren, *The Complete 'King Lear', 1608–1623* (Berkeley: University of California Press, 1989), Jesús Pérez Tronch (ed.), *A Synoptic Hamlet* (Valéncia: Sederi, Universitat de Valéncia, 2002), Paul Bertram and Bernice W. Kliman

(eds.), *The Three-Text Hamlet: Parallel Texts of the First and Second Quartos and First Folio* (New York: AMS Press, 1991).

13. See, for instance, Leah Marcus, *Unediting the Renaissance: Shakespeare, Marlowe and Milton* (London: Routledge, 1996), Randall McLeod, 'UnEditing Shakspeare', *Sub-stance* 33–4 (1982), 26–55, Randall McLeod (alias 'Random Clod'), 'Information Upon Information', *Text* 5 (1991), 241–81, and Michael Warren, 'Repunctuation as Interpretation in Editions of Shakespeare', *English Literary Renaissance* 7 (1977), 155–69, 'Textual Problems, Editorial Assertions in Editions of Shakespeare', in *Textual Criticism and Literary Interpretation*, ed. Jerome J. McGann (University of Chicago Press, 1985), pp. 23–37, 'The Theatricalization of Text: Beckett, Jonson, Shakespeare', in *New Directions in Textual Studies*, ed. Dave Oliphant and Robin Bradford, with introduction by Larry Carver (Austin: Harry Ransom Humanities Research Centre, 1990), pp. 39–59.

14. Robert Weimann, *Author's Pen and Actor's Voice: Playing and Writing in Shakespeare's Theatre* (Cambridge University Press, 2000), p. 41.

15. Barbara Mowat, 'The Reproduction of Shakespeare's Text', in *The Cambridge Companion to Shakespeare*, ed. Margreta de Grazia and Stanley Wells (Cambridge University Press, 2001), pp. 25–6.

16. Margreta de Grazia, *Shakespeare Verbatim: The Reproduction of Authenticity and the 1790 Apparatus* (Oxford University Press, 1991), Laurie Maguire, *Shakespearean Suspect Texts: The 'Bad' Quartos and Their Contexts* (Cambridge University Press, 1996).

17. Bowers, *Textual and Literary Criticism*, p. 18.

18. See, for instance, Greg's *Dramatic Documents from the Elizabethan Playhouses*, 2 vols. (Oxford University Press, 1931).

19. See W. W. Greg, 'The Rationale For Copy-Text', *Studies in Bibliography* 3 (1950–1), 19–36.

20. Werstine is building on important earlier work of his, notably 'Narratives About Printed Shakespeare Texts: "Foul Papers" and "Bad" Quartos', *Shakespeare Quarterly* 41 (1990), 65–86, and 'Post-Theory Problems in Shakespeare Editing', *The Yearbook of English Studies* 29 (1999), 103–17. Honigmann's seminal work in the field includes *The Stability of Shakespeare's Text* (London: Edward Arnold, 1965) and *The Texts of 'Othello' and Shakespearian Revision* (London: Routledge, 1996).

21. See D. F. McKenzie, *Bibliography and the Sociology of Texts*, the Panizzi Lectures 1985 (London: The British Library, 1986), and *Making Meaning: 'Printers of the Mind' and Other Essays*, ed. Peter D. McDonald and Michael F. Suarez, S. J. (Amherst: University of Massachusetts Press, 2002); and Jerome J. McGann, *The Textual Condition* (Princeton University Press, 1991).

22. See also Marcus's *Unediting the Renaissance*.

23. For disagreement over the specific question of whether authorial second thoughts (often believed to be indicative of 'foul papers') can be securely diagnosed or not, see Jowett (pp. 65–6) and Werstine (pp. 54–7).

24. See Michael Warren, 'Quarto and Folio *King Lear* and the Interpretation of Albany and Edgar', in *Shakespeare: Pattern of Excelling Nature*, ed. David

Bevington and Jay L. Halio (Newark: University of Delaware Press, 1978), pp. 95–107; Taylor and Warren (eds.), *The Division of the Kingdoms*; Warren (ed.), *The Complete 'King Lear', 1608–1623*; and Grace Ioppolo, *Revising Shakespeare* (Cambridge, MA.: Harvard University Press, 1991).
25. Bowers, *Textual and Literary Criticism*, p. 143.
26. Alan Dessen, *Rescripting Shakespeare: The Text, the Director, and Modern Productions* (Cambridge University Press, 2002), p. 237.

PART I

Establishing the text

CHAPTER I

The two texts of 'Othello' and early modern constructions of race

Leah S. Marcus

There has in recent years been a seismic shift in the way Shakespearean textual scholars view the early printed versions of the plays. Through much of the twentieth century, earlier-published, shorter quarto versions were generally viewed as derivative – pirated versions or 'memorial reconstructions' of the play in performance – while longer, later-published quarto and Folio versions were regarded as more authoritative, closer to the plays as Shakespeare originally wrote them, or at least closer to the form in which he envisioned them for performance on stage. More recently, as in the case of the quarto and Folio versions of *King Lear*, some scholars have been willing to argue for Shakespeare as a reviser and augmenter of his own work, so that shorter and earlier published versions could be understood as earlier stages in his own evolving conception of his creations.

In the heady early days of the paradigm shift, *Othello* was mentioned alongside *King Lear* as a two-text play whose early quarto and Folio printings should be regarded as distinct versions, each with its own artistic integrity and theatrical logic. Countering Alice Walker's definitive statement of the older view of the first quarto of *Othello* (1622) as a corrupt and vulgarizing perversion of Shakespeare's intentions for the play, which she saw as more nearly reflected in the First Folio version of 1623, E. A. J. Honigmann announced optimistically in 1982, 'A strong case can be made for the "revision" of *Othello* and of *King Lear*; the fact that Shakespeare is thought to have re-touched not one but two of his greatest tragedies, and to have strengthened both in similar (and unusual) ways, makes the "revision-theory" more compelling – and more exciting.'[1] In the case of *King Lear* the aftermath is well known: the 1986 Oxford edition of the *Complete Works* offers both the quarto and Folio versions separately and as equals, and that editorial decision is repeated in the more recent *Norton Shakespeare* (1997), based on the Oxford text, and in Michael Warren's *The Complete King Lear* (1989). The two-text theory of *King Lear* may fairly be said to have 'arrived' – no critic, director, or editor of the play can now afford to ignore it. What of the two-text *Othello*?

As I shall argue below, the differences between quarto and Folio versions of *Othello* are at least as important for interpretation as the differences between the two early versions of *King Lear*. And yet, Honigmann's optimistic assessment of the case for two separate texts of *Othello* was followed by little beyond silence. Even Honigmann's 1997 Arden edition of the play and his companion volume consolidating the case for Shakespeare as reviser of *Othello* do not further develop the interpretative questions that had interested him earlier.[2] In the last decade, there have been two new editions of the first quarto of *Othello*, but there is still, to my knowledge, no recent parallel-text edition to facilitate study of the differences between the two versions. Editors have generally skirted the tricky question of how Q1 *Othello* might mean differently than F1; with few exceptions they do not offer an apparatus that facilitates comparison between the two.[3] Even in the Oxford Shakespeare *Complete Works*, for reasons that had as much to do with lack of space as with the editors' preferences, Q1 was not printed separately or discussed as a separate entity.[4]

There are various possible explanations beyond publishing cost why the two-text *Othello* has died aborning while the two-text *King Lear* has flourished. Within the play, Othello sets himself resolutely, if futilely, against the doubling of meanings. In his destruction, engineered by a villain whose personal oath is 'by Janus' and whose virulent duplicity goes beyond anything to be found elsewhere in Shakespeare, the idea of a double text may carry a special stigma. But I will argue here that a more accessible, more intractable, explanation has to do with race. As recently as 1989, Michael Billington was able to write of the play in performance, '*Othello* is currently the least revived of all Shakespeare's tragedies and the reasons are not far to seek: casting problems and racial guilt.'[5] In the last ten years, however, *Othello* has been frequently performed and the subject of race in the play has engaged literally hundreds of critics in print. It is time we turned our editorial attention to a matter that has become central to the criticism.

Briefly summarized, my argument will run as follows: Q and F *Othello* offer markedly different constructions of race and its relation to other elements of the play, especially female purity. Most of the key passages critics have repeatedly cited to define the play's attitude towards blackness, miscegenation, and sexual pollution derive from the Folio version of the play, and do not exist in the quarto. To imagine 'gentle Shakespeare' as a reviser who began with a text resembling Q, then amplified and refocused it into a text resembling F, is to imagine a Shakespeare who deliberately intensified what look from our modern perspective like racist elements of the play. Ania Loomba and others have recently emphasized the relative indefinition of racial identities and boundaries in the early modern era by comparison with our own. Loomba characterizes Shakespeare's time as 'either the last period in history where ethnic identities could be understood as fluid, or as the first moment of the emergence of modern notions of "race"'.[6] Where we place *Othello* in this shifting calculus of difference will depend to a significant degree on whether we choose Q or F.

The quarto and Folio versions of *Othello* were published only a year apart, yet they are markedly unlike: Q contains numerous oaths that have been softened or eliminated in F, which suggests that Q may predate the 1606 'Acte to Restraine Abuses of Players'. Q has fuller stage directions, which may suggest an origin closer to the play in performance. The two texts contain numerous small variants of the type that we have come to expect from Shakespearean two-text plays. But the most interesting difference is that F contains approximately 160 lines of text that are not present in Q. Conversely, Q includes a few lines that are not present in F. Were the Folio-only lines in the play from Shakespeare's first composition of it, then cut, perhaps for a specific performance, or were they Shakespeare's own additions as part of a broader revision? The added lines are by no means innocuous: they contain some of the play's most racially charged language. Within the confines of the present chapter I cannot hope to address all of the areas of difference between the two texts, but will confine myself to a discussion of the most extended F-only passages. What would the play look like without them?

Answering that question is, of course, impossible because we have all been conditioned to define *Othello* as a play that contains them: even editors who prefer Q as their copy-text routinely graft the F-only passages onto the play, and that practice of conflation has been followed ever since the 1630 publication of the second quarto.[7] But, following a methodology that has become commonplace in studies of *King Lear*, we can, as a heuristic device for recovering difference, at least try to think our way back into imagining what one version might have looked like on stage, might look like even now for readers, in the absence of its textual supplement. The method is not without flaws: to choose to compare two texts through a rather clumsy, formalist mode of close reading is to sacrifice some of our ability to see how a given text differs from itself. Then too, what look on paper like marked contrasts between versions can usually be overcome through staging. But that does not mean that the differences should be ignored.

The first long F-only passage occurs during Iago and Roderigo's jeering encounter with Brabantio (1.1.81–157),[8] during which they attempt to convince the old man that his daughter has eloped with Othello. Both texts include Iago's scathingly clever, yet indirect, references to the coupling of Othello and Desdemona: they are a black ram and a white ewe making the 'beast with two backs', spawning coursers and jennets. But only in the Folio version does Roderigo chime in with his own much more explicit imagining of Desdemona's pollution (1.1.119–35). Here I cite the First Folio, using square parentheses to indicate the portions of the speech that are F-only:

Rod. Sir, I will answere any thing. But I beseech you
[If't be your pleasure, and most wise consent,
(As partly I find it is) that your faire Daughter,
At this odde Euen and dull watch o'th'night
Transported with no worse nor better guard,
But with a knaue of common hire, a Gundelier,
To the grosse claspes of a Lasciuious Moore:
If this be knowne to you, and your Allowance,
We then haue done you bold, and saucie wrongs.
But if you know not this, my Manners tell me,
We haue your wrong rebuke. Do not beleeue
That from the sence of all Ciuilitie,
I thus would play and trifle with your Reuerence.
Your Daughter (if you haue not giuen her leaue)
I say againe, hath made a grosse reuolt,
Tying her Dutie, Beautie, Wit, and Fortunes
In an extrauagant, and wheeling Stranger,
Of here, and euery where: straight satisfie your selfe.]
If she be in her Chamber, or your house,
Let loose on me the Iustice of the State
For thus deluding you.

(TLN 133–53)

The characterization of Othello as an erratic outsider, an 'extrauagant, and wheeling Stranger, / Of here, and euery where' is F only, as is the graphic depiction of the 'Lasciuious Moore' grossly clasping a 'faire Daughter' who has hired a common knave to transport her, in 'grosse reuolt' against her father's authority. The lines that critics most often rely on to establish Othello's (stereotypical) Moorish lust and his marginality to Venetian culture even at the beginning of the play, the lines they cite most often to demonstrate the normative culture's intolerance of miscegenation – these do not exist in the quarto, where Roderigo's speech reads in full,

> Sir, I will answer anything: But I beseech you,
> If she be in her chamber, or your house,
> Let loose on me the Iustice of the state,
> For this delusion.
>
> (B3r)[9]

It is easy to see why editors long considered the Folio version of Roderigo's speech as simply excised in quarto: except for the usual minor differences in spelling, punctuation, and wording, Roderigo's surrounding lines are identical in both versions. Those editors who have more recently argued for Roderigo's more extended speech as a Shakespearean addition have suggested that the new lines proved necessary because early audiences found the scene too confusing without them.[10] But surely the Q version of the scene is no more confusing than many another Shakespearean first act exposition, and all is made clear a few minutes later when Desdemona and Othello face the Senators and offer their own version of events. What the F 'additions', if such they are, accomplish is to give an almost pornographic specificity and negativity to the image of interracial love. But they do more than that: in Q it is possible to regard Iago's taunts about animal sexuality as his own twisted, personal vision, since Roderigo does not contribute to them, unless we count his earlier reference to Othello as 'thicklips' (1.1.65). By having Roderigo join and even best Iago in articulating this 'primal scene' of miscegenation, F establishes it as a community view, even if the community consists at this point of two men plus Brabantio, who responds to Roderigo, 'This accident is not unlike my dream, / Belief of it oppresses me already' (1.1.140–1). His speech exists in both Q and F, but only in F do we know exactly what dreadful things he has been dreaming. As though by contagion, Roderigo's speech in F taints our vision of their love even before we see them together in Scene 3 as a valiant general and his forthright wife.

Remarkably, the greater sexual explicitness created by Roderigo's speech in the Folio version of the play extends to its language in later scenes, where Q is often more general. As would be expected, the greater explicitness is concentrated in the last two acts of the play, when the F-only passages painfully intensify the debate about Desdemona's virtue. Othello's fit upon hearing Cassio's 'confession' of adultery from Iago (4.1.35–43) is much more extended in the Folio version, and introduces, as Honigmann has observed, 'sexual overtones that are peculiarly revolting and effective – conjuring up images of male and female sexual organs, thinly disguised'.[11] Especially in its longer Folio version, Othello's ranting is a tortured, fragmented elaboration of the 'gross' images from Act 1:

> *Othe.* Lye with her? lye on her? We say lye on her, when they be-lye-her. Lye with her: {at this point, Q adds 'Zouns',} that's fullsome: Handkerchiefe: Confessions: Handkerchiefe. [To confesse, and be hang'd for his labour. First, to be hang'd, and then to confesse: I tremble at it. Nature would not inuest her selfe in such shadowing passion, without some Iustruction. It is not words that shakes me thus, (pish) Noses, Eares, and Lippes: is't possible. Confesse? Handkerchiefe? O diuell.]
>
> (TLN 2412–20)

In the next extended F-only speech (4.2.74–7) Othello finally confronts Desdemona directly with his rage against her supposed infidelity:

> [What commited,
> Committed? Oh, thou publicke Commoner,
> I should make very Forges of my cheekes,
> That would to Cynders burne vp Modestie,
> Did I but speake thy deedes.] What commited?
>
> (TLN 2768–72)

After this powerfully incendiary language, Othello finally comes out and calls her 'Strumpet' a few lines later. The Q version of lines 2768–72 is only two words, 'impudent strumpet' (sig. K3v, p. 824), which are usually added on for good measure to the F-only insults in the conflated texts of modern editions, so that in our modern texts Othello is more extensively abusive than in either early text considered separately. At 4.2.85–7, Q has Desdemona protest in response, 'If to preserue this vessell for my Lord, / From any hated foule vnlawfull touch, / Be not to be a strumpet, I am none' (sig. K4r, p. 824). The F version of the passage reads instead 'any other foule vnlawfull touch' (TLN 2781), implying that Othello's touch is also unlawful: in F, her marriage is itself construed as whoredom.

In response to these F-only passages, Desdemona's speech of self-justification before Iago at 4.2.150–66 is fourteen lines longer in F and more precise about what she is accused of. Only in F does she kneel before him and explicitly articulate the charge against her:

> I cannot say Whore,
> It do's abhorre me now I speake the word,
> To do the Act, that might the addition earne,
> Not the worlds Masse of vanitie could make me.
>
> (TLN 2875–8)

Her kneeling before Iago is a gesture that increases both her abjection and the hideous irony of her situation – protesting her virtue to the very man who best knows her truth.

The best-known segment of F that does not exist in Q is most of the Willow Scene (4.3), which requires Desdemona to sing her song of abandoned love. The standard explanation for its absence from Q is that the play-text had to be adjusted quickly for a performance in which a boy singer was not available – perhaps because of a sudden adolescent change of voice. But some editors have made a case for the Willow Scene as a Shakespearean addition, noting that at other points towards the end of the play, Emilia's role is also expanded in F.[12] All of the most sexually explicit speeches of the scene are among its F-only lines: Emilia's affectionate banter about a 'Lady in Venice' who would walk barefoot to Palestine for a touch of Lodovico's 'nether lip' (TLN 3009–10), Desdemona's ventriloquizing of the lover's voice in the Willow Song: '*If I court mo women, you'le couch with mo men*' (TLN 3026), her questioning of Emilia about whether there can possibly be women who 'abuse their husbands / In such grosse kinde' (TLN 3032–3), and Emilia's extended declamation contending that 'it is their Husbands faults / If Wiues do fall', which claims for women the same passions and frailties as men have (TLN 3059–76). Lynda Boose and Michael Neill have emphasized the play's enlistment of the audience's capacity for a prurient, even pornographic, interest in the bedchamber of the two lovers – an interest that culminates in the eroticized sight of Desdemona's murder between her wedding sheets.[13] In F Iago even talks like the proprietor of a peep-show in his solicitation of Roderigo:

Didst thou not see her paddle with the palme of his hand? [Didst not marke that?]
Rod. Yes, [that I did:] but that was but curtesie.

(TLN 1035–8)

Did you get that? Yeah, yeah! The extra F-only words shape the passage in a way that suggests adolescent voyeurism. By hammering away at the topic of sexual transgression within the context of marriage between a Venetian and a Moor, by scratching away at a wound and continually reopening it, the formidable series of F-only passages outlined above helps to keep alive in the play an itch of sexual prurience that turns its audience much more decisively than does Q into complicitous voyeurs upon a scene of vice that is the more powerful because it is a figment of our (and Iago's, Roderigo's, and finally Othello's) imaginations.

What would Q look like without the sexual overlay of F? For one thing, the F-only passages put additional burdens on the tragic protagonist. As we have seen, in the F version of Act 1, Othello is defined as a deviant and lascivious outsider even before he appears on stage. Iago, Roderigo, and Brabantio constitute a miniature culture of xenophobia: while in Q it is possible to imagine Iago as the sole source of contagion, the effect in F is to intensify the social pressures against Othello's marriage. In the final two acts of the Folio version, the miniature culture of female domesticity and intimacy created by the Willow Scene, with its affectionate banter between the two women, and the concomitant expansion of Emilia's role at other points in the final scenes of F, similarly serve to create a society against which Othello is defined as aberrant. In Act 5 of the Folio version, Emilia protests much more vigorously against Othello's injustice and Iago's 'Villany' and threatens to kill herself 'for greefe' (TLN 3475–8); in F she dies addressing her dead mistress and echoing Desdemona's Willow Song, a telling reminder of the intimacy of the earlier scene:

Æmil. What did thy Song boad Lady?
Hearke, canst thou heare me? I will play the Swan,
And dye in Musicke: *Willough, Willough, Willough.*
(TLN 3545–7)

There is an important difference in functioning between the culture of xenophobia aimed against Othello at the beginning of the play and the fragile culture of female domesticity at the end of it. During the intervening acts, audience sympathies have been forced into realignment. The more Othello rants against Desdemona, the more he sacrifices the sympathy of bystanders within the play and also of the audience outside it. We have already noted how Roderigo's F-only speech defines the Moor as 'extravagant' and unsettled even before he comes on stage. It will come as no surprise that several other F-only passages serve to intensify our sense of Othello not as the urbane Venetian we briefly glimpse in 1.3 and at his arrival on Cyprus, but as a threatening outsider.

Much critical attention, especially in the last decade, has been devoted to the question of Othello's colour. Is he coal-black, as several lines from the play seem to suggest, or is he instead tawny or swarthy, like Shakespeare's 'Dark Lady' or like the Moorish ambassador to England whose portrait survives from his visit in 1600–1?[14] It has by now been established that there were numerous 'blackamoors' in England. For London audiences, the sight of black skin would not have been the monstrous anomaly earlier critics of the play assumed it would be. Queen Elizabeth's notorious edicts attempting to deport 'negars and blackamoors' – on grounds that they consumed scarce food needed by her own subjects in time of famine, that they were associated with the Spaniards at a time that England was at war against Spain, and that they were, in any case, Muslim or pagan infidels and therefore no part of the English Christian community – did not meet with success: many courtiers had black servants, and there are records of black property-holders and taxpayers in the period.[15] It is overwhelmingly likely that in seventeenth-century productions, Othello was portrayed as black, like Aaron in *Titus Andronicus*, for which we have Henry Peacham's sketched record of a scene as it appeared on stage, or like Queen Anne and her ladies when they appeared as blackamoors in *The Masque of Blackness*, which was performed at court on 6 January 1605, and which may well have been in rehearsal the previous November when *Othello* was performed at court.

Early audiences, it seems, liked their 'black' Moors to look black, but that leaves open the question of what stereotyped reactions they may have brought to the sight of that skin colour on stage. As part of the recent interest in race in *Othello*, critics have debated almost endlessly the potential associations of blackness in Elizabethan and early Jacobean culture.[16] It is easy to impose our own postcolonial, post-slavery associations of blackness with degradation upon a culture in which the constellation of structures that we view as constituting racism were only in process of coming together. What is less easy is to attempt to determine how a given cultural artefact might have functioned as part of an incipient discourse of racism.

The term 'racism' itself dates only from the 1930s, but the concept goes back much further. If we base ourselves upon George M. Fredrickson's recent definition, then Shakespeare's England was not quite racist. According to Fredrickson, racism exists when differences that 'might otherwise be considered ethnocultural are regarded as innate, indelible, and unchangeable' and are combined with efforts at exerting control over the stigmatized group. 'Racism, therefore, is more than theorizing about human differences or thinking badly of a group over which one has no control. It either directly sustains or proposes to establish *a racial order*, a permanent group hierarchy that is believed to reflect the laws of nature or the decrees of God.'[17] According to most readings of the play, *Othello* is not quite racist, in that it is capable of presenting, even if only briefly, a powerful portrait of a man who is marked by ethnocultural differences from the Venetians, but appears to be accepted by them because he has adopted the religion and ethos of the dominant group. In the words of the Duke to Brabantio,

'If virtue no delighted beauty lack / Your son-in-law is far more fair than black' (1.3.290–1).

In this view, Othello's black skin is a liability, but not a marker of 'innate difference' that demands subordination in a 'permanent group hierarchy'. What *Othello* does, and much more explicitly and powerfully in F than in Q, is enact a process by which skin colour comes to be associated even by Othello himself with innate differences that demand his subordination or exclusion. On this view, the play is a powerful laboratory in which many of the stereotyped racial attitudes that were to dominate later culture are allowed to coalesce. The play was enormously popular on stage during the seventeenth century, when imperial expansion and plantation slavery were becoming key elements of England's economic prosperity, and English racial attitudes were coming to be defined along colour lines. Small wonder that the controversy over quarto and Folio *Othello* has been placed on a back burner rather than receiving the attention it deserves as a parallel case to *King Lear*. If Shakespeare was the reviser who turned Q into F, then he revised in the direction of racial virulence.

The lines most frequently cited by modern critics to establish both the skin colour of Othello and its association with filth and moral turpitude exist only in the Folio version of the play. Here is the F passage from 3.3 in its broader context:

Oth. Nay stay: thou should'st be honest.
Iago. I should be wise; for Honestie's a Foole,
And looses that it workes for.
[*Oth*. By the World,
I thinke my Wife be honest, and thinke she is not:
I thinke that thou art iust, and thinke thou art not:
Ile haue some proofe. My name that was as fresh
As *Dians* Visage, is now begrim'd and blacke
As mine owne face. If there be Cords, or Kniues,
Poyson, or Fire, or suffocating streames,
Ile not indure it. Would I were satisfied.
Iago.] I see you are eaten vp with Passion:
                    (TLN 2026–37)

In Q, the issue is Iago's honesty – something that should indeed be subject to doubt – but in F, Othello expands the whole question of honesty into an interrogation of the relation between skin colour, reputation, and moral rectitude. In modern editions, 'My name' at TLN 2032 is almost always altered to 'Her name', following the second quarto of 1630, which has no particular textual authority but irons out the gender trouble of imagining a seasoned black warrior who can think of his name as resembling fair 'fresh' Diana's face. In this passage, an ugly demand for congruence between a 'fair' inside and a 'fair' outside begins to push Othello towards a mistaken self-imaging that blackens his name and nature to match his skin. Desdemona's purity is required for his own: if she is sullied, then what now look to us like racial stereotypes begin to click into place. In Q, by contrast, the language that associates 'black' with immorality is not reserved exclusively for Othello himself. One of the only passages in which Othello's language towards Desdemona in Q is harsher than it is in F – contrary to the pattern we have established above – is at 4.2.67, just before his accusations of 'whore' that we have already discussed. In Q Othello addresses Desdemona, 'O thou blacke weede, why art so louely faire?' (Sig. K4r, p. 824); the equivalent passage in F is 'Oh thou weed: / Who art so louely faire' (TLN 2762–3). Most modern editions follow the Folio and read simply 'weed'.[18] It is a minute difference, perhaps, but a key one in that it establishes a separability of blackness and skin colour in Q that does not exist in F.

Elsewhere in the Folio, what Fredrickson would call Othello's 'ethnocultural differences' are further negativized in ways that they are not in the quarto. Only in F does Brabantio reiterate to the Venetian Senate his conviction that Othello must have bound Desdemona in 'Chaines of Magick' in order to gain her love:

> Iudge me the world, if 'tis not grosse in sense,
> That thou hast practis'd on her with foule Charmes,
> Abus'd her delicate Youth, with Drugs or Minerals,
> That weakens Motion.
> (TLN 290–3)[19]

The 'foule Charmes' suggest heathen magic, but elsewhere in F Othello is strongly associated with the Muslim infidel. The famous lines in which he likens the icy current of his passion for revenge to the icy current of the 'Ponticke Sea' – running straight, swift, and 'compulsiue' through the Bosphorus past Istanbul into the Mediterranean – exist only in the Folio. They establish a connection to the Ottoman Turks whom his allegiance to Venice would require him to identify as the enemy (TLN 2103–12).

As Nevill Coghill was the first to notice, the F-only lines in the 'Ponticke Sea' speech, in which Othello kneels before Iago and protests the implacability of his lust for revenge, balance the F-only lines, cited earlier, in which Desdemona kneels before Iago to protest her innocence of the unspeakable crime of whoredom.[20] The parallel structure adroitly heightens our sense of utter contrast, to the point of disconnection, between the 'black' revenger and his 'fair' victim. Finally, at the very end of the play, as Othello attempts to justify his murder of Desdemona before the horrified Venetian onlookers, the Folio version alone includes lines that require the on-stage audience to recoil in horror from Othello's person, which by this point in the play has become dangerous, almost contagious. Only in F does he protest to his auditors, 'Be not affraid, though you do see me weapon'd' and again, three lines later, 'Do you go backe dismaid? 'Tis a lost feare' (TLN 3566, 3569). In Q, the primary focus of the speech is on his reaction to Desdemona's death – the pity of it! In F, the speech is divided between the lines on Desdemona and his perception of his own isolation from his erstwhile culture. As Arthur Little, Jr, has perceptively noted, *Othello enacts* Elizabeth's order for the deportation of 'negars and blackamoors' in that the tragic protagonist, who is at least tenuously accepted by powerful Venetians at the beginning of the action, dies in exile at the end, defined as irredeemably alien from it by a sequence of events that consolidate the audience's negative 'cognitive assonance to physical blackness'. Whatever it may have been at the beginning of the play, Othello's black skin at the end of it is indelibly associated with hypersexuality, predation upon white womanhood, demonism, and alien status.[21] And these connections are drawn with particular explicitness in the Folio. Through his suicide, Othello tries to undo the set of stereotypes that have so fatally clicked into place. But that action against the infidel 'Turk' he has become completes his 'exile' by relieving the dominant culture of the disturbing difference that his presence has represented.

Before the quarto version of *Othello* came to be viewed as Shakespeare's first version of the play, it was reviled in a language of miscegenation that demonstrates the unease textual scholars felt but could not directly express toward the more benign construction of racial difference offered in Q. Alice Walker, for example, records her dismay with the 'contamination' of the Folio, which has 'taken colour in linguistic forms' from the quarto: 'the pollution holds in the exchange'.[22] What she is subliminally reacting against, I would suggest, is the recognition that Q does not rein in the cultural danger represented by Othello's blackness and sexuality with anything like the virulence of F. Now, however, F is taken to be Shakespeare's revision of Q, and it is more common to encounter praise for the many felicities of F that are only embryonic in Q. We need to recognize the extent to which the more powerful language of F gains its special force through its strikingly concrete representations of the dangers of racial difference and its racheting up of racial conflict to – and some would say past – the limits of human endurance. It would, of course, be possible to rescue Shakespeare from the implications of this recognition, as Honigmann tried to do when he suggested that Shakespeare 'knew more about racism than modern critics have cared to admit',[23] the implication being that Shakespeare aired contemporary racial attitudes in order to critique them out of some greater and more refined sense of humanity. I have suggested, rather, that Shakespeare as a reviser of *Othello* was, in effect, himself written by shifting contemporary attitudes toward race. A similar shift takes place over time in the texts of *Titus Andronicus*: its Folio text includes a final four lines that do not exist in the first quarto of 1594. These four lines specify Aaron, the 'damn'd Moore / From whom, our heauy happes had their beginning' (TLN 2705–6) as the source of all the deaths, mutilations, and mutinies that Rome has suffered during the course of the play.

It is possible, of course, that the revision theory of *Othello* is in error, as Scott McMillin has recently contended, and that what have looked for the past several decades like additions to Q are instead cuts from an original Shakespearean version resembling F.[24] In that case, we are back in Alice Walker's territory, but able, we can hope, to view the issue of Q–F racial difference with a bit less obliquity and suppressed shame. If the F-only passages are cuts – and a strong argument can be made for that position – then someone – Shakespeare? his company? the Master of the Revels? – deliberately took out the most racially explicit passages of the play, presumably to meet the demands of a specific performance. One likely occasion might have been the inaugural performance of *Othello* at court in November 1604. There are numerous reasons why the King's Men might have wanted to tone down the racial virulence of the play at that particular time: *The Masque of Blackness* was about to be performed by the Queen and her ladies; James I had just formally concluded peace with Spain in August 1604, and an increased Spanish presence at court might make it wise to soften some of the play's most flamboyant language about Moors, blackness, and miscegenation.[25] What is most interesting about this alternative scenario is that it requires us to imagine Shakespeare or some other agent during the period as able to perceive and dampen the play's most virulent language of racial difference for the sake of a given performance while simultaneously preserving it for later performances, in which it might be expected to prove more palatable. Neither the reviser nor the cutter much resembles the 'gentle Shakespeare' we have been taught to know and love. But one thing is certain: we need to be able to study the Q–F differences in all their painful clarity in our modern editions, which presently obscure them.

NOTES

1. E. A. J. Honigmann, 'Shakespeare's Revised Plays, *King Lear* and *Othello*', *The Library* 6th series, 4 (1982), 142–73, 171.
2. Contrary to his usual pattern of thinking about the early quartos, W. W. Greg posited the Folio version of *Othello* as based on Shakespeare's own revisions of Q in *The Shakespeare First Folio* (Oxford: Clarendon Press, 1955), pp. 357–74. Nevill Coghill is credited by Honigmann with being the first reader to explain the Shakespearean revisions from Q to F in terms of their thematic implications in *Shakespeare's Professional Skills* (Cambridge University Press, 1964), pp. 164–202. Honigmann's *The Stability of Shakespeare's Text* (London: Edward Arnold, 1965), pp. 100–20 appeared too soon fully to acknowledge Coghill's arguments, which Honigmann treated in 'Shakespeare's Revised Plays', n. 1 above. See also Balz Engler, 'How Shakespeare Revised *Othello*', *English Studies* 57 (1976), 515–21, which extends Coghill's argument. For Honigmann's more recent work, which does not press the thematic arguments further, see his Arden3 edition of *Othello* (Walton-on-Thames: Thomas Nelson, 1997); and his *The Texts of 'Othello' and Shakespearean Revision* (London: Routledge, 1996).
3. The two recent editions of Q1 *Othello* are by Andrew Murphy (ed.), *The Tragoedy of Othello, The Moore of Venice* (Hemel Hempstead: Harvester Wheatsheaf, 1995); and Scott McMillin (ed.), *The First Quarto of Othello* (Cambridge University Press, 2001). McMillin, however, sees Q1 as an abridged performance version and Shakespeare's 'original' as more closely resembling F. Recent editors of the play who have made the differences between Q and F particularly accessible include Barbara A. Mowat and Paul Werstine (eds.), *Othello* (New York: Washington Square Press, 1993), which clearly marks Q-only and F-only passages in the text; and Norman Sanders (ed.), *Othello* (Cambridge University Press, 1984), which briefly summarizes Coghill and Honigmann's arguments in his 'Textual Analysis', pp. 193–207.
4. Stanley Wells and Gary Taylor, with John Jowett and William Montgomery, *William Shakespeare: A Textual Companion* (Oxford: Clarendon Press, 1987), p. 478.
5. Michael Billington in *The Guardian* (16 March 1989); as cited in Lois Potter, *Shakespeare in Performance: Othello* (Manchester University Press, 2002), p. 185.
6. Ania Loomba, '"Delicious Traffick": Racial and Religious Differences on Early Modern Stages', in *Shakespeare and Race*, ed. Catherine M. S. Alexander and Stanley Wells (Cambridge University Press, 2000), pp. 203–24, p. 203. See also Kim F. Hall, *Things of Darkness: Economies of Race and Gender in Early Modern England* (Ithaca: Cornell University Press, 1995); Margo Hendricks, 'Surveying "Race" in Shakespeare', in *Shakespeare and Race*, ed. Alexander and Wells, pp. 1–22; and Emily C. Bartels, '*Othello* and Africa: Postcolonialism Reconsidered', *The William and Mary Quarterly* 3rd series, 54 (1997), 45–64.

7. See Thomas L. Berger, 'The Second Quarto of *Othello* and the Question of Textual "Authority"', in *Othello: New Perspectives*, ed. Virginia Mason Vaughan and Kent Cartwright (London and Toronto: Associated University Presses, 1991), pp. 26–47.
8. Here and throughout, line numbers to the standard, conflated text of *Othello* are cited from Honigmann's Arden3 edition.
9. For parity with Folio citations, quarto citations are also given in facsimile, from Michael J. B. Allen and Kenneth Muir (eds.), *Shakespeare's Plays in Quarto* (Berkeley: University of California Press, 1981). Since this edition does not supply Through Line Numbers, citations are given by quarto signature number plus page number in the edition. The present citation is to p. 791.
10. See Coghill, *Shakespeare's Professional Skills*, pp. 180–2, Honigmann, 'Shakespeare's Revised Plays', 161, and Sanders (ed.), *Othello*, p. 203.
11. Honigmann, 'Shakespeare's Revised Plays', 164.
12. See especially Coghill, *Shakespeare's Professional Skills*, pp. 192–9.
13. See Michael Neill, 'Unproper Beds: Race, Adultery, and the Hideous in *Othello*', *Shakespeare Quarterly* 40 (1989), 383–412; and Lynda E. Boose, '"Let It Be Hid": Renaissance Pornography, Iago, and Audience Response', in *Autour d''Othello'*, ed. Richard Marienstras and Dominique Goy-Blanquet (Paris: Institut Charles V, 1987), pp. 135–43.
14. See Bernard Harris, 'A Portrait of a Moor' (1958), as reprinted in *Shakespeare and Race*, ed. Alexander and Wells, pp. 23–36; and Mythili Kaul's introduction to *Othello: New Essays by Black Writers* (Washington, DC: Howard University Press, 1997), pp. 1–19.
15. See, among many other studies, Peter Fryer, *Staying Power: Black People in Britain since 1504* (Atlantic Highlands, NJ: Humanities Press, 1984), pp. 1–32; Paul Edwards, 'The Early African Presence in the British Isles', in *Essays on the History of Blacks in Britain*, ed. Jagdish S. Gundara and Ian Duffield (Aldershot: Ashgate, 1992), pp. 9–29; and James Walvin, *The Black Presence: A Documentary History of the Negro in England, 1555–1860* (London: Orback and Chambers, 1971).
16. See, among many other studies, Loomba, '"Delicious Traffick"'; Hall, *Things of Darkness*; Fryer, *Staying Power*, pp. 135–46; Eldred D. Jones, *Othello's Countrymen: The African in English Renaissance Drama* (London: Oxford University Press, 1965); and Emily C. Bartels, 'Making More of the Moor: Aaron, Othello, and Renaissance Refashionings of Race', *Shakespeare Quarterly* 41 (1990), 433–54.
17. George M. Fredrickson, *Racism: A Short History* (Princeton University Press, 2002), pp. 5–6. I am also indebted to Kwame Anthony Appiah's review, *New York Times Book Review* (4 August 2002), 11–12, which agrees with Fredrickson's definition in general but urges more attention to the damage that racist ideology can do even in the hands of the powerless.
18. An exception is M. R. Ridley's Arden2 edition of *Othello* (London: Methuen, 1958), which, atypically for its time, uses the quarto as its copy-text and retains the reading 'black weed', p. 154.

19. See Coghill's discussion of thematically connected lines, *Shakespeare's Professional Skills*, pp. 183–5.
20. *Ibid.*, pp. 188–91.
21. See Arthur L. Little, Jr, *Shakespearean Jungle Fever: National–Imperial Re-Visions of Race, Rape, and Sacrifice* (Stanford University Press, 2000), pp. 85–6; and Michael Neill, '"Mulattos", "Blacks", and "Indian Moors": *Othello* and Early Modern Constructions of Human Difference', *Shakespeare Quarterly* 49 (1998), 361–74.
22. Alice Walker, *Textual Problems of the First Folio* (Cambridge University Press, 1953), p. 4.
23. Honigmann, *Othello*, p. 31.
24. See McMillin (ed.), *Othello*, pp. 13–44.
25. Jones, *Othello's Countrymen*, p. 30, notes that blackamoors, who commonly appeared as characters in other masques of the period, disappeared from the Tudor masque during the time of Spanish Philip and Mary Tudor, which suggests Spanish antipathy to the motif.

CHAPTER 2

'Work of permanent utility': editors and texts, authorities and originals

H. R. Woudhuysen

It is pleasantly appropriate for this collection of essays that the phrase quoted in the title, 'work of permanent utility', should be a reported one, perhaps even a memorial reconstruction or a shorthand note; for it is what W. W. Greg said that Alfred W. Pollard had said when the Malone Society was being set up in 1906:

> It was he [Pollard] who pointed out, what I believe to be the truth, that every generation will need to make its own critical editions to suit its own critical taste, but that work of permanent utility can be done by placing in the hands of students at large such reproductions of the original textual authorities as may make constant and continuous reference to those originals themselves unnecessary.[1]

Soon after the Malone Society was founded, Greg elaborated on the idea in a paper he read at a literary conference in Switzerland. Again, we only know at second hand what he said, and this time the reporter is Pollard. If the Malone Society carries out its programme, Greg argued, readers:

> will know that any serious student can work on the very materials they [the editors] themselves have used, not as now in a dozen different libraries, but in his own study. Each generation must be left to make its own critical editions according to its own taste and knowledge, but it ought not to be impossible to produce reprints of the original texts which shall be for practical purposes final.[2]

And this is more or less what the Malone Society has been trying to achieve for nearly a century. Even if we now might raise a quizzical eyebrow at the idea of 'texts which shall be for practical purposes final', it would be hard to maintain that the Society's hundred and sixty-five publications do not constitute 'work of permanent utility'.

The one major change of direction to its publishing programme has been a relatively recent one: since the 1984 volume which contained both *The Pardoner and the Friar* and *The Four Ps*, type-facsimiles of printed play-texts, in diplomatic or at least semi-diplomatic forms, have been more or less abandoned in favour of photo-facsimiles of printed plays. There are practical problems with type-facsimiles; it is difficult setting and proofing reprints of plays, especially ones originally printed in black-letter. But there is also something rather fake about type-facsimiles of plays: our modern desire for authenticity and originality feels embarrassed by something which is not really one thing or the other.[3] Photo-facsimiles, on the other hand, appear to give the reader the real thing – although we should be rightly sceptical of the cliché that the camera never lies. Yet this change of direction, which is meant to give members carefully chosen and edited photo-facsimiles, goes directly against what Greg reportedly said. He rejected using photography for the Society's volumes, because 'where an original is faulty it exaggerates its defects, often to the point of illegibility, whereas an editor by comparing two or more copies may be able to state the true reading quite decidedly'.[4] In other words, the editor's job was to edit, and Greg believed that publishing photographs of a printed book was not editing. Of course, in 1908 when he was speaking, some of the difficulties which we associate with photo-facsimiles, chiefly the problem of the variant forme with its different stages of press correction, were largely unexplored.[5] Later on, with his usual pithiness, Greg was to sum up the problems of facsimile reproduction: 'photographic reproductions are reliable but illegible, reprints are legible but unreliable'.[6] Yet Greg's arguments raise questions which it might be worth thinking about, not just in relation to the Malone Society and its publications but in relation to larger editorial and theoretical issues.

In a sense the Society has always had slightly divided aims. We do not know what Greg and McKerrow discussed as undergraduates at Trinity College, Cambridge, at the end of the nineteenth century, when they began to think about the problems of editing and annotating English Renaissance literature. So we must judge them on what they actually produced. It is Greg's hand which is so clearly behind the nearly ninety volumes – an astonishing number – which the Society produced in the thirty-three years that he acted as its general editor from 1906 to 1939, and I think that those volumes, as later ones do, reveal two strains. There is a concern with purely textual matters in printed and manuscript plays and dramatic pieces, but there is also a careful programme for the publication of documents and of material intended to allow the history of English drama to be written. What unites these two strains are the extraordinarily high standards of accuracy and correct scholarship that were brought to them, and which the Society still tries to maintain. The Malone Society's publications were particularly unusual and valuable because its concern with recording and reproducing the inked marks of a text was more elaborate and comprehensive than that of almost any other editions or series of the first half of the last century.

'Accuracy', as Housman dryly noted, 'is a duty not a virtue':[7] Malone editors and general editors have been more or less dutiful as their time, circumstances, and abilities allowed them. Greg himself was not always as impeccable as one might think: Trevor Howard-Hill has written about Greg's failure in his 1909 Malone edition of the manuscript of *The Second Maiden's Tragedy* to note marginal markings in the play. 'All this marginal pother', these 'marginal trivialities', as Howard-Hill calls them, are signs of Sir George Buc's reading of the manuscript in his role as Master of the Revels, and should have been recorded in his edition, but were not.[8] Greg's failure to note these marks touches on the Society's divided aims, which I have just mentioned. Unlike Howard-Hill ('His blindness was wilful'), I do not think Greg was deliberately suppressing evidence or merely being careless. Instead, he clearly saw the marginal markings as later, modern additions which were not part of the play's original purpose or function. Rather, they provided evidence of its subsequent reception history, and Greg was concerned with the manuscript play's textual transmission alone: he was editing the plays as literary works in manuscript, not as dramatic documents of the kind he was to examine in his two-volume study of *Dramatic Documents from the Elizabethan Playhouses* (Oxford University Press, 1931).

This incident raises the main question which I want to discuss here. When editors prepare texts of plays by Shakespeare and his contemporaries, what exactly are they editing? We may have become sceptical about the possibility, or even the wish, to get back to the 'original', to detect the 'true reading', but we still have a sense of wanting to own or to read the real thing, whatever it might be. As the title-pages of several plays show, this is not a new sense. The second quarto of *Hamlet*, for example, declares that it is printed 'according to the true and perfect Coppie'; *The Duchess of Malfi* in 1623 reproduces 'The perfect and exact Coppy', and in the same year *The Devil's Law Case* is similarly 'The true and perfect Copie from the Originall'. These, then, are true, perfect, exact, and authentic versions of the plays, but they are also just copies: they can never actually reproduce the original itself, but can only represent it in a more or less faithful way.

One of the last century's most valuable advances in our understanding of the transmission of Shakespeare's texts was our evolving sense of what constitutes that original of which printed and manuscript play-texts can only be copies. For Malone Society editors the answer to the question 'What is being edited?' is a fairly straightforward one: it is the physical object which embodies the play in manuscript or in print that is being edited. Other sorts of editors may not be able to give such a definite and straightforward answer. For like almost all works of literature, the text of a play is not the play itself, but simply a collection of instructions for how it might be reconstituted or performed – in the same way a musical score is not the piece of music itself, but a set of directions which suggest how the piece might be played.[9] If the Malone editor is editing a text, then the Shakespeare editor could be said to be editing a work – of course the work may be based on one or more texts, but it is the work as a sort of Platonic idea that is at issue.

'Text' and 'work': these are, of course, not uncomplicated terms and can be subject to a wide range of meanings and definitions (including Roland Barthes's neat inversion of them, 'The Work is in your hand, the text in the language').[10] Yet most people understand that reading an edition of *Hamlet* is different from reading an edition of the second quarto of the play, or for that matter a facsimile of it, or the original. As Trevor Howard-Hill has said, 'The great generality of readers – and I would include university teachers as well as students in that category – wish to read works, not editions.'[11] The distinction can be elaborated in G. Thomas Tanselle's discussions of the subject. 'Historians', he has written, 'may more often find themselves producing diplomatic texts of particular *documents* . . . and scholars of literature (both ancient and modern) may more often be engaged in constructing critical texts of *works*.'[12] Texts, he argues, are 'made up of inked marks that conform to the notation scheme for a particular language'; documents are the physical embodiment of what passes between author, scribe or compositor, and the reader. The text of a document is tangible, whereas the text of a work is intangible, existing only in the author's or the reader's mind.[13]

To some this may all be rather elementary stuff, expressed in characteristically carefully chosen words, but it does touch on a real difficulty. For, while trying to reproduce the work, editors of plays necessarily have to put all their faith in one or sometimes two or more documents. So it is not surprising to see inexperienced, and even some experienced editors, printing 'Finis' or 'The End' at the end of plays – a feature of the document, not the work – because the word or words are present in a quarto or folio; I myself plead guilty to doing this. There is more to this problem than just looking to see whether the editor does go in for faithfully reproducing such a feature of a text or not, but it is a convenient way of thinking about it. Furthermore, while torn between the work and the document, editors have gone through terrible contortions in trying to define what sort of version of the work they are or should be editing. The usual answers to the question of what editors are editing range from the play as it left the author's hands in his own manuscript, to the play as it might have been performed by his contemporaries, to the play as it is preserved in one or more printed or manuscript forms, to the play as it might be made accessible for reading and/or performance at the present time.

All of these theories of editing have, and have had, their advocates (as well as their critics), and there is a sufficient demand for different types of editions of plays for editors to produce editions based on some or all of them. For example, in the Oxford Shakespeare Stanley Wells and Gary Taylor set the fashion for performance-based editions of the plays, which usually draw on the so-called 'promptbook' texts preserved in the First Folio. This was a reaction to the more traditional approach of the Arden2 and New Cambridge Shakespeare, which sought to return to the author's (equally) so-called 'foul papers'. The current single-volume editions of plays published in the Oxford, Cambridge, and Arden3 series all more or less follow the Wells–Taylor Oxford Shakespeare approach, and seek to establish performance-based texts. This reaction may seem a reasonable one; after all, Shakespeare was a man of the theatre and it is more or less sensible to argue that his plays were written for performance, and that it is in performance that they are most fully realized as works of art.

This preference for performance-based texts has not gone unchallenged. Shakespeare the engaged and sociable man of the theatre is as much a projection of our age and tastes as is, or was, Shakespeare the aloof and cold poet for whom no performance of any of his plays could ever adequately represent them. We can never know for certain whether he really was content with changes made to his scripts in the course of rehearsal or performance. What we take to be the performance texts that have come down to us may not represent what was 'usually' performed in Shakespeare's time, but be specific versions for specific casts, places, and occasions.[14] There is a further nagging difficulty: if we are really going to opt for Folio texts of, say, *Hamlet* or *Troilus*, are we to suppose that these long plays were performed in their Folio texts completely uncut? If we truly want to embrace performance texts, would it not be more realistic to suppose that these plays (and others) were never, or not always, or only sometimes performed in their entirety, so that strictly speaking an editor should print shortened versions of them? This point was made, rather more elegantly, by McKerrow in his *Prolegomena for the Oxford Shakespeare*, when he argued that: 'it is very doubtful whether, especially in the case of the earlier plays, there ever existed any written "final form" . . . We must not expect to find a definitive text in the sense in which the published version of the plays of a modern dramatist is definitive.'[15] The plurality of different Shakespeare editions, a plurality which is being extended to Jonson and may one day even reach to Middleton, allows some of these difficulties to be avoided. 'No one critical text', Tanselle has pointed out, 'can be the best one from everyone's point of view or for all purposes.'[16]

If all editions can only ever be approximate, if they can only ever be copies of an unrecoverable original, then all editions, and for that matter all performances, betray the work itself. The editorial task is to lay the materials as faithfully as possible before the reader, so that a text can be constructed according to differing sets of uses and requirements. This approach has found particular favour with editors of poems from the Romantic period. There is no 'right' or 'correct' text of a work, only greater or lesser betrayals of it. The editorial choices which lie behind editions of plays, and the material forms which those editions take, of necessity falsify the plays themselves. This is, more or less, the argument of those – among them, Margreta de Grazia, Peter Stallybrass, and, of course, Leah Marcus – who find what has become known as 'unediting' so attractive. 'Unediting' is based on a variety of versioning, and in a supposedly radical and democratic way takes authority away from the editor, returning it to the reader who is free to choose whatever sort of text he or she may want. The editorial pessimism of the 'uneditors' leads them to take advantage of what Jack Stillinger has wittily called '"no-fault" editing', or what Tanselle might rather more soberly dub 'noncritical' scholarly editions.[17]

What seems to lie behind the reasoning of the proponents of unediting is a fairly simple equation between editing and literary theory. Since we no longer believe that any edition can be faithful to the supposed original, let alone be 'definitive', we adopt the view that no edition is or can be better than any other – and this is not unlike literary theory's assault on literature and value, its attempted abolition or revision of the canon. But I also think that the new technology has had an influence on this nervousness about editing. Electronic texts can make a whole range of different versions accessible, and even allow the user to create a new or different version at will.

Despite the superficial attraction of the idea, I wish to argue that there can be no such thing as an 'unedited' text. As a solution to the question of what is being edited, advocates of 'unediting' appear to take the problem away from the editor, who may be presumed to have some expertise and even, occasionally, a mild interest in the theoretical and practical problems involved, and place it in the hands of a user who may not know how to proceed. If we look at electronic archives and websites, at the simplest level they inevitably involve choices and hierarchies of some kind: there is bound to be some controlling design which makes certain assumptions, pushing the user in certain directions. Electronic texts are too obviously manipulated to convince most people that they are 'unedited'; the growing availability of Early English Books Online will, perhaps, play some part in making us rethink our attitudes to the possibilities offered by electronic editions.

Instead, it is the allegedly obsolete technology of the book which seems at first to offer 'uneditors' the greatest opportunities. Here the name that springs to mind is that of Michael Warren and his magnificent work on *King Lear*.[18] Despite some valiant rearguard fighting by R. A. Foakes and Richard Knowles among others, all the bickering and squabbling over whether Shakespeare did revise *King Lear* has led to a too rarely articulated sense that *Lear* as a work can never be recovered (because it never was a single work), and that only the relevant documents which preserve versions of it can be edited. So we are lucky enough to have been offered facsimiles of Q and F, old-spelling as well as modernized versions of them, and parallel-text editions: Stephen Greenblatt in his Norton volume can slip in a conflated version of the play, and in the Arden3 series R. A. Foakes has produced an 'edition that seeks to give an idea of the work, while making the major differences between the versions easily recognizable'.[19] Yet the question remains, slightly altered, but still there: when editors prepare these editions of particular documents, what exactly are they editing? This takes us back to the Malone Society and its move away from semi-diplomatic type-facsimiles to photo-facsimiles.

In several of his later writings Fredson Bowers touched on some of these problems. Cheaper and better forms of reproduction, he argued in 1987, mean that 'the convenience of diplomatic reprints of printed texts has been diminished and that of type-facsimiles destroyed'. But then in the same footnote, he neatly modified this view: 'for reading but not for most bibliographical investigations a careful diplomatic reprint of an early printed text has some virtues missing in a photographic reproduction'.[20] We might say that the editor of Dekker, Beaumont and Fletcher, and Marlowe would think that, wouldn't he: photo-facsimiles are useful for some bibliographical work, but real editing involves diplomatic reprints. Of course, what lies behind this argument is what Tanselle said, which I have already quoted, and am paraphrasing here: that historians produce diplomatic texts of particular *documents*, but literary scholars construct critical texts of *works*.[21] The editor of a facsimile cannot and must not alter the text of the play being reproduced to construct a critical edition; the editor of a type-facsimile or a semi-diplomatic edition of a play can and perhaps must do so.

The difficulty lies in how far an editor should go in emending or tidying up a text. This was the problem which faced editors of the older Malone volumes: to preserve a misprint seems unhelpful, but to correct it is to move away from editing the document to constructing a critical text of the work. In addition to misprints, there remains the irritating problem with those variant formes (corrected or uncorrected?), and the even more awkward occasions of missing speech prefixes and stage directions or the correction of obvious errors. An editor can – Malone editors have – printed lists of errors that would have been corrected if it were that sort of edition, but who wants to read a play whose evident nonsense can only be sorted out by looking elsewhere in the volume? Yet if errors are to be corrected, where should the editor stop and how confident can we be that *this* is an error but *that* is not?

The answer to that opens, I suspect, another can of worms. The late Kenneth Muir asked 'whether it is really possible to establish a reliable text without being able to explain every line of it', and Bowers wrote of 'the necessity [for the editor] to paraphrase every line of an Elizabethan dramatist (and particularly, Shakespeare)'.[22] Paraphrasing a line and explaining what it means are not always quite the same thing, but the fact remains that despite three centuries of work by some of the greatest literary geniuses and scholars of several continents, there are numerous passages in Shakespeare's plays and poems whose meaning is still not fully understood or has been silently passed over and awaits some explanation. If this is so for Shakespeare, what hope can there be for, say, *Dick of Devonshire* or *The Hog Hath Lost his Pearl*? If you refuse to explain why a reading is wrong, then you cannot really change it: this was a conundrum Bowers faced in his editions of Renaissance dramatists, one which some of his critics felt he never quite successfully resolved.

The document, then, must be left just as it is and, in theory at least, a photo-facsimile interferes less with the original than a type-facsimile: authenticity comes as standard. I am not at all certain of this, but will return to it below. Instead I would like to take up the question of what is being edited by turning again to Tanselle. 'If one is interested in a text as it appeared at a particular time to a particular audience,' he has written, 'a diplomatic or facsimile edition of it serves the purpose best.'[23] This is a more suggestive remark than it might at first appear, for it implicitly leaves out the author or what we may want to call the author-function from the process. So that, during all these years the Malone Society has been producing editions which have been at the cutting-edge of literary and editorial theory. For, in a sense, by reproducing documentary texts in facsimiles of various kinds, the Society has been reproducing socialized not authorial ones.[24] And this is exactly what has been advocated by scholars as distinguished as the late D. F. McKenzie and Jerome J. McGann.

Although addressing slightly different audiences, and although their published comments on each other's works were surprisingly few, McGann's and McKenzie's approaches to the socialization of the text are broadly similar. Their versions of materiality necessarily play down the idea that there is something special about the role of the author: they are anti-intentionalists. All authors are, we have to remember, more or less dead. The theatre emerges as *the* site for the production of socialized and collaborative works – that is why, following the Oxford Shakespeare, we like 'promptbooks' not 'foul papers'. Although the sense that plays must be thought about as socialized collaborative performances has never been stronger, it remains legitimate to ask what a socialized edition of one of Shakespeare's plays would actually look like. David C. Greetham, who might be thought naturally sympathetic to such a project, has argued, 'you cannot actually *produce* a social textual edition'.[25] I am no longer entirely sure about this, and wonder in fact whether the facsimile is not exactly just such 'a social textual edition'. For if, in what has become known as early modern England, the theatre is *the* site for the production of socialized and collaborative works, the other site is the printing shop. That is largely due to the work of D. F. McKenzie who, in his celebrated article 'Printers of the Mind' and elsewhere, pointed out the fallacy of looking at the single book on its own as it passed through the printing shop. Printed books, he argued, are produced out of a series of complicated and overlapping operations located within a highly developed social and economic network of relations.[26]

It should follow that the closest we can come to the supposed ideal of 'a social textual edition' is, if not the original document, then an exact facsimile of it. However, photographic facsimiles are notoriously unreliable. Photographs may distort and obscure; printers may clean up and even alter text (as in the notorious Kökeritz Yale facsimile of the First Folio); the wrong edition, even a nineteenth-century reprint, may be chosen for reproduction; the very paper on which a facsimile is printed may alter the work's appearance.[27] Even if these traps for the unwary are avoided, there is still the problem of what to do about those variant formes. Every facsimile poses textual and editorial problems: from the selection of the copy or copies to be reproduced, to how to deal with its distinctive features and faults. What do you do about blank pages? Are the lines of the text to be numbered, and if so how and where? In this light the facsimile looks slightly less attractive as the perfect vehicle for the 'unedited' and socialized text. For facsimiles are themselves editions, involving a whole range of editorial and critical choices, and the dream of an unmediated text is no more than a dream.

It gets worse. In a very good, but too little known, article Joseph A. Dane has pointed out some of the fallacies and problems associated with facsimile editions. 'A "book" is a material object,' he states, and 'by its very nature non-reproducible. The only part of a book that is reproducible is a text.'[28] His point is a simple one, that a facsimile can only describe the paper, the ink or the minute individual characteristics of particular types used in the making of a book: it cannot reproduce them. In this sense books themselves cannot be facsimiled; like paintings only certain features of their appearance can be reproduced, and the copy remains no more than partial. Dane takes a step back from the usual argument about corrected as against uncorrected formes, and points out that in the most famous and widely used Shakespeare facsimile, Hinman created a First Folio which was essentially a made-up copy, of a kind that a bibliographer should hate: it conforms to no known copy and so does not represent a historical record of something that ever existed. This is because Hinman took the single page from a wide range of Folger copies as his unit for reproduction. At least Michael Warren in his *King Lear* took the forme, and so produced an ideal copy of a kind which the printer might have actually made. Warren's facsimiles are rooted in some sort of reality, even if it is the reality of what just happens to have survived.[29]

What seems to me the strongest objection to the thinking that facsimiles are the way forward for those who want to unedit the Renaissance comes from David Bevington's review of the Hinman facsimile. Bevington pointed out that facsimiles tend to transfer what the author intended to write to what the printer intended to create.[30] Of course these terms will seem suspicious to some, and for them the double socialization of theatre and printing shop is, presumably, doubly attractive. But it can only be attractive to someone who is interested in a play from a bibliographical or from a reception-history point of view. It is a nice irony of our times that it is the name of that poor old author-function Shakespeare which sells series rather than the socialized and collaborative elements in his dramatic texts.

Facsimiles are immensely useful for certain specific purposes, but we should constantly bear in mind the limitations of what they are and what they can do. The material features of an early quarto or folio will always be of great interest to readers, scholars, and editors, but a facsimile can only

Editors and texts, authorities and originals 47

reproduce some of these. It certainly cannot in itself bring the user closer to what the author may be supposed to have written. Facsimiles are editions, and there can be no such thing as 'no-fault editing'. However, facsimiles can only reproduce the texts of documents created at a particular moment, by a particular group of men, directed at a particular audience. There is still another world, and space enough in it for the critical editing of works.

NOTES

1. W. W. Greg, '"Facsimile" Reprints of Old Books', *The Library* 4th series, 6 (1925–6), 321; the passage is quoted in part by F. P. Wilson, 'The Malone Society: the First Fifty Years, 1906–56', in *Collections* IV (Oxford: The Malone Society, 1956), p. 2, and again by John Russell Brown, 'The Rationale of Old-Spelling Editions of the Plays of Shakespeare and his Contemporaries', *Studies in Bibliography* 13 (1960), 50.
2. A. W. Pollard, 'Notes of Books and Work', *The Library* n.s., 9 (1908), 111.
3. Cf. James McLaverty, 'Facsimiles and the Bibliographer: Pope's *Dunciad*', *Review* 15 (1993), 1.
4. Pollard, 'Notes of Books and Work', 111.
5. Fredson Bowers, 'The Problem of the Variant Forme in a Facsimile Edition', *The Library* 5th series, 7 (1952), 262–72.
6. Greg, '"Facsimile" Reprints', 322.
7. A. E. Housman, *Collected Poems and Selected Prose*, ed. Christopher Ricks (London: Allen Lane, The Penguin Press, 1988), p. 386.
8. T. H. Howard-Hill, 'Marginal Markings: the Censor and the Editing of Four English Promptbooks', *Studies in Bibliography* 36 (1983), 176, 177; the following quotation occurs on p. 171.
9. Cf. G. Thomas Tanselle, 'Editing without a Copy-Text', *Studies in Bibliography* 47 (1994), 1–22, reprinted in *Literature and Artifacts* (Charlottesville: The Bibliographical Society of the University of Virginia, 1998), pp. 236–57, esp. p. 240.
10. See Louis Hay, 'Does "Text" Exist?', *Studies in Bibliography* 41 (1988), 64–76, esp. 67–8.
11. T. H. Howard-Hill, 'Modern Textual Theories and the Editing of Plays', *The Library* 6th series, 11 (1989), 114.
12. G. Thomas Tanselle, 'Classical, Biblical, and Medieval Textual Criticism and Modern Editing', *Studies in Bibliography* 36 (1983), 27–8.
13. G. Thomas Tanselle, 'Textual Instability and Editorial Idealism', *Studies in Bibliography* 49 (1996), 1–60, esp. 43 and n.76.
14. See, for example, George Walton Williams's review of the Oxford Shakespeare in *Cahiers Elisabéthains* 35 (1989), 107, and Janette Dillon, 'Is There a Performance in this Text?', *Shakespeare Quarterly* 45 (1994), 74–86.
15. Ronald B. McKerrow, *Prolegomena for the Oxford Shakespeare: A Study in Editorial Method* (Oxford: Clarendon Press, 1939), p. 6.

16. G. Thomas Tanselle, 'Historicism and Critical Editing', *Studies in Bibliography* 39 (1986), 36.
17. Jack Stillinger, *Multiple Authorship and the Myth of Solitary Genius* (Oxford University Press, 1991), p. 82; cf. G. Thomas Tanselle, 'Recent Editorial Discussion and the Central Questions of Editing', *Studies in Bibliography* 34 (1981), 23–65, esp. 60–2.
18. *The Complete King Lear 1608–1623*, prepared by Michael Warren (Berkeley: University of California Press, 1989).
19. R. A. Foakes (ed.), *King Lear* (London: Thomas Nelson, 1997), p. 119.
20. Fredson Bowers, 'Readability and Regularization in Old-Spelling Texts of Shakespeare', *Huntington Library Quarterly* 50 (1987), 221 n.4.
21. Tanselle, 'Classical, Biblical, and Medieval Textual Criticism', 27–8.
22. Muir is quoted by S. Schoenbaum in *Shakespeare and Others* (Washington and London: Folger Books, 1985), p. 268; Fredson Bowers, 'The Problem of Semi-Substantive Variants: an Example from the Shakespeare–Fletcher *Henry VIII*', *Studies in Bibliography* 43 (1990), 89.
23. Tanselle, 'Classical, Biblical, and Medieval Textual Criticism', 48.
24. Cf. G. Thomas Tanselle, 'Textual Criticism and Literary Sociology', *Studies in Bibliography* 44 (1991), 83–143, esp. 142–3.
25. D. C. Greetham, *Theories of the Text* (Oxford University Press, 1999), p. 396; one of the best considerations of the practical editorial consequences of these problems is Peter L. Shillingsburg, 'An Inquiry into the Social Status of Texts and Modes of Textual Criticism', *Studies in Bibliography* 42 (1989), 55–79, esp. pp. 60–8; see also Tanselle, 'Textual Criticism and Literary Sociology', esp. pp. 140–2.
26. D. F. McKenzie, 'Printers of the Mind: Some Notes on Bibliographical Theories and Printing House Practices', *Studies in Bibliography* 22 (1969), 1–75.
27. Cf. F. B. Williams, 'Photo-Facsimiles of *STC* Books: a cautionary Check List', *Studies in Bibliography* 21 (1968), 109–30; Fredson Bowers, 'The Yale Folio Facsimile and Scholarship', *Modern Philology* 53 (1955), 50–7.
28. Joseph A. Dane, '"Ideal Copy" versus "Ideal Texts": the Application of Bibliographical Description to Facsimiles', *Papers of the Bibliographical Society of Canada* 33 (1995), 32.
29. *Ibid.*, 42, 44.
30. David Bevington, review of the Hinman facsimile of the First Folio, *Modern Philology* 68 (1970), 98–100.

CHAPTER 3

Housmania: episodes in twentieth-century 'critical' editing of Shakespeare

Paul Werstine

In 1903 appeared an obscure edition of the first book of *M. Manilii Astronomica* published at his own expense by the Professor of Latin at University College, London, A. E. Housman. Its introduction often descended to the 'scurrilous' (to use its editor's own later characterization of his tone),[1] particularly in its polemic against editorial methods then current in Germany, where editors faced with different manuscript traditions of the same work sought to establish their text of the work by following the superior manuscript tradition. Comparing such an editor to 'a donkey between two bundles of hay' who 'confusedly imagines that if one bundle of hay is removed he will cease to be a donkey', Housman denounced as arbitrary any editorial decision to regard one manuscript as better than another:

> he [the editor as donkey] pretends that they [the manuscripts] are not equal: he calls one of them 'the best MS' . . . He adopts its readings when they are better than its fellow's, adopts them when they are no better, adopts them when they are worse: only when they are impossible, or rather when he perceives their impossibility, is he dislodged from his refuge and driven by stress of weather to the other port.[2]

By 1942, the reputation of Housman's once obscure edition had been much enhanced by his subsequent long and industrious career as a textual critic and editor, so that W. W. Greg, looking back on the words I have quoted, could then characterize them as Housman's 'famous assault upon the ineluctable authority of the "best" manuscript'.[3] This is only one of several references in Greg's work to Housman's views, to which Greg appears to have been, on the whole, rather cool, recognizing that Housman sometimes obscured textual problems in his efforts to open up within texts as many places as he could for the exercise of his own often dazzling yet intuitive judgement in the act of emendation.[4] To praise him, Housman's fellow classicists linked him to Richard Bentley (1662–1742), long highly regarded as an earlier brilliant emender;[5] Greg too introduced his extensive comment on Housman's method by invoking Bentley, but, for Greg, as a student of vernacular texts, the association was, if anything pejorative: 'as Pope rewrote Shakespeare, ... Bentley re-wrote Milton'.[6] While Greg opposed free play of editorial judgement, his frequent reference to Housman indicates the pressure he felt to devise an editorial method for Shakespeare that could escape the great classicist's strictures against best-text editing.[7] Greg's efforts, however, to squirm from the lash of Housman's polemic brought him, by the late 1930s, into collision with 'the most formative influence on his life', R. B. McKerrow.[8] Their opposition can still be read today by juxtaposing McKerrow's 1939 *Prolegomena for the Oxford Shakespeare* (the preface to which is dated 22 December 1938)[9] with Greg's 1942 *The Editorial Problem in Shakespeare*, based on lectures first delivered in the early spring of 1939, only two or three months after McKerrow completed *Prolegomena*. In the preface to *Prolegomena*, McKerrow notes his debt 'to my friend W. W. Greg, who very kindly read this introduction in its first form as long ago as 1933 or 1934, and with whom I have since discussed many of the matters of editorial practice with which it is concerned',[10] thus alerting his readers to the places in *Prolegomena* where he takes issue with Greg. This controversy between scholarly friends would be of merely historical interest were it not that it is being replayed, with a difference, in the present volume, as Greg's innovation in response to Housman, sharply challenged by the more conservative McKerrow, is again, after a long ascendancy, being challenged and, in response, defended by those who seek to conserve it. Study of this controversy will also enable us to avoid imposing on early twentieth-century Shakespeare textual scholarship the false unity and uniformity of F. P. Wilson's label 'the New Bibliography'.[11]

Departing from the 'best-text' editing reviled by Housman, while at the same time shunning the uncontrolled eclecticism Housman practised, Greg devised an editorial method that has subsequently been dignified by the name 'critical' editing. Although not fully articulated until Greg's 'The Rationale for Copy-Text' published in 1950–1, the method is already in evidence in Greg's Clark Lectures as published in *The Editorial Problem*. Greg's editorial method depends upon the identification, in quite specific terms, of the now lost manuscript copy that once lay behind an early printing of a Shakespeare play as either Shakespeare's 'foul papers' or a 'promptbook'. As Greg would write in 1956, looking back, 'it came gradually to be assumed, perhaps without much critical investigation, that these [now lost manuscripts that served as printer's copy] were as a rule either prompt copies or else what were called "foul papers"'; he then went on to distinguish between his two categories by declaring that 'foul papers' contained 'the text substantially in the shape in which the author intended it to stand, but not in fair enough form to serve as a promptbook'.[12] In 1939 as he delivered the lectures that were to become *The Editorial Problem in Shakespeare*, his confidence in an editor's ability to distinguish between Shakespeare playtexts printed from 'foul papers' and from 'promptbooks' depended entirely on 'Dover Wilson['s] . . . monograph on *The Manuscripts of Shakespeare's 'Hamlet'* . . . [,] by far the most exhaustive and penetrating study of the authoritative texts'; in the case of other plays surviving in multiple early printed versions, 'there is, so far as I am aware, no obvious clue to the relative authority of the editions, but this may of course only be due to their having been less closely studied'.[13]

In practising what would come to be called 'critical' editing as Greg conceptualized it, editors would emulate Wilson, choosing as the basis for an edition not the text that was more or most free of obvious error, as the 'best-text' editorial method would require, but the text that seemed from an inferential reconstruction of its history to preserve Shakespeare's 'foul papers'. Inevitably, at least in some cases, Greg's 'critical' method would lead to a different choice of early printed text from the 'best-text' method because, ironically, the very obvious errors that caused texts to be shunned by 'best-text' editors constituted the distinctive marks of a text printed from 'foul papers'. As Greg wrote,

If a play was printed from the author's original draft, we may expect to find in it contradictions and uncertainties of action and unresolved textual tangles; if, on the other hand, a play was printed from a theatrical fair copy, we may indeed expect to find such contradictions and tangles smoothed out, but we have no assurance that this was done by the author himself.[14]

Nevertheless, according to Greg in 'The Rationale', one would not be obliged to throw away, like Housman's donkey's second bundle of hay, the text thought to derive from the 'theatrical fair copy'; instead one could evaluate its variant readings and emend the 'foul papers' text whenever a reading from this 'fair copy' appeared in one's editorial judgement to be worthy of attribution to Shakespeare in the course of what might be inferred to be his revision of the play.[15] Thus Greg sought to curb but not eliminate the operation of editorial judgement so prized by Housman.

Greg's conversations with McKerrow on these issues must have been lively, for McKerrow took pains in his *Prolegomena* to reject the very notion of 'foul papers' and to repudiate Wilson's study of *Hamlet* upon which Greg so heavily relied. For McKerrow, an editor would have to be credulous to believe he could attain 'any close approach to the author's manuscript' because Shakespeare wrote his plays not to be printed as literature but to be performed in the theatre, where they must be supposed vulnerable to 'modification' and 'revision' by 'others'.[16] In addition, McKerrow was profoundly sceptical about accepting 'errors and inconsistencies', which Greg took to be the signs of 'foul papers' lying behind a printed text, as certain evidence of an author's 'mere carelessness or indifference'. McKerrow knew that other agents in the playhouse and the printing house stood between Shakespeare and the Shakespeare books we read, and he knew that these other agents were just as likely to be responsible for the mistakes that Wilson and Greg after him sought to visit on the author alone.[17] Undeterred by the possibility of having Housman's scurrility quoted against him, McKerrow determined that when confronted with multiple early printed texts (none of them simply reprints), an editor's duty, as a rule, would be to choose as the basis for an edition 'the most careful copy of its original and the most free from obvious errors', and to depart from this copy only when its readings 'appear to be certainly corrupt'.[18] Sadly, whatever further debate with Greg McKerrow may have provoked by taking this stand against his friend was silenced by McKerrow's death on 20 January 1940.

Greg's bitter disappointment at his inability to persuade his newly lost friend to agree with Wilson's conclusions regarding the *Hamlet* texts and to believe in the method by which Wilson arrived at them is registered in Greg's 1941 attack on *Prolegomena*, rhetorically masked as a correction of McKerrow's views. Greg declared that it was 'a blemish in McKerrow's work' that McKerrow had abandoned 'investigations into the relationship of extant texts to one another and into the nature of their immediate sources'.[19] This failure had led him, according to Greg, to the 'unsatisfactory' principle of preferring as the basis for an edition whatever text was 'the most careful copy of its original'. Greg opined that adherence to such a principle would have required McKerrow to select 'a carefully edited "report", accurately printed' over 'a careless print of difficult "foul papers"' – or over precisely what Greg sought to elevate to the text of choice for a 'critical' editor.[20] It took much time and effort before Greg's model for 'critical' editing became the standard. As late as 1955 Fredson Bowers, who, together with G. Thomas Tanselle, deserves the lion's share of the credit for elevating 'critical' editing to the status it once enjoyed, found it worth his time again to attack McKerrow's *Prolegomena* for the same alleged faults that Greg had noted.[21]

To gauge the success of the late twentieth century's experiment with 'critical' editing is to evaluate the validity of editorial identifications of the manuscript copy that is alleged to lie behind particular early printed texts.

The practice, insofar as Greg endorsed it, begins, as I said above, with Wilson's study of *Hamlet*, and Wilson begins by comparing specific places in the second quarto of 1604–5 (Q2) to their counterparts in the Folio of 1623 (F). According to Wilson, some places in Q2 self-evidently preserve both Shakespeare's first shot at an expression and his second thought, both produced in such careless haste as to leave the first shot unerased or, in the perception of the printer, unclearly erased. Wilson's prominent example consists of these Q2 lines:

> For women feare too much, euen as they loue,
> And womens feare and loue hold quantitie,
> Eyther none, in neither ought, or in extremitie
> (sig. H2r)

The counterpart in F is briefer:

> For womens Feare and Loue, holds quantitie,
> In neither ought, or in extremity
> (sig. oo6r–6v, TLN 2036–7)

To Wilson, it is obvious that the first line in Q2 is a Shakespearean first shot that, standing as a single unrhyming line in a passage of couplets, was always meant to be abandoned (as it is in F) and replaced (as in Q2 and F) by the more successful attempt at a couplet that immediately follows it. It is equally obvious to Wilson that the complete couplet in Q2 does not represent Shakespeare's final intention, for the extrametrical 'Eyther none' appears to Wilson another first shot that was abandoned, as again it is in F, in favour of 'in neither ought'.[22] The force of Wilson's claim for the self-evidence of his reading of Q2 lies in his vividly imagining himself encountering (through the medium of Q2) Shakespeare's original halting composition and inscription of the play – and encountering Shakespeare's papers in exactly the same way the transcriber of F's printer's copy had encountered them, this despite the fact that we know nothing of the identity of such a transcriber or of the exemplar of *Hamlet* he copied. It scarcely matters that Wilson is thus begging the question about what stood as printer's copy for Q2; what matters more is Wilson's omission of the rest of *Hamlet*'s textual tradition beyond Q2 and F. Q2 stands at the head of a long tradition of successive reprints, all of them reproducing the Q2 passage as quoted above – a signal that Q2 did not in this place print self-evidently extraneous text. Wilson is also silent about the source of his interpretation of Q2, which is to be found in the Cambridge Shakespeare of 1863–6, whose editors, unlike Wilson, summarize the variety of earlier editorial opinion about Q2's lines. This opinion, like McKerrow's objection to Greg's reliance on Wilson, allows for extra-authorial agency in the construction of printed texts. Both Samuel Johnson in 1765 and Charles Jennens in 1773 conjectured that a line written to rhyme with Q2's 'For . . . loue' had been dropped from Q2's copy, a possibility the Cambridge editors think worthy of elaboration, as they note that since the extant unrhymed line appears at the top of a page, a line could have been dropped from the bottom of the preceding page. Edmond Malone in 1790 supposed that 'Eyther none' may have been the beginning of that lost line. George Steevens in 1773 thought perhaps that Shakespeare had ended the line unique to the quarto tradition with 'lust', not 'loue', so that the line originally formed a triplet with the two preceding lines, which end with 'distrust' and 'must'.[23] Wilson and the Cambridge editors, Clark and Wright, are as likely to be correct about the source of evident difficulties in Q2 as are Johnson, Jennens, Malone, or Steevens, but no more likely to be correct, since the history of Q2's reception shows the matter to be one of interpretation, hardly the basis for establishing a text of the play.

The most ambitious of 'critical editors' working in the tradition of Wilson and Greg have been indefatigable in their search for unresolved textual tangles to interpret as signs of the use of Shakespeare's 'foul papers' as copy for both Q2 *Hamlet* and other early printed texts. In the New Cambridge *Hamlet*, Philip Edwards offers three more examples interpreted according to Wilson's paradigm (words cut from F appear in square brackets):

> Giues him three[score] thousand crownes in annuall fee.
> (Q2 sig. E3v; F sig. oo2v, TLN 1098)

. . . you could for neede study a speech of some dosen [lines], or sixteene lines (Q2 sig. F4v; F sig. oo4v, TLN 1580–1)

> Both heere and hence pursue me lasting strife,
> If once [I be] a widdow, euer I be [a] wife.
> (Q2 sig. H2v; F sig. oo6v, TLN 2088–9)[24]

For Edwards, these are examples of Shakespearean first shots and second thoughts, but, as McKerrow anticipated, other interpretations for these QF variants present themselves; in these cases they had already presented themselves to Wilson in 1934. He thought Q2 correct in the first example.[25] In the second example, he thought that the Q2 error could have arisen either through the compositor's anticipation of the word 'lines' later in his copy, or through the compositor's miscorrection of successive foul proofs:

after omitting the word 'lines' altogether at first, the compositor, when first directed by the proof-reader to correct the error, then inserted 'lines' in the wrong place (after 'dosen'), but having his attention called to his miscorrection, then placed the word in its proper place, forgetting, however, to delete it after 'dosen'.[26] Wilson also invoked a similar pattern of compositorial miscorrection to account for the third example.[27] As the disagreement between Edwards and Wilson shows, self-evident Shakespearean first shots and second thoughts are hard to locate in Q2 *Hamlet*.

They are equally hard to locate in, for example, Folio *Henry V*, although editors have followed Greg in identifying it too as set into type from Shakespeare's 'foul papers'. Unlike other recent editors of *Henry V* who list imprecision in the designation of characters in speech prefixes and stage directions as well as positive error in some stage directions as if these could be interpreted as evidence that 'foul papers' served as printer's copy,[28] Gary Taylor knows that

> None of these deficiencies and inconsistencies would in itself rule out the use of [F's printer's copy] as an Elizabethan promptbook [*sic*]; such theatrical manuscripts as have survived make it clear that the theatres of that age did not require the standard of precision and regularity found in, for instance, a Royal Shakespeare Company promptbook of today.[29]

Instead, Taylor seeks to found his inference about 'foul papers' behind F *Henry V* on grounds similar to Wilson's for Q2 *Hamlet*. Taylor interprets the exchange between Pistol and his French prisoner at the beginning of 4.4 as Shakespeare's first shot,

Pist. . . . What is thy Name? discusse.
French. O Seigneur Dieu.
Pist. O Signieur Dewe should be a Gentleman: perpend my words O Signieur Dewe . . .

(sig. i4, TLN 2390–3)

and the following later exchange as Shakespeare's second thought, on the assumption that if the first exchange were meant to stand in the text, Pistol would not seek the French soldier's name again:

Pist. . . . aske me this slaue in French what is his Name.
Boy. Escoute comment estes vous appelle?
French. Mounsieur le Fer.
Boy. He sayes his Name is M.Fer.
Pist. M. Fer: Ile fer him, and firke him, and ferret him . . .

(sig. i4, TLN 2405–10)

Duplication is so far from self-evident in these passages, however, that Taylor wisely does not omit the first from his edited text, although, in other not insignificant ways, he does rely, in part, upon this interpretation of F as a 'foul-papers' text.[30]

Wilson's method of construing textual tangles survives until nearly the end of the twentieth century, but by then it no longer inspires its practitioners with the confidence to treat it as a basis for 'critical' editing. E. A. J. Honigmann explicitly emulates Wilson in approaching the *Othello* printed in quarto in 1622. There Honigmann hits upon alleged Shakespearean first shots in a number of half-lines, also to be found in F – lines that, he says, 'could be deleted without loss' or 'are not strictly necessary and are just as easy to remove', but concludes that 'metrical irregularity must not be taken too seriously, even when the removal of a loose half-line yields a clean cut'; he thus lets all of the half-lines stand in his text.[31] His more extensive example is a joke made by Emilia at Desdemona's expense:

Des. Wouldst thou doe such a deed, for all the world?
Em. Why would not you.
Des. No, by this heauenly light.
Em. Nor I neither, by this heauenly light,
I might doe it as well in the darke.
Des. Would [F: Would'st] thou doe such a thing [F: deed] for all the world?
Em. The world is a huge thing, it is a great price,
For a small vice.
Des. Good troth [F: Introth] I thinke thou wouldst not.
(Q sig. L2v; F sig. vv3v, TLN 3035–43)

Honigmann interprets the precise repetition in F of Desdemona's question five lines after she first asked it as a clue that Shakespeare intended the first five lines of this passage to be struck from his *Othello* as a rejected first shot but that he did not mark his intention clearly enough for those who transmitted the play-text to follow this intention. Such an interpretation of repetition has a long history in textual criticism. And this particular interpretation is most attractive because, if it could somehow be validated, it would spare Emilia from the charge of harsh insensitivity in asking 'Why would not you' of a Desdemona who has already shown her horror at being accused of marital infidelity.[32] Of course, there is no way in which to validate Honigmann's interpretation, as he recognizes when he, like Taylor in editing *Henry V*, does not cut the alleged first shot from the edited text. Indeed so prudent is Honigmann that even though his Wilson–Greg analysis of textual tangles leads him to construe the 1622 quarto of *Othello* as the printed text that stands in closer relation to Shakespeare's 'foul papers', he properly chooses to set aside such an analysis and instead bases his edition on F.[33]

The story I've been narrating so far may seem to be one about the rise and fall of optimism among editors from the last century. Wilson, later endorsed by Greg, was able to set aside best-text editing in a surge of optimism about the validity of interpreting tangles in early printed texts as sure signs of the use of Shakespeare's 'foul papers' as printer's copy. The strength of this optimism allowed Wilson and later Greg to sweep aside the more involved and cumbersome accounts of these tangles inherited from the editorial tradition and also to withstand McKerrow's withering pessimism about divining features of Shakespeare's own manuscripts from places in printed texts. As the twentieth century rounded to a close, such optimism waned, and even though such editors as Edwards, Taylor, and Honigmann could rival their predecessors in construing printed passages as indices to the process of Shakespeare's halting composition and therefore to the presence of his papers immediately behind the print, nonetheless one after another of these later editors began to lose the confidence enjoyed by Wilson and Greg in the reliability of this particular construction of tangles that has always been the foundation of 'critical' editing. Presumably, in terms of this narration, if such optimism could wane, it might also wax again at other times and with other editors.

Editorial practice, though, need not be based on optimism or pessimism. No matter whether we are by nature optimistic or pessimistic, there are documents surviving in the form of dramatic manuscripts from the time of and around Shakespeare's career that can instruct us about what we can know, rather than feel, about the validity of inferring the use of 'foul papers' as printer's copy from the appearance of unresolved difficulties in print. One of these is BL MS. Add. 18653, the 'Tragedy of Sr Iohn Van Olden Barnauelt', a play now attributed to the collaboration of John Fletcher and Philip Massinger. This manuscript copy is in the hand of the scribe Ralph Crane, well-known for his association with the King's Men, once the company to which Shakespeare belonged.[34] In 2.1, a scene attributed to Massinger, we find a line that, if it appeared in print, would cry out to be construed as an authorial first shot followed by a second thought, both now still standing in the putative printing; that is, the line that would require a follower of Greg or Wilson to read it much as Edwards interpreted the line 'some dosen lines, or sixteene lines' from Q2 *Hamlet*. In the Crane transcript the line reads 'I know you love the *Prince* valiant *Prince* and yet' (line 679).

Surely, a follower of Greg would have to say, Massinger first wrote 'the *Prince*' and then decided to introduce the complimentary epithet 'valiant' before '*Prince*', but after he had added 'valiant' followed by a second '*Prince*', he forgot to erase his first '*Prince*'. Thus, if this manuscript were printed, a 'critical' editor would be compelled to conclude that printer's copy was authors' 'foul papers' and equally compelled to choose the printing of it as the basis for a 'critical' edition, if there were a choice of texts and if the rival texts did not contain equally reliable evidence, as is sometimes the case, that they were also printed from 'foul papers'.

This conclusion about printer's copy and the editorial method founded on this conclusion would both be wrong, since the manuscript is no one's 'foul papers' but the scribe Ralph Crane's. What appear to be the authorial first shot and second thought are nothing of the kind. Massinger, if we can trust the attribution of 2.1 to his authorship, wrote a line that Crane initially transcribed as 'I know you love the *Prince* of *Orange*, yet'. When the Master of the Revels, Sir George Buc, read Crane's transcript to determine if it was in his view suitable to be staged, he employed his distinctive brown ink not only to place one of his typical crosses before the line, but also to rule out 'of *Orange*', leaving the line incomplete in both sense and metre. To repair the lacuna, the scribe Crane, rather than any author, interlined the words 'valiant *Prince* and' to produce the line as it now stands in the manuscript: 'I know you love the *Prince* valiant *Prince* and yet'. Editors and textual critics who now refuse to accept such printed lines as 'some dosen lines, or sixteene lines' in Q2 *Hamlet* as constituting evidence that Q2 was printed immediately from Shakespeare's own 'foul papers' and who therefore decline to practise Gregian 'critical' editing are not necessarily being governed by some quirk in their dispositions that makes them chronically pessimistic about finding Shakespeare immediately behind his printed plays. Instead they are simply acquainted with documentary evidence that proves invalid any inferences about the nature of printer's copy that are based on unresolved textual tangles in printed texts.

Now that 'critical' editing of Shakespeare has had its day, it is possible to observe that it may never have constituted a theoretical position that one might occupy to secure oneself from Housmanian scurrility. In his famous essay 'The Application of Thought to Textual Criticism', Housman fashions as one of his targets a hypothetical editorial rationale that, while not identical to Greg's, is all too close to Greg's for comfort, Greg's 'prompt-book' matching up with Housman's MS. A (which is 'the more correct but the less sincere' manuscript) and Greg's 'foul papers' approximating Housman's MS. B (which is 'the more corrupt but the less interpolated' manuscript). To choose, as Greg does, a text like MS. B is to open oneself to Housman's attack:

> I ask this scholar... who says that the more sincere of the two MSS. is and must be the better – I ask him to tell me which weighs most, a tall man or a fat man. He cannot answer; nobody can; everybody sees in a moment that the question is absurd. *Tall* and *fat* are adjectives which transport even a textual critic from the world of humbug into the world of reality, a world inhabited by grocers, who depend on their brains for their bread. There he begins to understand that to such general questions any answer must be false; that judgment can only be pronounced on individual specimens; that everything depends on the degree of tallness and the degree of fatness.[35]

However, to be pushed off Gregian 'critical' editing is not for today's editors of Shakespeare to be pushed back onto McKerrow's preference for 'best-text' editing. McKerrow differs from many of today's Shakespeare editors because his explicit goal was to 'present Shakespeare's work as nearly in the form in which he left it as the evidence which we have permits' and, as a 'best-text' editor, his method for achieving this goal was to select as the basis for his edition the printed text that is 'the most careful copy of its original and the most free from obvious errors'.[36] Many of today's Shakespeare editors have rightly abandoned McKerrow's stated goal of establishing the text of a metaphysical 'work' that transcends its evidently imperfect printed states. Instead these editors are content to strive for the humanly possible goal of editing one or more of the early printed texts, without claiming to locate either author or work in relation to these printed versions. Perhaps the most spectacular consequence of this shift in editorial direction will be the three-text *Hamlet* forthcoming in the Arden3 series. Yet as early as 1993 with, for example, *Othello*, the editors of the New Folger series have indicated theirs is an edition, not of the 'work', but of the Folio printing of *Othello*, and therefore neither a 'best-text' edition nor a 'critical' one.[37]

The failure of Wilson, Greg, and their numerous followers to establish the provenance of early printed Shakespeare plays in terms of 'foul papers' and 'prompt-books' does not mean that one cannot determine anything about the provenance of these texts. By minute comparison of ten First Folio comedies to extant manuscripts in the hand of Ralph Crane, T. H. Howard-Hill was able to demonstrate the strong probability that five of them were printed from Crane transcripts.[38] If one compares even one of the striking features of the 1599 quarto of *Romeo and Juliet*, namely its stage direction '*Enter Will Kemp*' (sig. K3v), to extant dramatic manuscripts, one can learn, against all received Gregian wisdom about this text's origin in 'foul papers', that the provenance of this text is theatrical. As Greg himself observed in 1931 from his fine study of such manuscripts, a study conducted before he fell under Wilson's spell, 'in every instance in which an actor's name appears in a manuscript play it is written in a different hand from the text, or at any rate in a different ink and style, showing it to be a later addition and not part of the original composition'.[39] Subsequent study of other manuscripts has done nothing to overthrow Greg's conclusion;[40] thus there are good grounds for believing that printer's copy for the 1599 *Romeo and Juliet* came from the playhouse to the printing house. In no way then is the end of 'best-text' and 'critical' editing the end of editing; it's a new beginning.

NOTES

1. A. E. Housman (ed.), *M. Manilii Astronomica Liber Qvintvs* (Londinii: The Richards Press, 1930), p. v.
2. *M. Manilii Astronomica Liber Primvs*, p. xxxi.
3. W. W. Greg, *The Editorial Problem in Shakespeare* (Oxford: Clarendon Press, 1942), p. 182.
4. 'Whether an original reading can survive only in what is generally an inferior tradition depends entirely upon the genetic relationship of the manuscripts, a matter concerning which Housman was less explicit than one could wish' (*ibid.*).
5. Norman Page, *A. E. Housman: A Critical Biography* (London: Macmillan, 1983), p. 163.
6. W. W. Greg, 'Bibliography: an Apologia', *The Library* 4th series, 13 (1932), 128–9.
7. Greg also invoked Housman at the beginning of *Principles of Emendation in Shakespeare* (Oxford: Clarendon Press, 1928), p. 1.
8. F. P. Wilson, 'Sir Walter Wilson Greg, (1875–1959)', in *Dictionary of National Biography 1951–1960*, ed. E. T. Williams and Helen M. Palmer (London: Oxford University Press, 1971), p. 431.
9. Ronald B. McKerrow, *Prolegomena for the Oxford Shakespeare: A Study in Editorial Method* (Oxford: Clarendon Press, 1939), p. x.
10. *Ibid.*
11. F. P. Wilson, *Shakespeare and the New Bibliography* (Oxford: Clarendon Press, 1945). In *Theories of the Text* (Oxford: Clarendon Press, 1999), p. 227, D. C. Greetham notes McKerrow's affinity to post-structuralists, an observation close to mine, arrived at independently in a paper read at the 1999 meeting of the Society for Textual Scholarship, New York City, subsequently published as 'Editing Shakespeare and Editing Without Shakespeare: Wilson, McKerrow, Greg, Bowers, Tanselle, and Copy-Text Editing', *Text* 13 (2000), 27–53, in which I discuss in a great deal more detail relations among these figures that are merely alluded to in the following paragraphs.

12. W. W. Greg, 'Review of *On Editing Shakespeare and the Elizabethan Dramatists* by Fredson Bowers', *Shakespeare Quarterly* 7 (1956), 101–2. For notice of the anachronism of the term 'promptbook' as used by Greg for manuscripts from Shakespeare's era, as well as for analysis of the precise meanings that Greg attaches to both 'promptbook' and 'foul papers' as flagrantly anachronistic, see my 'Plays in Manuscript', in *A New History of Early English Drama*, ed. John D. Cox and David Scott Kastan (New York: Columbia University Press, 1997), pp. 483–92, and 'Post-Theory Problems in Shakespeare Editing', *Yearbook of English Studies* 29 (1999), 106–11.
13. Greg, *Editorial Problem*, pp. 64, xxiv–xxv n. 2.
14. *Ibid.*, p. ix.
15. W. W. Greg, 'The Rationale of Copy-Text', *Studies in Bibliography* 3 (1950–1), 19–36.
16. McKerrow, *Prolegomena*, pp. 6–7.
17. *Ibid.*, p. 9.
18. *Ibid.*, pp. 14, 20.
19. W. W. Greg, 'McKerrow's "Prolegomena" Reconsidered', *Review of English Studies* 17 (1941), 144.
20. *Ibid.*, 147.
21. Fredson Bowers, 'McKerrow's Editorial Principles for Shakespeare Reconsidered', *Shakespeare Quarterly* 6 (1955), 309–24.
22. J. Dover Wilson, *The Manuscript of Shakespeare's 'Hamlet' and the Problems of its Transmission*, 2 vols. (Cambridge University Press, 1934), vol. I, p. 27.
23. William George Clark and William Aldis Wright (eds.), *Works of Shakespeare*, 9 vols. (Cambridge University Press, 1863–6), vol. VII, p. 603.
24. Philip Edwards (ed.), *Hamlet, Prince of Denmark* (Cambridge University Press, 1985), pp. 10–11. I have previously discussed these passages in a quite different way in 'The Textual Mystery of *Hamlet*', *Shakespeare Quarterly* 39 (1988), 1–26.
25. J. Dover Wilson, *Manuscript*, vol. II, p. 274.
26. *Ibid.*, vol. I, pp. 55, 143.
27. *Ibid.*, vol. I, p. 143.
28. Andrew Gurr (ed.), *King Henry V* (Cambridge University Press, 1992), p. 216; T. W. Craik (ed.), *King Henry V* (London: Routledge, 1995), p. 24.
29. Gary Taylor (ed.), *Henry V* (Oxford: Clarendon Press, 1982), p. 14. Taylor had read at a 1979 Shakespeare Association of America seminar the paper published by William B. Long as 'Stage Directions: a Misinterpreted Factor in Determining Textual Provenance', *Text* 2 (1985), 121–37.
30. Taylor (ed.), *Henry V*, p. 16.
31. E. A. J. Honigmann, *The Texts of 'Othello' and Shakespearian Revision* (London: Routledge, 1996), pp. 36–7.
32. *Ibid.*, pp. 34–5.
33. *Ibid.*, p. 146. For a sensitive but incisive response to Honigmann's book, see Scott McMillin, 'The *Othello* Quarto and the "Foul Paper" Hypothesis', *Shakespeare Quarterly* 51 (2000), 67–85.

34. T. H. Howard-Hill (ed.), '*Sir John Van Olden Barnavelt*' *by John Fletcher and Philip Massinger* (London: The Malone Society, 1980).
35. A. E. Housman, 'The Application of Thought to Textual Criticism', in *The Classical Papers of A. E. Housman*, 3 vols., ed. J. Diggle and F. R. D. Goodyear (Cambridge University Press, 1972), vol. III, p. 1063.
36. McKerrow, *Prolegomena*, pp. 1, 14.
37. Barbara A. Mowat and Paul Werstine (eds.), *Othello* (New York: Washington Square Press, 1993), p. xlvi. I choose this edition for my example, rather than, say, the two texts of *King Lear* published in the Oxford *Complete Works*, because what is needed is an example of 'editing one or more of the early printed texts, without claiming to locate either author or work in relation to these printed versions'. It is well known from both the title and some of the contents of *The Division of the Kingdoms: Shakespeare's Two Versions of 'King Lear'*, ed. Gary Taylor and Michael Warren (Oxford: Clarendon Press, 1983) that Wells and Taylor did claim 'to locate [their] author... in relation to [the] printed versions' of *King Lear*.
38. T. H. Howard-Hill, *Ralph Crane and Some Shakespeare First Folio Comedies* (Charlottesville: University Press of Virginia, 1972).
39. W. W. Greg, *Dramatic Documents from the Elizabethan Playhouses*, 2 vols. (Oxford: Clarendon Press, 1931), vol. I, pp. 215–16.
40. J. W. Lever, editor of the Malone Society reprint of *The Wasp* (London: The Malone Society, 1976), cautiously draws attention to the possibility that the author of this holograph play wrote the actor's name 'Iorden' (line 522) into his manuscript. However, we are entitled, says Lever, to suspect that the author probably did so, not in the act of composition, but only after the book-keeper had already, in his own annotation, assigned the role of the 'Capt' to Iorden (p. xiii).

CHAPTER 4

Addressing adaptation: 'Measure for Measure' and 'Sir Thomas More'

John Jowett

This paper discusses two-text editing as that term can be applied, with some extenuation, to two editorial projects. The first is my editing of *Measure for Measure* for the forthcoming edition of Thomas Middleton's *Collected Works*.[1] No doubt still to the surprise of many readers, the play will make its appearance there on the basis that the Folio text is printed from an adapted version of the play prepared by Middleton in 1621.[2] The second project, an edition of *Sir Thomas More* for Arden3, takes its beginning in this paper. Despite their manifest differences as texts, these two plays demand attention to the same editorial issue. *Sir Thomas More* too is an adapted text. That indeed is its most definite characteristic, seen in its fundamental material construction as a manuscript comprising an 'Original Text' in Anthony Munday's hand and a complex set of revisions on separate leaves in a number of other hands.

It is, of course, the process of adaptation that gives the play its claim to a place in the Arden3 series, for it is 'Hand D', the writer and author of a segment of the revisions, that has been identified as Shakespeare's. I will not be addressing here the question of whether Hand D is indeed the hand of Shakespeare, but it seems to me far more probable than not.[3] Building on that unprovable but likely assessment, the play's inclusion in Arden3 will mark its first appearance in the context of a Shakespeare series.[4] In this respect there is a striking parallel with the inclusion of *Measure for Measure* in a Middleton edition, in that both plays are transported into new authorial environments that are defined by the process of adaptation.

The task of editing both plays evolves from the starting-point that adaptation is an issue that in these circumstances needs presenting to the reader within the edited text itself. Despite the fact that Arden3 and the Oxford Middleton are modernized critical editions, each of these plays will be treated exceptionally in order to present the text in both its pre-adaptation and post-adaptation states. Neither state will be relegated to an appendix. Instead, the process of adaptation will be presented on the text pages themselves. As the adaptations are localized, affecting some parts of the texts but not others, the editions will shift to and fro between single-text presentation and two-text presentation as the reader moves through them.

Many of the essays in this volume debate the problems inherent in departing from the reproduction of copy-text. The contribution of the present essay to the debate is to identify two areas in which the logic of copying copy-text breaks down. Both concern the relation between verbal text and physical document. *Measure* as it is printed in the 1623 Folio is an undifferentiated and continuous single text. If the hypothesis of adaptation is right, it achieves this appearance by preserving a passage after 1.2.79 that was intended to be replaced by new material, printing it without differentiation as though it were part of the sequential text:

Clo. Yonder man is carried to prison.
Baw. Well: what has he done?
Clo. A Woman.
Baw. But what's his offence?
Clo. Groping for Trowts, in a peculiar Riuer.
Baw. What? is there a maid with child by him?
Clo. No: but there's a woman with maid by him:

It is clear too that it effaces many details of the Shakespearean pre-adaptation version. In other words, it combines superficially unrecognizable synopsis with superficially unrecognizable occlusion. Editors who ground their practice in conservatively reproducing copy-text will be strongly tempted to disbelieve the hypothesis of adaptation for the simple reason that it throws down a startling challenge to their editorial practice. If one were to persist with copy-text rationale in a case such as *Measure*, one would mediate to the reader none of the things that an editor usually mediates: neither the original text, nor the revised text, nor the text as it seems to have been performed. The text can be preserved in its familiar shape only in the name of preserving the features of the document: in other words, by a logic that would imply an unemended edition in original spelling or even a facsimile. In this situation it is hard to recover a rationale for the standard editorial treatment of the play, as emendation of local textual cruxes elsewhere in the play would bring the text out of line with the printed document without bringing it into line with its authorial or theatrical precedents.

Both the plays under consideration illustrate that the text is by no means necessarily coterminous with or identical to its materialization in a specific document. And this can be seen without resort to the competing claims of other substantive texts as potential contributors to an edited text or components of the work. In the case of *Measure*, the document is textually singular (or rather the printed copies are more or less identical), whereas the text, viewed as something represented rather than simply existent in the document, is divisible. Whether editing should address the material document or the text is a major question in itself. But in the cases in view it is effectively decided by the nature of the editions in which I am engaged as critical editions with an orientation to authoriality and to theatre – to the substance, therefore, of the text in a different state, or different states, from the documentary text.

The editorial disambiguation of text within a single document to identify it as belonging to one of two or more stages of production is a standard procedure, though the results are more typically presented in the collation line than in the edited text. It happens in established cases where textual scholars identify duplication in a manuscript, as manifested in the printed book for which it served as copy. In the relatively unproblematic case of Q2 *Romeo and Juliet*, for example, the single-text document has in modern editions been effectively fractured into two texts at the points where Q2 (1599) prints a first draft followed by lines that replace it. In Q2, one speech spoken by Romeo at the end of one scene is virtually repeated, now spoken by Friar Laurence, at the beginning of the following scene:

> *Ro.* Would I were sleepe and peace so sweet to rest
> The grey eyde morne smiles on the frowning night,
> Checkring the Easterne Clouds with streaks of light,
> And darknesse flected like a drunkard reeles,
> From forth daies pathway, made by *Tytans* wheeles.
> Hence will I to my ghostly Friers close cell,
> His helpe to craue, and my dear hap to tell.
>   *Exit.*
>   *Enter Frier alone with a basket.*   (night,
> *Fri.* The grey-eyed morne smiles on the frowning
> Checking the Easterne clowdes with streaks of light:
> And fleckeld darknesse like a drunkard reeles,
> From forth daies path, and *Titans* burning wheeles:
>   (D4^v)

Editors have debated vigorously which of these versions supersedes the other, but few if any have expressed any doubt that there is a duplication. The copy manuscript may well have displayed the signs of supersession: for instance, a deletion mark, or the placement of the revised text in the margin. But even if it were as visually seamless as the printed text, in which the two states of the text are presented sequentially and without any signal of textual layering, there can be little doubt that the passage exists in two distinct and alternative states, and that any appearance of linearity would be misleading with respect to both the genesis of the text and its realization on the stage.

Editors rightly emend,[5] as they do in another passage from the same play in which a short passage is reworked at greater length. In the transcript below, the first sketch is underlined and the closely equivalent phrases in the longer reworking are printed in bold; the phrase 'where ere thou tumblest in' is reworked less directly in the image of the 'seasick weary barke':

> <u>Depart againe, come lye thou in my arme,</u>
> <u>Heer's to thy health, where ere thou tumblest in.</u>
> <u>O true Appothecarie!</u>
> <u>Thy drugs are quicke. Thus with a kisse I die.</u>
> **Depart againe**, here, here, will I remaine,
> With wormes that are thy Chamber-maides: O here
> Will I set vp my euerlasting rest:
> And shake the yoke of inauspicious starres,
> From this world wearied flesh, eyes looke your last:
> Armes take your last embrace: And lips, O you
> The doores of breath, seale with a righteous kisse
> A datelesse bargaine to ingrossing death:
> Come bitter conduct, come vnsauoury guide,
> Thou desperate Pilot, now at once run on
> The dashing Rocks, thy seasick weary barke:
> **Heeres to my Loue. O true Appothecary:**
> **Thy drugs are quick. Thus with a kisse I die.**
>
> (L3)

Here too the diagnosis is secure, and the editorial response of deleting the superseded lines as underlined above is well established. There are similar passages elsewhere in Q2 *Romeo and Juliet*, in Q1 *Love's Labour's Lost*, and in other texts.

In such cases, to represent the text editorially as breaking into Draft A and Draft B might be both valid and purposeful. An objection that would apply at least to the second passage, and perhaps to the first as well, is that in the case of immediate and sequential revision the Draft A alternative would be superseded by the time the single-track text resumed. In such a case the textual structure is that of a fold, with the precedent text flowing underneath the revision. There is no comparable limitation in the case of a text where the original text is entirely separable from the alterations, because those alterations were made at a substantially later date. This is indeed the situation in adapted texts, such as *Macbeth* and *Measure* are believed to be. It is also the situation in manuscript plays such as *The Lady's Tragedy* (*Second Maiden's Tragedy*) and my other text under consideration, *Sir Thomas More*.

The fact that I am discussing here presentation of text rather than presentation of document does not diminish the significance of the material document, but simply recognizes that the document does not necessarily deliver the stratified text adequately and in a way intelligible to the modern reader. The responsibility of the editor, as I understand it, is to respond first and foremost to the content and structure of the text, reluctantly letting the bibliographical codes of the document fall back. Q2 *Romeo and Juliet* and the Folio texts of *Macbeth* and *Measure* present themselves as continuous, *The Lady's Tragedy* contains pasted-in revision slips, and *Sir Thomas More* contains a series of problematically placed additional leaves that are sometimes resistant to straightforward assimilation; other play manuscripts have marginal insertions. These material differences have to be taken into account in establishing the structure of the text and explaining it to readers. But the document can, as it were, fail to interpret itself, to distinguish between superseded and new text, by failing properly to accommodate added slips, leaves, and marginal or interlined inserts to the text into which they fit. Or, through transcription or printing, it can reproduce the complex and stratified text on which it is based as a linear text, without overtly signalling the transformation that has taken place.

In the case of *Sir Thomas More* the manuscript, for once gloriously extant, needs considerable interpretation and textual correlation before it begins to reveal even the possibility of a text of the revised version. W. W. Greg's Malone Society Reprints edition, which aims to preserve the characteristics of the manuscript, nevertheless drastically reorganizes its structure to make it manageable to the reader. The interleaved additional leaves from the Original Text are separated out and printed after it.[6] The headings Greg supplies of 'Original Text' and 'Additional Passages' (as opposed to, say, 'Original Manuscript' and 'Added Leaves') say something about the text as distinct from the manuscript. And necessarily so: this document cannot be edited *as a text* without a considerable measure of editorial interpretation and organization.

In the case of *Measure*, the continuity of the overlaid text as printed in F has been preserved in almost all editions to date. The exception is the Oxford Shakespeare *Complete Works* which, paradoxically but out of necessity, chooses the more readily recovered version dated at 1621 rather than the occluded Shakespearean original; it therefore removes to an appendix the short Shakespeare passage in 1.2 on the basis that Middleton's new opening to the scene is evidently designed to replace it. The unfamiliarity of the approach of distinguishing an original text from an adapted text partly lies in the relative novelty of the theory of adaptation itself. It partly depends on a tradition of continuous-text presentation that resists multiple text. Continuous-text or clear-text presentation accepts the impression of textual stability and monolinearity, and by doing so it generates that impression in the reader. As D. C. Greetham puts it, 'A clear-text eclectic or "exclusive" edition thus encourages the horizontal, singular axis of contiguity over the vertical axis of substitution.'[7]

I do not endorse the view that it is intrinsically worthwhile to disrupt the linearity of the text at all costs and wherever possible. This can lead to the editor's insistence that the issue of textuality must take precedence over all other critical practices. Drawing attention appropriately to issues of text is one thing; imperilling the very possibility of continuous literary or theatrical reading is another. There are, however, situations where the issue of text is unignorable, and can be dealt with in ways that will enable it to feed into the edition in a way that is compatible with its broadest pedagogical purposes. In the texts under discussion, the disruption of the continuous text signals more than the textualization of textuality. It signals that *here* is the place where the text divides, and divides in a way that pertains urgently to the text's inclusion in the larger collected edition or series.

After all, readers finding *Measure* in an edition of Middleton's works will be curious as to why it has been dislocated from its usual Shakespearean context. The meaning and scope of this conspicuous act of appropriation need to be established within the edition as clearly as possible. It is important to assert that, as far as is known, Shakespeare wrote the play without collaborating with another dramatist, that the texture of the writing is still overwhelmingly Shakespearean, and that Middleton's contribution is confined to specific additions and reorganizations belonging to 1621.

This offers a unique opportunity for the editor to place less emphasis than usual on the responsibility to present the text for unpredetermined and various practices of reading and criticism. The familiarity of *Measure* in another context – the context of the Shakespeare canon – means that few readers will encounter the play in the Middleton edition for the first time. The situation is far from that of, for example, *More Dissemblers Besides Women*, where the editor is faced with the primary need to reproduce and disseminate a rarely read and straightforwardly Middletonian text.

The decision to include *Measure* within a Middleton edition that as a matter of general editorial policy presents entire texts rather than

Middletonian fragments therefore shapes all that follows in terms of the editor's orientation of the text to the reader. It justifies a form of presentation that highlights the process of adaptation, distinguishing between the text of 1603–4 and the adaptation of 1621. And I use these terms to identify the two textual strata that concern us here in order to make the point that the issue is not simply authorial. Authorship provides the lever whereby the question of versions is prised into view and assumes its own interest. What might it mean to think of an adapted version of the play as belonging to 1621; in what ways might it belong to this cultural environment and speak differently as a result?

For these reasons, I present a text marked up with the features of 1621 clearly distinguished from the features of 1603–4, in full recognition that the agents involved may not exclusively be Middleton and Shakespeare, but acceptance too that in practice they appear mostly to be so. The typographical presentation that has been adopted for the Middleton *Collected Works*, on the advice of the electronic general editor John Lavagnino, has been to mark the deleted text in grey type and the added text in bold (figure 1). Thus the superseded text is placed under erasure.[8] The design provides a sufficient degree of differentiation for even single words printed in grey or bold to be differentiated from normal text, while allowing longer passages to be presented without overemphasis. The faded presentation of the grey text leaves it still legible. The rules for reading are simple. To follow the adaptation, read normal text plus bold, ignoring grey. To follow the original, read normal text plus grey, ignoring bold.

The textualist bias of this presentation is reduced insofar as the text follows the usual procedure of the volume in being modernized. As with the choice of variations in typeface over special sorts and symbols, the effect is to lower the temperature of editorial interference and avoid making the presentation appear technical and experimental as it were for its own sake, beyond the immediate requirements for making the adaptation evident.

Yet in one respect, editorial intervention is maximized. It is part of the logic of two-text editing that where there is a measure of doubt as to whether a variant is a product of error or an example of valid alterity, the doubt should be resolved in favour of the two-text alternative. This principle is expressed strongly by Gary Taylor, who states as his aim in editing *The History of King Lear* to respond to Quarto readings 'as though F did not exist'.[9] As applied to the adaptation-oriented editing of *Measure*, which is based on a general hypothesis about the text and is sustained by a number of conjectural separations and reconstructions, the principle of two-text

            hours since and he was ever precise in promise-keeping.
          SECOND GENTLEMAN Besides, you know, it draws something
            near to the speech we had to such a purpose.
          FIRST GENTLEMAN But most of all agreeing with the proclam-
75   ation.
          LUCIO Away; let's go learn the truth of it.
                                              Exit [Lucio, with Gentlemen]
          BAWD Thus, what with the war, what with the sweat,
            what with the gallows, and what with poverty, I am
            custom-shrunk.
                                 Sc. 2
                          Enter Clown [and Bawd, meeting]
79a   [BAWD] How now, what's the news with you?
79b   CLOWN Yonder man is carried to prison.
79c   BAWD Well! What has he done?
79d   CLOWN A woman.
79e   BAWD But what's his offence?
79f   CLOWN Groping for trouts in a peculiar river.
79g   BAWD What, is there a maid with child by him?
79h   CLOWN No, but there's a woman with maid by him.
80   [CLOWN] You have not heard of the proclamation, have
            you?
          BAWD What proclamation, man?
          CLOWN All houses in the suburbs of Ferrara Vienna must
            be plucked down.
85   BAWD And what shall become of those in the city?

          CLOWN They shall stand for seed. They had gone down
            too, but that a wise burgher put in for them.
          BAWD But shall all our houses of resort in the suburbs be
            pulled down?
          CLOWN To the ground, mistress.   90
          BAWD Why, here's a change indeed in the commonwealth.
            What shall become of me?
          CLOWN Come, fear not you. Good counsellors lack no cli-
            ents. Though you change your place, you need not
            change your trade. I'll be your tapster still. Courage,   95
            there will be pity taken on you. You that have worn
            your eyes almost out in the service, you will be con-
            sidered.
                                 [A noise within]
          BAWD What's to do here, Thomas Tapster? Let's withdraw!
                    Enter Provost, Claudio, Juliet, officers, Lucio
                               and two Gentlemen
          CLOWN Here comes Signor Claudio, led by the Provost to   100
            prison; and there's Madam Juliet.
                                              Exeunt Bawd and Clown
                                 Sc. 3
                          Enter Provost, Claudio
          CLAUDIO
          Fellow, why dost thou show me thus to th' world?
          Bear me to prison, where I am committed.
          PROVOST
          I do it not in evil disposition,

77–9 Thus...custom-shrunk Compare the Bawd's similar complaint that he is ruined by the 'poverty', the Devil's lengthy sceptical response, and the Bawd's insistence 'What with this long vacation...Pierce was never so penniless as poor Lieutenant Frig-beard', in *Black Book* ll. 126–333. The same passage also includes an allusion to syphilis comparable with the Bawd's reference to its cure by 'the sweat', in 'Monsieur Dry-bone the Frenchman' (ll. 322–3). See also commentary to 4.3.17.

78 poverty The adaptation was prepared at a time of the severest economic depression in living memory. As the depression was fuelled by a slump in exports, it was largely an effect of trade with Europe, and so the allusion fits in with the European consciousness of the episode.

79 custom-shrunk Middleton repeatedly uses the verb *shrink* to indicate male withdrawal from, or incapacity for, sexual activity (*No Wit* 7.1.120, *Weapons* 1.1.240, *Women Beware* 3.1.100).

99–101 BAWD...Juliet Probably added for the adaptation. JAGGARD's 'and there's Madam *Juliet*' has to be an addition if Juliet is herself an addition, and this brings both speeches into question. The clumsy sequence of a natural exit point ('you will be considered'), then an interruption leading to a new exit point ('let's withdraw'), then speech suggesting interest in the approaching figures ('Here comes...'), then an exeunt, is more likely to result from the disjunctions of a revised staging than to belong to the original text. In the fuller, more complex staging of the adapted text, the added lines establish the identities of the three characters entering for the first time.

99.1–2 Enter...Gentlemen The adaptation creates much more of a public shaming ritual. Lucio and the Gentlemen have no part in the 1603–4 text, and serve in the adapted text only to change the emphasis of the staging. Without them, Lucio is redundant until he greets Claudio.

99.1 Juliet She has no part in the scene other than to appear visually as the observed, in a manner that contrasts in appearance and gender with the similarly silent but observing Gentlemen. Her theatrical function must be to be inscribed as visibly pregnant, 'With character too gross', and she may well have worn the gown of penance imposed on detected fornicators. It seems characteristic of the adaptation to add to and emblematize the presence of women: the expanded Bawd's role and Juliet in 1.2, Mariana (accompanied by a singing boy-actor) in 4.1, and Juliet in 5.1, where she makes another silent appearance. Pregnant unmarried women appear on stage to supply a visual and sometimes silent serio-comic comment on their misdeeds in *No Wit* (Grace), *Witch* (Francesca), *Quarrel* (Jane), *Nice Valour* (the 'Cupid') and *Dissemblers* (the 'Page').

officers The officers merely accompany Juliet and are unmentioned in the dialogue. The Clown announces that Claudio is simply 'led by the Provost', and at the end of the scene Claudio tells a single officer—the Provost again—'Come, officer, away'.

101 Madam Juliet The word 'madam' is found elsewhere in the play only in the Middletonian part of 1.2: when the Bawd is mocked as 'Madam Mitigation' at 1.2.43 and when Juliet herself is mentioned as 'Madam Julietta' at 1.2.68–9.

101.2 *Sc. 3* Noting the continuity of action, editors have removed the scene break printed in JAGGARD. Given the staging in the adapted text, it makes sense for the entry to happen before the Clown and Bawd withdraw, so that the Clown can identify the newcomers more effectively for the audience. But in JAGGARD, as marked in the present text of the original version, the entry follows the clearing of the stage that makes the scene-break. In the original staging the two speeches that establish continuity preceding JAGGARD's scene-header were probably absent.

1 *Measure for Measure* 1.2.71–104, as it will appear in the Oxford edition of Thomas Middleton's *Collected Works*.

separation means that the criteria are not as stringent as would be the case in the usual editorial emendation of error. To say this is to recognize the instability of the whole process of editing when it is based on distinguishing two textual strata within a single text.

The case that can be made for many original/adaptation variants is, however, compelling. As Taylor has brilliantly argued, it was Middleton who evidently made the location Vienna, changing from the original Italian setting, which was probably Ferrara.¹⁰ There is, of course, no proof, but neither is there any effective rebuttal of the strong case Taylor makes. The editorial responsibility is therefore clearly to mark Ferrara in grey and Vienna in bold wherever the Folio text reads 'Vienna'. More conjectural is the extent to which F needs emending to restore the profanity that has been removed to bring the text into line with the 1606 Act to Restrain Abuses of Players. There is bound to be an area of doubt as regards both the identification of expurgation and the form in which the expurgated phrase should be restored. But it is hard to doubt that the level of profanity must have differed substantially between the pre-1606 and post-1606 performance texts, and it can be shown that many of the profanity-substitutes are unShakespearian in idiom.¹¹

The variants mentioned here, arising from the change of location and the expurgation of profanity, account for most of the differences that involve single words and short phrases. At the other extreme lie the major alterations identified in *Shakespeare Reshaped* of 1993, in which Gary Taylor and I explore how Shakespeare's texts were modified through their circulation in the theatre in the years before the publication of the First Folio: the addition of the opening passage in 1.2, and the alterations around the act-break at the beginning of Act 4 that include the transposition of the Duke's soliloquies at the end of 3.1 and in 4.1, and the insertion of a song by John Fletcher with some accompanying dialogue at the beginning of 4.1. Intermediate in substance are other passages where research undertaken since 1993 has confirmed the presence of Middleton's hand or revealed it for the first time. These include the exchange between Escalus and the Justice at the end of 2.1, the presence of Lucio in 2.2, and the clown Pompey's catalogue of the prisoners at the beginning of 4.3, all to some extent under suspicion already in 1993.¹² Mistress Overdone is named in the last of these episodes, and textual dislocations in the other two passages naming her reveal Middleton's hand here, locally, as well.

In short, the original/adaptation split readings, though most heavily represented in two sections, are unevenly scattered throughout the play. This has implications for other aspects of editorial presentation. Taking advantage once again of the availability of well-annotated editions of the play in the Shakespeare context, the editor can dedicate the commentary at the foot of the page to matters relating to the adaptation. This causes the commentary to disappear entirely on some pages, but to fatten considerably in the adapted passages. Quite apart from its content, the very physical substance of the commentary acts as a focusing device. Alongside the typographical variety within the text of the play, the commentary makes the page visually busy. And it makes the adapted sections occupy a disproportionate number of pages. The intent of the edition will not be in doubt.

This is, then, a form of specialized and motivated editing, one might even say polemical editing. Such an approach emphatically is not applicable generally. In this respect the purpose of the edition differs from the Arden3 *Sir Thomas More*, where a large part of the objective must be to establish an authoritative and usable text that will make the play accessible to a relatively broad readership. There are other differences between the two projects. Whereas *Measure* comes to us as a printed text, *Sir Thomas More* survives as a manuscript in which all the variation that is discovered through inference in *Measure* is here laid out before us in incontrovertible form and detail. What is discovered in the manuscript corresponds, as it happens, with some of the features detected in *Measure*. There is an original version, though it has become disrupted as the result of leaves being lost or destroyed. Then there are the Additional Passages, which variously rework and replace material in the Original.

In both examples, in contrast, say, with Langland's *Piers the Ploughman* (even as conceptualized as a three-text work as in Walter W. Skeat's pioneering edition),[13] or with Joyce's *Ulysses*, the textual situation can be considered in terms of binary alternatives. This entails some simplification, in that it would be possible to argue for interim stages of development in either text. For instance, the Master of the Revels Edmund Tilney's censorship of *Sir Thomas More* could be said to establish its own textual stratum, but its characteristics are either negative (instructions for omission) or textually unrealized (as with the instruction to write a summary report of the insurrection). Though Tilney's marks are textual, there would be no basis on which to present a separate play-text based on them. The two-text model is adopted largely because it situates the reviser within the text, but it also reflects a genesis that can be no more helpfully and accurately described than as happening in *two* crucial stages in which the text is originated and then radically altered.

The textual similarities that lie behind the documentary differences between *Measure* and *Sir Thomas More* raise the possibility that a similar editorial strategy could be pursued in both cases. My rejection of such an option is based not on the nature of the physical documents from which the texts are edited, but above all on considerations of presentation and layout within the two editions. The strength of the *Measure* solution lies in its ability to highlight variant texts over a short span of text, and to deal with single-word variants alongside those variant passages. However, when the length of the variant passage extends to several hundred lines, as in parts of *Sir Thomas More*, a linear, sequential presentation will be of little help to the reader. It will be apparent too that the extent to which passages effectively can be correlated by the reader when presented in a sequence depends heavily on the format of the edition. The Middleton *Collected Works* will have a double-column layout similar to the Oxford Shakespeare *Complete Works* but with a commentary at the foot of the page. The relatively large volume of text presented on a single opening allows the distribution of typographically differentiated text to be seen as a pattern on the page. This does not apply to the Arden3 format, where there are sometimes so few lines on an opening that the text can no longer be visualized in blocks, and typographical discrimination in variant passages of any length is not a particularly functional option. To put the matter another way, readers are distinctly inconvenienced if not confused when they need to skip several pages in order to resume their reading of the text; and this applies whether 'the text' is considered to be the original or the adapted version.

The option of printing the Original Text as the main edited text and the Additional Passages as an appendix, on the model of the Malone Society Reprints edition, or, for example, typical critical editions of *The Spanish Tragedy*, has little appeal in the context of the Arden3 series. It would keep the Shakespearean sections out of the text of the play, and would make it difficult to experience the revision to which they contributed. Yet to apply the standard single-text procedures to this exceptional manuscript play is fundamentally misleading. It would mean cutting out sections of the Original Text and implanting the Additional Passages as though they had always belonged there, and as though (as is not the case) we can have any certainty that there was ever such a thing as a completed revised text.

The editorial form most appropriate to *Sir Thomas More* as to be presented in the Arden3 series is one that exploits that most fundamental binarism of the book format, the two-page opening. That is to say, the passages where the Original Text is superseded by an Additional Passage will, I anticipate, be presented in parallel text format. I will be urging that *Sir Thomas More* is a special case that, on account of the fragmentary nature of Shakespeare's supposed contribution and the empirical fact of the editor's copy being a manuscript of complex organization, demands to be treated as an exception to the series' usual, but not universal, policy of presenting a single text.[14] It is only a partial exception, in that most of the play exists only in the one state represented by the Original Text.

The parallel text solution is not entirely straightforward. To begin with, the degree to which the passages run in line-to-line correspondence varies considerably, and in some cases the Additional Passage would better be described as loosely correspondent rather than in any exact sense parallel. Moreover, some of the Additional Passages are literally additions, without any equivalent in the Original Text. The two longest additions replace leaves that are lost from the Original Text. Where there actually are equivalent texts to range alongside each other, the line-by-line and even speech-by-speech sequence often does not run in parallel. Where lines are correlatable, they can occur in non-parallel contexts, or in passages of different length. Thus it will be the exception rather than the rule to find the kind of close parallelism that is usual in, for instance, *King Lear* or *Bussy D'Ambois*. The purpose of a parallel layout is therefore often not to facilitate a reading of microscopic textual adjustment. It is rather to define a much broader picture of alternative strategies for dramatizing an episode.

Comparably with the treatment of *Measure for Measure*, the aim is to represent textual process without disproportionate detriment to such continuity of the text as can be determined. If the procedure disturbs the reader to some extent, it is no more than is necessary to offer a reminder of the documentary foundations of the edition and provide an immediate *in situ* choice of versions. If it alters the physical organization of the manuscript, it does so necessarily, in that no edition of the play could both preserve it and be readable. Moreover, the alteration is far more limited than is the case with the Revels edition, where a synthetic revised version weaves seamlessly between Original Text and Additional Passages.[15]

I have been describing an area of editorial choice that concerns the level of manifest intervention that disrupts what would, according to the usual tenets of critical editing, be presented as a plain and continuous text. In the cases I have been considering, this is tantamount to saying that I have been considering the extent to which textual process should be presented alongside textual product. I have taken a strong view that in both plays the process is something that needs to be seen. The two examples differ profoundly in that the copy-text for *Measure* is in the first instance an undisrupted text in which the process is not seen, whereas the disruptions within *Sir Thomas More* are major, and constitute an unignorable obstacle to reading. In both cases, however, the relationship between the text as outcome and the text as process is dependent on editorial interpretation. To regard the text as process is to look both at and beyond the available documents, whose presence as objects freezes the text into immobility. The edition is, of course, equally immobile, but it can provide a vehicle for a reading that achieves a coherent mobility.

As anticipated in my opening comments, one of the strongest reasons for this emphasis for these particular texts is the urgency of the issue of canonicity. Both editions are playing initiatory roles in redefining canons. In both plays, the dramatist in question played a minor role, acting as a reviser in a second stage of the text's development. I would not go as far as to suggest that the editorial presentation depends entirely on these circumstances for its justification. Indeed, given the complexity of the *Sir Thomas More* manuscript, and given its extraordinary richness as a documentation of process, an editorial approach that does some justice to that process is, I believe, the best outcome in the context of any editorial series. But the fact that these texts are being deliberately and conspicuously moved into a new context correlates meaningfully with the textual mobility that will be seen within these editions. In each case this text is not as it once was, because it has been adapted. It is on account of the difference adaptation makes that *Sir Thomas More* becomes Shakespearean and *Measure* becomes Middletonian.[16]

To this extent, the two-text editing of these plays is a mark of the problematic nature of authorial canons. Two-text editing says that these plays can be securely placed neither within nor without authorial canons as they are usually conceptualized. It defines an authorial penumbra. It suggests a practical, concretized image of authoriality not as a set of sealed containers but as an intercanonical network. Paradoxically, in order to sustain this image that erodes the authorial boundaries, the local markers of authorship within the text, as far as they are understood by scholars, must always be clear to the plays' readers.

NOTES

1. General editors Gary Taylor and John Lavagnino (Oxford University Press, forthcoming).
2. Gary Taylor and John Jowett, *Shakespeare Reshaped, 1606–1623* (Oxford University Press, 1993), pp. 107–236 and 296–321; John Jowett, 'The Audacity of *Measure for Measure* in 1623', *Ben Jonson Journal* 8 (2001), 229–47; Gary Taylor, 'Shakespeare's Mediterranean *Measure for Measure*', paper presented at the Seventh World Shakespeare Congress, Valencia, 2000, to appear in Thomas Clayton, Susan Brock, *et al.* (eds.), *Shakespeare and the Mediterranean* (forthcoming); Middleton, *Collected Works*.
3. For a recent assessment in favour see Brian Vickers, *Shakespeare as Co-Author* (Oxford University Press, 2002), pp. 67–72. For a recent assessment against, see Paul Werstine, 'Shakespeare More or Less: A. W. Pollard and Twentieth-Century Shakespeare Editing', *Florilegium* 16 (1999), 125–45.

4. Note, though, that the full text is in *The Complete Works* edited by C. J. Sisson (London: Odhams, 1954).
5. In the shorter Q1 text (1597) the speech is given to the Friar, and the words are closer to the Friar's version in Q2. This is consistent with the simplest interpretation of Q2, that the sequence of the text corresponds with the sequence of writing, and that the Friar's version supersedes the Romeo version.
6. *The Book of Sir Thomas More*, ed. W. W. Greg, rev. Harold Jenkins (Oxford: Malone Society, 1961).
7. D. C. Greetham, *Theories of the Text* (Oxford University Press, 1999), p. 305.
8. Compare Greetham, *Theories*, p. 365, citing Jacques Derrida and Martin Heidegger; 'where, in both cases, the problematic signifier is put under erasure so that its traces can still be seen – like a palimpsest – while it is not accorded full ontological presence in the *current* discourse' – the current discourse here being constituted by Middleton's works.
9. In Stanley Wells and Gary Taylor, with John Jowett and William Montgomery, *William Shakespeare: A Textual Companion* (Oxford University Press, 1987), p. 510.
10. Taylor, 'Shakespeare's Mediterranean'.
11. Taylor and Jowett, *Shakespeare Reshaped*, pp. 51–106.
12. As discussed in Middleton, *Collected Works*.
13. *The Vision of William concerning Piers the Plowman, in Three Parallel Texts, together with Richard the Redeless*, ed. Walter W. Skeat, 2 vols. (Oxford University Press, 1886).
14. One of the differences between Arden3 and the earlier Arden2 series is Arden3's greater flexibility in responding to the variety of textual situations. Jonathan Bate's edition of *Titus Andronicus* (London and New York: Routledge, 1995) uses a variant type-face to highlight material present only in the Folio text. R. A. Foakes's *King Lear* (Walton-on-Thames: Thomas Nelson, 1997) surrounds readings unique to the quarto with superscript 'Q' and readings unique to the Folio with superscript 'F'. Where appropriate, highly variant short quartos are reproduced photographically as an appendix.
15. Anthony Munday *et al.*, *Sir Thomas More*, ed. Vittorio Gabrieli and Giorgio Melchiori (Manchester University Press, 1990).
16. In the case of *Sir Thomas More* the same editorial considerations might apply to an edition in the context of an edition of Thomas Dekker's or Thomas Heywood's works: the revision is far from exclusively 'Shakespearean'. No other hand has been identified in the adaptation of *Measure*, and indeed *Collected Works* will consolidate the evidence for Middleton's authorship of a passage that was suggested in *Shakespeare Reshaped* to be possibly in a third hand. But, as noted above, the words of the song are by Fletcher.

CHAPTER 5

The New Bibliography and its critics

Ernst Honigmann

Often referred to now as if it stood for a clearly defined programme at a particular moment in time, the New Bibliography would be more justly described as a journey of discovery undertaken by a group of colleagues who could not know exactly where they were going and who regarded every halt in their progress as temporary. The leaders of the group – A. W. Pollard (1859–1944), R. B. McKerrow (1872–1940), W. W. Greg (1875–1959) – attracted a good deal of criticism, including criticism from the present writer, but their most important critics were undoubtedly the other members of their group. As they re-edited major documents of the 'Elizabethan' period they constantly challenged the findings of previous generations, and then modified their own in the light of criticism from each other: I see the New Bibliography and its critics as an evolutionary process with significant staging-posts, a process which I shall divide (very roughly) into four generations – 1900–20; 1920–50; 1950–70; 1970– .

FIRST GENERATION, 1900–1920

Two societies issued many of the publications of the New Bibliography in the early twentieth century: the Bibliographical Society (1892–) and the Malone Society (1906–). I shall concentrate in this paper on the analysis and classification of dramatic texts, so it will be as well to mention immediately that much else was accomplished in these early years. To name some of the outstanding achievements, Greg edited *Henslowe's Diary* (2 vols., 1904, 1908) and the *Henslowe Papers* (1907), McKerrow edited Thomas Nashe (5 vols., 1904–10), and others engaged in team-work such as *A Short-Title Catalogue of... English Books (1475–1640)*, ed. A. W. Pollard *et al.* (1926). F. P. Wilson, a central figure behind the scenes and also the author of brilliant articles and shorter books, chronicled the rapid advances of the first years in 'Shakespeare and the "New Bibliography"',[1] and concluded that 'if one man is to be chosen as the hero, then it is clear who that man is'. Looking back half a century later, we can say that Wilson's tribute to Greg was wholly justified. A man of private means,[2] Greg devoted his entire life to the New Bibliography and to helping friends with the same interests.

The story of the modern re-examination of Elizabethan dramatic texts begins, however, with A. W. Pollard, the author of *Shakespeare Folios and Quartos* (1909). Unlike Sidney Lee, whose *Life of William Shakespeare* (1898) had become a standard work, Pollard defended the good faith of Heminges and Condell in their First Folio, arguing that 'stolen and surreptitious copies' in the Folio epistle referred not to the majority of quartos (some of which were actually reprinted in the Folio) but only to the first quartos of *Romeo and Juliet*, *Henry V*, *Merry Wives*, *Hamlet*, and *Pericles*. Although not the first to take this view Pollard, it seemed at the time, firmly established the distinction between 'good' and 'bad' texts. Where Lee considered all the quartos, and hence at least some of the Folio texts, to be corrupt, Pollard brought to the editor's task a 'healthy and hardy optimism' (Preface), and this optimism inspired the New Bibliography to think again about the 'copies' used by Shakespeare's first printers.

For instance, Pollard and Dover Wilson returned to Shakespeare's 'bad' texts in a series of articles published in 1918 and 1919.[3] Collaboration of one kind or another became an almost regular phenomenon in the early phases of the New Bibliography, and we may assume that collaborators are also critics – often the best critics – and pushed each other forward. Even if Greg's name did not appear on the title-page, Pollard's *Shakespeare Folios and Quartos* benefited so significantly from Greg's criticism that the 'respective responsibilities for [our results] have become hopelessly entangled' (Preface).

F. P. Wilson traced the progress of these early provisional theories with exemplary care: I shall not try to compete with him but want to illustrate how the New Bibliography and its critics interacted by glancing at some of their arguments about dramatic texts, especially 'good' texts.

SECOND GENERATION, 1920–1950

The good texts were classified in five categories: (i) foul papers; (ii) promptbooks; (iii) private transcripts; (iv) players' parts; (v) plots. We assume that most of Shakespeare's plays once existed in the form of (i), (ii), (iv), and (v), and no doubt some as (iii), yet Shakespeare's editors are chiefly concerned with (i) – (iii) (and of course with 'bad' texts). Greg's indispensable *Dramatic Documents from the Elizabethan Playhouses* (2 vols., 1931) made available facsimiles, transcriptions, and commentaries.

(i) Foul papers

Greg thought it 'hardly surprising that among the waifs and strays of theatrical manuscripts that have come down to us, there is not much that we can confidently claim as foul papers. Most of the additions in the manuscript of *Sir Thomas More* may be reasonably regarded as such.'[4] The play of *Sir Thomas More* afforded the New Bibliography one of its greatest triumphs. Edited by Greg for the Malone Society (1911) it is in several hands, one of which (D) 'has been thought to be Shakespeare's' (Greg, p. ix). In 1923 Pollard gathered a small band of colleagues who contended on various grounds (handwriting, spelling, bibliographical links with the good quartos, the expression of ideas) that Hand D must be Shakespeare, a view that prevailed for many years. Nevertheless some dissent was heard, and more biting criticism has followed of late.

Shakespeare's Hand in 'The Play of Sir Thomas More', the 1923 collection edited by Pollard, gave the New Bibliography sensational publicity and also what appeared to be a reliable foundation for future editions of Shakespeare. No other sample of his handwriting is known, apart from the six signatures: the three pages by Hand D allow us a glimpse of his 'unblotted papers' and editors have found them invaluable when, in F. P. Wilson's words, they asked themselves 'what happened between composition and publication'.

(ii) Promptbooks

Whereas only a small number of Elizabethan dramatic manuscripts may be tentatively labelled foul papers, more manuscripts survive that we can more confidently describe as promptbooks. Some of them are scribal copies, a few are authorial. Of the scribal copies, several are in hands that can be identified as a playhouse book-keeper's. So here we stand on less shaky ground. As one might expect, the book-keeper sometimes added actors' names or stage directions. Yet, Greg warned, such features 'may be introduced by the book-keeper into the foul papers if he annotates them with a view to transcription';[5] characteristically, Greg devoted much space to similar warnings against hard-and-fast criteria for distinguishing foul papers from promptbooks, almost all of which he thought suggestive rather than definitive.

(iii) Private transcripts

Several of the transcripts that still survive are in the hand of Ralph Crane, a scrivener who worked for the King's Men before and after 1623. Thanks to splendid detective sleuthing by F. P. Wilson on Crane's manuscripts,[6] it was possible to identify Crane's idiosyncratic spellings, punctuation, and layout of dramatic texts, and thus to show that some of Shakespeare's Folio plays were printed from Crane transcripts – *The Tempest, Two Gentlemen, Merry Wives, Measure for Measure, The Winter's Tale*, and, I have suggested, *Othello*.[7] Transcripts, in short, were not only prepared for wealthy patrons but also to serve as printer's copy. Crane tidied and 'improved' his transcripts: we now know more about his writing habits than about those of others closely concerned with the transmission of dramatic texts, and this helps to clarify our general understanding of scribes and compositors and their faithfulness to 'copy'.

(iv), (v) Players' parts, plots

Although players' parts and plots must have existed for each of Shakespeare's plays, not one has survived. Greg edited non-Shakespearean plots and Alleyn's part in *Orlando Furioso*: the plots, sometimes in the hand of a playhouse book-keeper, can throw light on promptbooks, and Alleyn's part, compared with the printed version of the whole play, illustrates how unstable dramatic texts were at this time.

The ceaseless sifting of textual evidence and revaluation of theory continued for about fifty years from 1909, when the New Bibliography was most active. We may illustrate its shifts in thinking from McKerrow's papers on 'The Elizabethan Printer and Dramatic Manuscripts' (1931) and 'A Suggestion Regarding Shakespeare's Manuscripts' (1935).[8] McKerrow, following Pollard, again encouraged editorial optimism, arguing that the very untidiness and frequent corruptions of Shakespeare's good quartos, as compared with some other Shakespearean texts and other books of the same period, indicate that such good quartos must have been printed from the author's original drafts, not from a fair copy or promptbook; and in 1935 McKerrow added that Shakespeare's confusing use of different names for the same character in the good quartos would have been unacceptable in a promptbook and also points to foul-paper provenance (e.g. Lady Capulet is '*Lady of the house*', '*Old Lady*', '*Wife*', '*Mother*' etc.). Greg, Dover Wilson, F. P. Wilson etc. immediately welcomed McKerrow's conclusions; more recently, however, they have been challenged (see below, p. 89).

Let us finish with the 1920s, when E. K. Chambers rather than Greg may have seemed to dominate the 'Elizabethan' scene. Chambers (1866–1954) was nine years older than Greg; he published his monumental *Elizabethan Stage* (4 vols., 1923) and toiled at his equally valuable *William Shakespeare* (2 vols., 1930), but I do not see Chambers as a central figure of the New Bibliography, though he knew the leaders of the group and commented perceptively on their work. He served as first President of the Malone Society (1906–39) while Greg was general editor (also 1906–39). F. P. Wilson, who knew and admired both men, said of Chambers that contemporaries 'regard him as the very pink of orthodoxy and paragon of caution'; not so Greg, whose scholarship impressed others as 'adventurous' and 'profoundly influenced current theory and practice'.[9] Theirs must have been a strange relationship.

Greg's work was truly innovative, and he also stimulated others to innovate. For example, Peter Alexander identified *The Contention* (1594) and *True Tragedy* (1595) as 'bad' texts in *Shakespeare's 'Henry VI' and 'Richard III'* (1929). He also suggested that *The Taming of A Shrew* (1594) be redefined as a bad quarto and hinted that *The Troublesome Reign of John* (1591) might have to be included as well.[10] At the same time he implicitly questioned Pollard's division of the quartos into good and bad, urging that the quarto of *Richard III* must have had a more complicated history than that of a normal 'good' text. In short, the simplicity of 'Pollard's binarism', as Paul Werstine later called it, already began to worry textual critics in the 1920s. Madeleine Doran agreed with Alexander's view of the Henry VI plays, as did Chambers in 1930,[11] and Doran went on to argue, against Chambers, that Q *King Lear* was not a 'bad' quarto – an issue disputed for some time to come.[12] Meanwhile D. L. Patrick argued that Q *Richard III* must be a report of an abridged acting version.[13] *King Lear*, and to a lesser extent *Richard III*, refused to conform to the good–bad binarism, and every possible and some improbable theories were advanced to explain the text of Q *King Lear*. Pollard's 'good' texts spawned so many sub-categories that the division into either good or bad became almost meaningless.

Alexander focused on plays that Pollard had taken little interest in – the Henry VI plays, the Shrew plays (*A Shrew* and *The Shrew*) and the King John plays (*Troublesome Reign* and *King John*). As an undergraduate at Glasgow (1944–8) I heard Alexander speak of the King John plays 'for which no certain solution has yet been established', and later I returned to them in my Oxford B.Litt. thesis, 'Studies in the Chronology of Shakespeare's Plays' (1950) and my edition of *King John* (Arden2, 1954). One of the examiners of my thesis was F. P. Wilson, and I believe it influenced his thinking when he declared in 1951 that 'the fact is that the chronology of Shakespeare's earliest plays is so uncertain that it has no right to harden into an orthodoxy'.[14]

Already in the 1920s, and increasingly thereafter, the New Bibliography felt obliged to refine upon Pollard's division of Shakespeare's texts into either good or bad. We notice this in Alexander's book of 1929, where the index refers to *A Shrew* as a bad quarto, and Greg later added that it 'is not a "bad" quarto of the usual type'.[15] At much the same time as Greg's demurrer I used the term 'derivative play' to describe *Troublesome Reign* and *A Shrew*, works apparently not intended, like bad quartos, as reconstructions of popular plays but rather as independent plays that closely followed successful models. Alexander no doubt believed, as I did later, that the existence of a second derivative play dating from the same period (viz. *Troublesome Reign* and *A Shrew*) strengthened the case for both. And while it would be astonishing if Shakespeare followed a 'source-play' line for line, speech for speech, and scene for scene, it would not be at all surprising if this were to happen in a derivative play based on Shakespeare since we know that post-Shakespearean reconstructions or bad quartos were cobbled together in precisely this way.

THIRD GENERATION (1950–1970)

In the 1950s criticism of the New Bibliography grew more self-confident, especially in the person of Fredson Bowers. Bowers attacked where he thought the New Bibliography weakest, in its speculations about foul papers and theatrical fair copies:

> In my own opinion the present-day tendency to the mass assignment of any printer's copy as foul papers, when there is some presumed evidence in the printed text of authorial characteristics and none of theatrical prompt copy, has gone too far...I am not so convinced as some critics that the perfection of Shakespeare's plays was achieved in only a single act of composition, and that this 'original draft' was thereupon the manuscript turned over to his company.[16]

Bowers thought that the New Bibliography restricted its search for the 'copy' behind printed plays too exclusively to foul papers and promptbooks. 'Fouler papers' might lie behind the complete foul papers, 'intermediate manuscripts' may also have existed, and Greg, according to Bowers, assumed too readily that when the copy for a text cannot be a promptbook it must be foul papers. 'The evidence may not be so strong for foul-papers printer's copy as has been thought...I am far from sure that various of

Shakespeare's so-called foul papers were not close to what we might reasonably denominate worked-over fair copies.'[17]

The argument about Shakespeare's foul papers rested in part on the assertion of Heminges and Condell that 'we have scarce received from him a blot in his papers'. The New Bibliography took this more literally than did Bowers; reviewing Bowers, Greg replied that 'we have Ben Jonson's word for it that this [the "unblotted papers"] was no casual flower of speech but an habitual boast of the players. And unless Professor Bowers can point to earlier examples of the like claim, what business has he to assert that in making it Heminge and Condell were merely following a fashion, rather than setting one that Moseley followed a quarter of a century later?'[18]

Greg spoke for the past, Bowers for the future. Nevertheless I regard Bowers as a product of the New Bibliography as well as its most important mid-century critic. And other critics also appeared. C. T. Prouty's *'The Contention' and Shakespeare's '2 Henry VI'* (1954) returned to the Henry VI plays and argued that Alexander's hypothesis (cf. p. 81) might after all be incorrect.

> The alternative to memorial reconstruction is revision and since we have seen that a reporter does not explain the variations between our two texts, it will be well to examine known examples of revision to see what changes are introduced, and to see if these are analogous in any way to the case in hand.

He concluded, as others have done more recently, 'that a good many "Bad Quartos" are original plays, not reported texts'.[19] Hardin Craig's *A New Look at Shakespeare's Quartos* (1961) took the same route: he attacked 'the current "bibliographical school" of Shakespearean textual criticism', contending that the bad quartos 'were neither derived by stenography nor reconstructed from memory', and that most of them represent 'the author's original or "foul" papers'. The tight grip of the New Bibliography on the textual criticism of Shakespeare seemed about to loosen (and hence, perhaps, Greg's impatience in his review of Bowers).

Like Prouty and Craig, but starting from different premises, I had also noticed that the signs of corruption and revision are disturbingly similar. Might one be confused with the other? I was driven by a growing conviction that Shakespeare's editors, including the New Bibliography, had built their textual theories on a fallacy. Plays that survive in two or more substantive versions – such as *Hamlet*, *Othello*, *King Lear* – contain many hundreds of variant readings: the editors stigmatized most of these as corruptions and at the same time thought that a few must have been authorial revisions. Impressed as I was by the insistence of the New Bibliography that theorizing about printed texts should be checked, where possible, against extant manuscripts of the same kind and period, I was struck by the fact that authorial second thoughts can be quite indistinguishable from textual corruption. I first noticed this in later literary manuscripts, which included many variants similar to those found in corrupt texts – synonym substitution, singular–plural substitution, tense changes (spoke–spake, name–namde), transposition, graphically related substitution (lipping–sipping). Some of these authorial changes seemed to be deliberate and others unconscious – for an author transcribing his own work might suffer from fatigue just like a scribe or compositor. To be certain that such substitution could be safely ascribed to the author I needed to locate two holograph texts of the same work. Fortunately Middleton's *A Game at Chess* (1623) survives in two authorial fair copies, at Trinity College, Cambridge, and in the Huntington Library, California (partly in the author's hand). Middleton being a fluent and successful dramatist, we could hardly hope for a more appropriate author to compare with Shakespeare: and the variants in Middleton's fair copies bear a remarkable resemblance to the variants in Shakespeare's printed quartos and Folio.[20]

Manifest misprints in the quartos and Folio made it impossible to suppose that other variants in these texts were *all* authorial afterthoughts. Yet if an editor believes that the two texts of a Shakespeare play include *some* authorial substitution, how can he distinguish authorial substitution from corruption in the hundreds of remaining variants? This was a nettle that the New Bibliography had not grasped – or rather, it seemed to me a form of dynamite that could blow up the foundations of most editions of Shakespeare. In my earlier work on the King John plays I thought of myself as following in the footsteps of the New Bibliography: my new project brought me into collision with Pollard, Greg, and Alexander, greatly though I admired them.

Greg's *The Shakespeare First Folio* had to be my principal target because he now personified the New Bibliography and because he wrote so positively about Shakespeare's 'second thoughts'. He identified 'an unquestionable false start' in *Troilus and Cressida* (4.5.97) and claimed, of the opening lines of *A Midsummer Night's Dream*, Act 5, that 'There is no escaping the conclusion that in this we have the original writing',[21] and much more in the same vein. Greg's *The Shakespeare First Folio* was really the launching-pad for *The Stability of Shakespeare's Text* (1965), so I want to emphasize that much of my book had been drafted by 1959, when Greg died: he may have been eighty in 1955 but his mental powers were still dazzling. Yet, wonderfully alert as he was to the fallacies of his predecessors and contemporaries, Greg did not see that when he diagnosed 'second thoughts' in two-text plays as authorial, this brought into question a host of other readings.

In 1909 Pollard announced that the text of Shakespeare was not as corrupt as others had assumed; in 1923 he described himself as an 'incurable optimist', and in 1955 Greg endorsed 'the soundness of Pollard's optimism'. In 1965 I ended on a different note:

> If the two texts of a play like *Troilus and Cressida* contain first and second shots, as is generally admitted, a glance at authorial substitutions in holograph manuscripts will warn us to proceed with extreme caution, and to announce that scores of variants leave us completely in the dark... 'Optimistic' editors skim airily over too many unknowables in their corrective and eclectic labours, especially when dealing with plays probably resting on two arch-texts.

A realistic attitude to the unknowables in Shakespeare's text, I said, forces us to 'veer away from Pollard towards pessimism or, at any rate, scepticism'.[22]

FOURTH GENERATION (1970–)

Optimism suffered other blows in the fourth generation. A further phase of the revolt against the New Bibliography, and indeed against the editorial tradition generally, opened with Michael Warren's short paper on the revision of *King Lear* (1976).[23] This led to *The Division of the Kingdoms* (ed. Gary Taylor and Michael Warren, 1983), a collection of essays by eleven colleagues, most of them arguing that Shakespeare revised his play, and this in turn encouraged the editors of the Oxford Shakespeare (Stanley Wells, Gary Taylor, with John Jowett and William Montgomery, 1986) to publish two versions of *King Lear*:

> *King Lear* first appeared in print in a quarto of 1608. A substantially different text appeared in the 1623 Folio. Until now, editors, assuming that each of these early texts imperfectly represented a single play, have conflated them. But research conducted mainly during the 1970s and 1980s confirms an earlier view that the 1608 quarto represents the play as Shakespeare originally wrote it, and the 1623 Folio as he substantially revised it. He revised other plays, too, but usually by making many small changes... and adding or omitting passages, as in *Hamlet*, *Troilus and Cressida*, and *Othello*. For these plays we print the revised text in so far as it can be ascertained. But in *King Lear* the revisions are not simply local but structural, too... so we print an edited version of each text.[24]

Several points in this introductory note call for comment.

(1) The statement that the two texts of *King Lear* were wrongly thought to represent imperfectly 'a single play' omits to mention that all plays existed

in a state of constant evolution – from the original conception and preliminary discussions with actors, to rough drafts, fair copies, 'promptbooks', afterthoughts during performance, revivals, etc.; viz. the notion of the 'single play' had at this time to be elastic. Inevitably, more so in the theatre than in the bookshop. As Humphrey Moseley explained in 1647,

> When these comedies and tragedies were presented on the stage, the actors omitted some scenes and passages, with the authors' consent, as occasion led them; and when private friends desired a copy, they then, and justly too, transcribed what they acted. But now you have both all that was acted and all that was not, even the perfect full originals without the least mutilation.[25]

Bearing in mind that the actors might perform their plays at the Globe or Blackfriars, at court, at private houses, on provincial tours, that their company might be depleted by illness or death or by sudden departures, we see that the 'single play' had to be infinitely adjustable. The revision of *King Lear* may be more far-reaching than that of Shakespeare's other plays that we know of, but are we to imagine that *Hamlet* and *Othello* were always produced in a full text, lasting four hours or more, without adjustments such as we observe in the two texts of *King Lear*?

(2) Did Shakespeare revise *King Lear* 'substantially'? Would it not be true to say that so many characters, ideas, episodes, and speeches are very nearly the same in both versions, especially when we discount obvious misprints and alterations very probably due to scribes and compositors – would it not be equally true to describe the Q and F texts as 'substantially' the same play?

Readers and editors are more likely to think of a play as a text, or an ideal text ('the author's fair copy') frozen in time; Shakespeare's colleagues thought of it as a time-traveller, a living organism which adjusts to changing circumstances yet remains, essentially, the same play – just as a living body grows new cells all the time and nonetheless can be thought of as the same body. A body may lose an arm or a leg, or may acquire an artificial limb, a play may suffer 'mutilation' in its normal life in the theatre (so said Heminges and Condell, and Humphrey Moseley): how can we come to terms with this sameness and plurality?

We may wish to argue that every performance of *Hamlet*, by the same actors from the same 'book', will give us a slightly different experience and therefore a different play: every experience of the play, privately read or publicly performed, must be different. A small number of revised passages, or a single word changed by the author, constitutes a 'different' play, in theory. But where shall we draw the line? In my opinion the Oxford editors are (just) entitled to offer us two versions of *King Lear*, although the conflated text of the Arden3 editor, R. A. Foakes (1997), seems to me equally valid; on the other hand, the editing of other Shakespeare quartos, as if they are not very substantially the same play as the Folio version, seems – as I shall try to show – very questionable.

(3) It has become fashionable to dismiss conflated texts as obsolete. The editor, we are told, must do his best with each version of a two-text play, treating Q and F *King Lear* as distinct and separate. Insofar as some speeches and episodes in *King Lear* are alternatives, F replacing Q, this policy must be the right one – for such alternative passages. But is it right for the play's hundreds of other variants? How shall the editor distinguish authorial second thoughts from post-authorial corruption? Let the Oxford Shakespeare explain: 'Q [*King Lear*] contains many readings which are obviously nonsensical or inadequate, and the chief problem for an editor is the extent to which it should be corrected by reference to F. Naturally, we have retained Q wherever we could make defensible sense of it.'[26] The classic rebuttal of this position came long ago from the formidable A. E. Housman. To believe that wherever a text gives possible readings it gives true readings, said Housman,

and that only when it gives impossible readings does it give false readings, is to believe that an incompetent editor is the darling of Providence, which has given its angels charge over him lest at any time his sloth and folly should produce their natural results and incur their appropriate penalty. Chance and the common course of nature will not bring it to pass that the readings of a [text] are right wherever they are possible and impossible wherever they are wrong: that needs divine intervention.[27]

Because there are so many manifest errors in Q *King Lear*, where the editor must emend, I conclude that other improbable and some quite 'possible' readings in Q will be corruptions as well, and that editions of Q *King Lear*, and of all other Q versions of two-text plays edited on the principle proposed by the Oxford Shakespeare and denounced by Housman, will incorporate just as many false readings as old-fashioned conflated texts.

And, strangely, editors committed to an anti-conflation policy still persist in conflating! They hang on to improbable Q readings, yet replace Q with F when Q is 'obviously nonsensical or inadequate'. Is this not conflation? Where Goneril protests that she loves her father 'As much a child ere loued, or father friend' (1.1.54, Q), the Oxford editors (1986) prefer F's 'As much *as* child', and the Cambridge editor of Q, Jay Halio (1994), preferred two F readings, 'As much *as* child e'er loved, or father *found*'. Conflation appears to be unavoidable: the question is not whether to conflate or not, but rather how much to conflate.

(4) The editor's problem is aggravated by his inability to identify authorial revision. Consider two lines from the holographs of *A Game at Chess*:

> (a) this of all others beares the *hiddest* Venom
> the *smoothest* poyson, – *I am* an Arch-Dissembler S^r,
>
> (b) this of all others beares the *hiddenst* Venom
> the *Secretst* poyson; *Im'e* an Archdissembler (Sir)

Which is the earlier version? Which the better? Most of the other authorial variants are equally opaque, that is, hard to choose between – so how should an editor proceed? Let me repeat a caution equally relevant to Middleton and Shakespeare: 'I picture, then, not so much a fastidious author's determined attempts to improve passages that fail to satisfy as an author so unconceited with himself and so fluent that little verbal changes, *not necessarily always for the better*, ran quite freely from his pen when the process of copying refired his mind.'[28] Hence 'the instability of Shakespeare's text'. We may encounter hundreds of variants in the two texts of *King Lear* and most of them will defy our best efforts to decide which came first. And even if some variants in one text suggest that this text is the later one, we cannot simply adopt all the variants of this text, because, again, authorial revision and post-authorial corruption are so often indistinguishable. Editors of the fourth generation, whether of fully or partly conflated texts, have not taken on board this simple fact and its serious implications.[29]

The New Bibliography took more knocks when some of its basic concepts were challenged in the 1980s and 1990s, particularly its account of promptbooks and foul papers. 'Promptbook', first recorded by the *Oxford English Dictionary* in 1809, and 'foul papers', a term used by the scribe Edward Knight referring to Fletcher's *Bonduca* probably in or after 1625, may have been unknown before these dates – did Greg and the others transfer these words to an earlier period and describe promptbooks and foul papers 'unhistorically', as if the Elizabethan theatre anticipated the professional practice of later centuries?

I had better acknowledge a special interest. I argued in 1965 that Greg wrongly identified two play-texts as foul papers – his two most plausible examples – and that

> this term and its congeners (foul sheet, draft, etc.) do not signify an exclusive type of theatrical manuscript but any rough draft throughout the world of letters... The definition of terms will one day require more thought: for the time being, however,

no great harm will be done if we use 'foul papers' to denote any kind of draft preceding the first fair copy and define more circumspectly as the need arises.[30]

So, too, we may continue to use the word 'promptbook', as long as we remember that little is known for certain about promptbooks in the Elizabethan period. William B. Long, however, made an important contribution in 1985 when he observed that

> Greg strongly believed, in spite of evidence published in his own researches, that a finished promptbook had to be carefully inscribed and meticulously written ... so that the prompter could follow the text word-for-word, and that all ambiguities in stage directions would be resolved ... [whereas extant manuscript promptbooks] are by no means invariably neat and orderly; authorial stage directions are very seldom changed ... speech-heads are not regularized.[31]

While Long here offers less documentation than I would like – he argues from 'very seldom' and 'very often' and 'by no means invariably' – he does, I think, establish that we must beware of jumping to 'unhistorical' conclusions.

Paul Werstine has asked equally awkward questions, this time about foul papers. Do any dramatic foul papers still survive? What were the characteristics of foul papers? Is it certain that the good quartos were printed directly from Shakespeare's foul papers?[32] Since I disagreed with Greg on similar grounds long ago, partly following Bowers, it may seem quixotic if I now speak up on the other side. I do so because I think that the pessimism of the 'fourth generation' has gone too far, and requires qualification.

First, let us be clear that most performed plays must once have existed as foul papers and promptbooks, however we name and define these texts. No other full-length text need have existed. This is not to claim that a single quarto was ever printed directly from foul papers or a promptbook (though McKerrow and Greg thought so), only that, directly or indirectly, either foul papers or promptbooks will lie behind many of the printed texts that survive, perhaps at one or two removes. Greg may have leapt prematurely to 'crude binarism', from the thought that 'if the copy wasn't foul papers, it must have been a promptbook' (and vice versa), but his emphasis on these two kinds of text, though too exclusive, is not surprising.

Second, though the criteria used to identify promptbooks are open to criticism, those used for foul papers are less vulnerable. 'In general, and *a priori*, we should expect an author's foul papers to show a lot of deletion, alteration, interlining, false starts, and the like, and the thoroughness and clearness with which corrections were made would be likely to vary much with the care ... of the writer.'[33] Thus Greg, and I take his account of foul papers seriously even though I do not accept that two of the very few 'waifs and strays' identified as such by Greg are likely to have been foul papers. Why so? Because Greg, a life-long student of literary manuscripts and editor of *English Literary Autographs* (3 vols., 1925–32), knew what he was talking about. The 'foul' features that he described ('In general, and *a priori* ...') are found in dramatic and non-dramatic texts and must have been as common in the seventeenth century as later. Only when we move on to the specifically dramatic features of foul papers – stage directions, speech prefixes, *dramatis personae* lists – does an element of guesswork intrude. Werstine thinks that McKerrow 'simply asserted that variations in the naming of characters'[34] point back to Shakespeare. McKerrow had said that a promptbook 'would surely, of necessity, be accurate and unambiguous in the matter of the character-names',[35] and Long has convinced me that the official 'book' could include such confusion. Who, then, was responsible for these irregularities and confusions?

Here we must relate the bibliographical to the 'literary' evidence. By this I mean all the clues in the plays that indicate Shakespeare's free-wheeling writing habits, his intense concentration on what is important and, comparatively speaking, his indifference to the peripheral. Hence many mysteries and inconsistencies: how old is Hamlet? how many children had Lady Macbeth? double time in *Othello*, Claudius and Claudio in *Hamlet*, different titles for the same person (King–Duke, Queen–Princess in *Love's Labour's Lost*, 1598). Sometimes Shakespeare took trouble with names, pinning down a character with a name at his first entry, then forgetting it (Solinus, Eskales, Lamprius, Claudius, Innogen, Vincentio);[36] at other times he rushed on with the dialogue and left the names of minor characters to be sorted out later (cf. the speech prefix *other* in Hand D of *Sir Thomas More* and in *Hamlet*, Q2, 5.1). As Keats put it, a great poet is 'capable of being in uncertainties', a quality 'which Shakespeare possessed so enormously'.[37] Uncertainty about names, and ghosts in stage directions, would not normally be introduced by professional scribes but may be seen, in the light of the 'literary evidence', as characteristic of Shakespeare and his creative momentum.

Third, consider how many printers were involved in the good quartos: *Love's Labour's Lost* 1598 (W. White); *Romeo and Juliet* 1599 (T. Creed); *Merchant of Venice* 1600 (J. Roberts); *Much Ado* 1600 (V. Simmes); *Troilus and Cressida* 1609 (G. Eld), and so on. These texts share characteristics identified by the New Bibliography: omitted stage directions, ghost characters, different names for the same speaker, false starts, deletions, uncertainty about the number of minor characters ('two or three', 'and the rest'), underpunctuation, abnormal and unstable spelling. Werstine has found exceptions (post-authorial confusion probably introduced by a scribe or censor) and of course there will be exceptions. The important thing is not that some supposed 'foul paper' characteristics might be carried over into later texts, but the total picture. And the total picture, as it emerges from the good quartos produced by so many printing houses and confirmed by the 'literary evidence', is always very much the same. What is the common factor? A playhouse scribe was not paid to generate confusion: all the evidence points back to the same cause, Shakespeare's indifference to inconsistency.

Fourth, while we may not know for certain that a good quarto was printed *directly* from foul papers, does it matter? Not greatly, in my opinion. Editors would rejoice, of course, if they could prove that good quartos were based on autograph copy, since every transcript would spawn conscious and unconscious changes, that is, a new stratum of error. What is more important is that we should be able to guess, more or less confidently, that the copy belonged to a family of texts, viz. (1) foul papers or transcript; (2) author's fair copy or transcript; (3) scribal copy or transcript; (4) promptbook or transcript (leaving aside bad quartos as a separate problem). I believe that so many texts from group 1 survive, with so many striking similarities, that we may be reasonably confident about them; and sometimes the evidence for groups 2 and 3 is also quite positive.[38]

To sum up the four generations: if the optimism of the New Bibliography now seems a little excessive, its critics are no less vulnerable – since their theories are still in the process of evaluation. I feel less pessimistic than Werstine about the good quartos and what we may learn from them, among other things because I am convinced by the published and some unpublished evidence for Shakespeare's hand in *Sir Thomas More*.[39] The truly impressive achievement, we may say, has been the steady advance of scholarship and knowledge over a period of almost a hundred years – an international advance led by Greg, who remains, for me, the hero of the movement. Other heroic figures followed – Fredson Bowers, Charlton Hinman, D. F. McKenzie, Jerome J. McGann – but no one else intervened so often and so decisively, pointing to new avenues of research and almost invariably leading the way himself.

NOTES

1. F. P. Wilson, 'Shakespeare and the "New Bibliography"', in *The Bibliographical Society 1892–1942: Studies in Retrospect* (London: The Bibliographical Society, 1945), pp. 76–135.
2. See F. P. Wilson, 'Walter Wilson Greg', in *Shakespearian and other Studies* (Oxford: Clarendon Press, 1969), p. 226.

3. See J. Dover Wilson in *The Library* 3rd series, 9 (1918), 153–85, 217–47; A. W. Pollard and Dover Wilson, 'The "Stolne and Surreptitious" Shakespearian Texts', *Times Literary Supplement*, 13 March, 7 August, 14 August 1919.
4. W. W. Greg, *The Shakespeare First Folio* (Oxford: Clarendon Press, 1955), p. 108.
5. *Ibid.*, p. 142.
6. F. P. Wilson, 'Ralph Crane, Scrivener to the King's Players', *The Library* 4th series, 7 (1926), 194–215.
7. See T. H. Howard-Hill, *Ralph Crane and Some Shakespeare First Folio Comedies* (Charlottesville: University of Virginia Press, 1972); E. A. J. Honigmann, *The Texts of 'Othello' and Shakespearian Revision* (London: Routledge, 1996), chap. 6 ('The Folio Scribe and Text').
8. R. B. McKerrow, 'The Elizabethan Printer and Dramatic Manuscripts', *The Library* 4th series, 12 (1931), 253–75; 'A Suggestion regarding Shakespeare's Manuscripts', *The Review of English Studies* 11 (1935), 459–65.
9. Wilson, *Shakespearian and other Studies*, pp. 214, 242n., 235.
10. Peter Alexander, *Shakespeare's 'Henry VI' and 'Richard III'* (Cambridge University Press, 1929), p. 202.
11. Madeleine Doran, *'Henry VI, Parts II and III': Their Relation to the 'Contention' and the 'True Tragedy'* (University of Iowa Press, 1928); E. K. Chambers, *William Shakespeare: A Study of Facts and Problems*, 2 vols. (Oxford: Clarendon Press, 1930), vol. 1, p. 281.
12. See R. A. Foakes (ed.), *King Lear*, Arden Shakespeare (Walton-on-Thames: Thomas Nelson, 1997), pp. 110–46.
13. See Greg, *First Folio*, pp. 190–1.
14. F. P. Wilson, *Marlowe and the Early Shakespeare*, the Clark Lectures, Trinity College, Cambridge, 1951 (Oxford: Clarendon Press, 1953), p. 113.
15. Greg, *First Folio*, p. 210.
16. Fredson Bowers, *On Editing Shakespeare* (Charlottesville: University of Virginia Press, 1955, rev. edn 1966), pp. 12–13, 21, 29–31, 186–90.
17. *Ibid.*, p. 190.
18. *Shakespeare Quarterly* 7 (1956), 103. See my *The Stability of Shakespeare's Text* (London: Edward Arnold, 1965), pp. 22–33, where I argue, against Greg, that Heminges and Condell were merely following a fashion in praising Shakespeare's 'unblotted papers'.
19. C. T. Prouty, *'The Contention' and Shakespeare's '2 Henry VI'* (Stanford University Press, 1954), pp. 107, 119.
20. See my *Stability*, pp. 59–62, 63–77.
21. Greg, *First Folio*, pp. 346, 242.
22. Honigmann, *Stability*, pp. 169–71.
23. Michael Warren, 'Quarto and Folio *King Lear* and the Interpretation of Albany and Edgar', in *Shakespeare, Pattern of Excelling Nature*, ed. David Bevington and J. L. Halio (Newark: University of Delaware Press, 1978), pp. 95–107.
24. The Oxford Shakespeare, modern spelling edn, 1986, p. 1025.
25. See Chambers, *William Shakespeare*, vol. 1, p. 97 (spelling modernized).
26. Stanley Wells, Gary Taylor *et al.*, *William Shakespeare: A Textual Companion* (Oxford: Clarendon Press, 1987), p. 510.

27. See A. E. Housman, Preface to *Juvenal* (1905), and Honigmann, *Texts of 'Othello'*, pp. 144–9.
28. See Honigmann, *Stability*, pp. 61, 63.
29. The great difficulty for editors of two-text plays is the presence of 'indifferent variants' (this–that, singular–plural, tense variants etc.), but it is sometimes possible to make a reasoned choice: see Honigmann, 'On the Indifferent and One-Way Variants in Shakespeare', *The Library* 5th series, 22 (1967), 189–204; and *The Texts of 'Othello'*, pp. 68–9, on has–hath variants.
30. See Honigmann, *Stability*, pp. 17–18.
31. William B. Long, 'Stage Directions: a Misinterpreted Factor in Determining Textual Provenance', *Text* 2 (1985), 121–37; see also Long, '"A bed / for woodstock": a Warning for the Unwary', *Medieval and Renaissance Drama in England* 2 (1985), 91–118.
32. Paul Werstine, 'Narratives About Printed Shakespeare Texts: "Foul Papers" and "Bad" Quartos', *Shakespeare Quarterly* 41 (1990), 65–86; see also Werstine, 'McKerrow's "Suggestion" and Twentieth-Century Shakespeare Textual Criticism', *Renaissance Drama* 19 (1988), 149–73.
33. Greg, *First Folio*, p. 110.
34. Werstine, 'McKerrow's "Suggestion"', 151.
35. McKerrow, 'A Suggestion', 464.
36. *Errors*, 1.1.1; *Romeo*, 1.1.87; *Antony*, 1.2.1; *Hamlet*, Q2, 1.2.1; *Much Ado*, 1.1.1; *Measure for Measure*, dramatis personae list.
37. Keats to George and Thomas Keats, 21 December 1817.
38. See Honigmann, *The Texts of 'Othello'*, pp. 98–9 (arguing for an authorial fair copy of *Othello*, against Greg); pp. 59–76 (arguing for a scribal copy by Ralph Crane).
39. See 'Shakespeare, *Sir Thomas More* and Asylum Seekers' (forthcoming in *Shakespeare Survey* 57).

CHAPTER 6

Scholarly editing and the shift from print to electronic cultures

Sonia Massai

The change from paper-based text to electronic text is one of those elementary shifts – like the change from manuscript to print – that is so revolutionary we can only glimpse at this point what it entails.
(Jerome J. McGann)[1]

It is easy to become entranced by the abstract *possibilities* of electronic text . . . to the extent that the practical issues of editing seem about to vanish entirely. They will not. New editorial issues emerge, and they do not simply displace the old ones.
(John Jowett)[2]

A growing awareness of different types of textual instability and variation both *within* and *between* early printed editions of Renaissance play-texts has led to a crisis in editing for the medium of print. This essay explains how genuinely revolutionary possibilities offered by the electronic medium can help editors overcome the present impasse. Paradoxically, the electronic medium allows editors to present peculiar types of textual instability and variation in early modern printed drama more effectively than the codex form. The way in which textual evidence is presented, in turn, changes the way in which electronic editors and users think about texts. Having access to multiple variant versions of a play-text necessarily calls into question the very idea of a definitive edition. Crucially though, multiplicity does not override the need to assess the relative textual authority of each available version. Although editors can now exploit the versatility of the electronic medium to present multiple textual authorities, they still need to make informed decisions on how textual evidence should be presented, and to explain what complex textual evidence actually represents. After exploring some of the new possibilities offered by the electronic medium to represent textual instability and variation, this essay will consider how the representational powers of the electronic medium challenge the role of the editor. Far from making the editorial task redundant, the advent of the electronic medium is helping editors reconsider their methods and practices. In other words, the impact of the electronic medium on the scholarly editing of Shakespeare and early modern drama can best be assessed by glancing, Janus-like, both forwards to the revolutionary changes envisaged by McGann and backwards at the legacy of the editorial tradition invoked by Jowett.

One specific type of textual instability has given contemporary editors of Shakespeare and early modern drama much cause for reflection. Considering the early modern practice of stop-press correction, Stephen Orgel has usefully pointed out that 'the idea of a book embodying the final, perfected text was not a Renaissance one' and that 'the text in flux, the text as process, was precisely what Renaissance printing practice preserved'.[3] Even textual scholars like Randall McLeod, who opt for photographic facsimiles as the only form of textual reproduction and transmission which does not erase the rich complexity and instability of the early editions, have therefore been accused of misrepresenting the fluidity of the early modern text. 'If edited versions... usually idealize the activity of authorship', David Scott Kastan points out, 'facsimile versions work to idealize the printed text.' 'Facsimile', Kastan continues, 'performs... its own act of idealization [by] reif[ying] the particulars of a single copy of the text, producing multiple copies of a textual form that would have been unique.'[4]

New technology, as explored by Michael Best, allows electronic editors to 'take advantage of the capacity of the medium for animation by recreating a semantic field where the text dances between variant readings'.[5] Best uses animation to show how the electronic medium can visualize the complexity of semantic fields generated by variant spellings in the original textual authority. Taking his cue from Margreta de Grazia and Peter Stallybrass, who believe that cognates of 'weird' support both semantic fields of 'perversion and vagrancy' (weyard–weyward) and 'the world of witchcraft and prophecy' (weird),[6] Best uses animated type to visualize the verbal indeterminacy associated with Shakespeare's weyard–weyward–weird–wayward sisters in *Macbeth*. Similarly, Best shows how animated stage directions can help editors avoid simplifying the often ambiguous moments when characters enter or exit the stage. Animation is a flexible tool, which can be effectively used to foreground other types of textual instability. My new Internet Shakespeare Edition of *The Reign of King Edward the Third*,[7] for example, provides a diplomatic transcription of the first quarto edition of 1596 (Q1) and draws attention to textual instability within it by allowing press-variants to flicker on screen.[8] The application of new technology obviously requires the electronic editor to undertake the same labour-intensive task of collating all the extant copies of the original textual authority which editors carry out while editing for the medium of print. Once the electronic editor has completed this task, though, Best's technology provides a powerful tool to visualize the results. Electronic animation, in other words, can overcome the limits of the codex form which prevent even photographic facsimiles from reproducing textual instability as found in early modern texts. Needless to say, animation does not replace the sophisticated level of annotation through which editors have traditionally explained the complexity of textual variation. Users of electronic editions still need guidance to understand what exactly it is that is flickering on their computer screens!

If animation helps electronic editors highlight several types of textual instability and variation *within* the original textual authority, the electronic medium can also be used to foreground variation *between* different textual authorities. The popularity enjoyed in the last quarter of the twentieth century by the theory that Shakespeare revised some of his plays has focused attention on authorial agency. Users of several electronic projects, like the Shakespeare Electronic Archive[9] or the Internet Shakespeare Editions,[10] can already compare substantially variant texts of plays such as *King Lear*, *Hamlet*, and *Othello* by opening several windows at the same time or switching between them. The electronic medium thus provides an effective alternative to the attractive but costly solution offered by Michael Warren's *The Complete King Lear*,[11] where variant textual authorities are available in unbound photographic facsimiles, or to Bernice Kliman's *Enfolded Hamlet* and Jesús Tronch's *Synoptic Hamlet*, which replace multiple-*text* with multiple-*reading* editions through the use of a coded system of brackets, and superscript and subscript type, thereby presenting alternative readings to a single version of a multiple-text play.[12]

Animation can also be used to foreground non-authorial agency. The emphasis recently placed on authorial revision as the most significant source of variation between different textual authorities has reinforced the notion of Shakespeare as an author in control of his works, extending that control to multiple versions of some of his plays. As a result, textual variation that does not seem to derive from a manuscript or printed text of independent authority or from fresh consultation of copy is dismissed as derivative and confined to the textual apparatus. However, this type of variation should be carefully considered because it often reveals that non-authorial agents including printers, publishers, editors, and professional correctors prepared manuscript copies of play-texts for press, thus contributing to constructing the printed texts from which 'Shakespeare' emerged as an early modern dramatic author.

Recent studies have started to undermine the assumption that 'plays as a class were generally less competently printed than other books',[13] that printed play-texts were regarded as mere ephemera,[14] and that the stage and the page represented competing sites of cultural production.[15] Evidence drawn from Shakespearean and other early modern printed drama suggests that play-texts were often deemed worthy of editorial attention. More specifically, variation between some early printed editions of Renaissance play-texts sometimes shows that when authors were unwilling or unavailable to prepare copy for press some other professional associated with the printing house carried out this task on their behalf.

One such professional was the printer and publisher Richard Jones. Jones's contribution to the establishment of English drama in print is particularly significant because he represents a crucial link between Italianate literary drama, which grew out of fashion in the early 1590s, and the printing of dramatic texts written for the public stage, which became popular around the same time. Some of the play-texts printed and/or published by Jones reveal that a considerable amount of editorial attention was bestowed on the preparation of dramatic manuscripts for press. In his address to the reader in Whetstone's *Promos and Cassandra* (1578), Jones candidly explains that Whetstone failed either to prepare copy or 'to geue [him] apt instructions' on how to print 'so difficult a worke, beyng full of variety, both matter, speache and verse'. Jones takes responsibility for turning Whetstone's 'fyrst coppy' into a book and hopes that his 'paynes' will be compensated by the readers' approval of his efforts (A3v). Similarly, Jones's famous address to the reader in the first edition of Marlowe's *Tamburlaine* (1590) reveals an editor keen to prepare his text for the benefit of his discerning gentlemen readers:

I haue (purposely) omitted and left out some fond and friuolous Iestures, digressing (and in my poore opinion) far vnmeet for the matter, which I thought, might seeme more tedious vnto the wise, than any way els to be regarded, though (happly) they haue bene of some vaine cōceited fondlings greatly gaped at, what times they were shewed vpon the stage in their graced deformities. (A2r)

This address shows that, once purged of 'fond and friuolous Iestures', Jones deems a play originally written for the public stage worthy of his gentlemen readers' attention.

Further evidence drawn from the three editions of *Tamburlaine* published by Jones reveals that he not only omitted 'friuolous Iestures' but that he is also likely to have corrected the text of the play before each subsequent edition was issued from his press. Editors often comment on the 'remarkably clean' quality of the text preserved in Jones's 1590 edition,[16] but little agreement has been reached on the origin of the changes introduced in the second and the third octavo editions printed by Jones in 1593 and 1597. Albrecht Wagner and Una Ellis-Fermor, for example, argued that the second and the third editions derived independently from the first and that neither enjoys fresh and substantive authority.[17] Ethel Seaton was the first to question their conclusions:

> [N]either [Wagner] nor Miss Ellis-Fermor explains how it is that O2, sometimes alone of all [the early editions], gives the correct reading or spelling in more than half a dozen instances.... Other changes from O1 in shades of expression or meaning seem to point to a desire for greater nicety, and thereby to suggest themselves as author's variants.[18]

Although Marlowe might have prepared copy for the second edition of *Tamburlaine*, the second edition introduces new mistakes, which would seem to discount authorial involvement. Seaton therefore concludes that Marlowe is more likely to have sent Jones an annotated copy of the first edition, but that he failed to supervise the impression and to correct the proofs. However, several factors suggest editorial rather than authorial intervention in the second and third editions of *Tamburlaine*. First, Seaton overlooks the fact that the third edition of *Tamburlaine the Great* printed by Jones after Marlowe's death in 1597 emends as many substantial mistakes as the second edition.[19] Secondly, Richard Edwards's *Damon and Pithias*, the only other play which Jones prints more than once (in 1571 and 1582), exhibits a similar range of seemingly authorial emendations respectively five and sixteen years after its author's death in 1566.[20] Thirdly, Jones's omission of the 'fond and friuolous Iestures' from the first edition of *Tamburlaine* might amount to extensive cuts,[21] thus pointing to Jones as a likely candidate for the other changes introduced in the later editions of 1593 and 1597.

Richard Jones's commitment to preparation of copy suggests that when authors, unlike Gascoigne, Daniel, or Jonson, failed to prepare their works for publication, the 'perfecting' of the 'fyrst copy' was sometimes undertaken either by the publisher himself or by a third party, often a professional corrector. Textual scholars have recently abandoned the notion that Shakespeare, like the majority of playwrights who worked for the early modern public stage, was indifferent as to whether his play-texts ever reached the printing house and how they were printed.[22] Some scholars have even suggested that Shakespeare might have instructed his printers very carefully in terms of what specific layout and typographical features should be used in order to help readers appreciate the subtle use of off-stage playing areas, modes of delivery of complex speeches, and rhetorical emphasis.[23] However, although Shakespeare probably prepared some of his plays for publication, it is unlikely that he supervised their impression or that he was directly involved in the preparation of copy for subsequent editions.[24] Besides, the claim on some title-pages that early Shakespearean editions were 'newly corrected', 'emended', or 'augmented' is sometimes supported by internal evidence, which argues for editorial rather than authorial intervention. John Jowett and Lynette Hunter, for example, have recently drawn attention to instances of editorial intervention in the early quarto editions of *Romeo and Juliet*. Jowett believes that Chettle annotated the printer's copy of Q1 and that his 'interests lay in embellishing the text as a script from the theatre as well as solving mechanical printing house difficulties'.[25] Jowett therefore concludes that 'any account of Q1 that sees it as an entirely theatrical text – or as an almost entirely Shakespearian text – needs to take account of a contribution emanating from the printing house'.[26] Lynette Hunter similarly believes that an 'intelligent' editor or editors annotated both Q3 and Q4 and that 'we may have misjudged the role of the corrector in the printing house [which] may be far more extensive and engaged than we have previously thought'.[27] In his Oxford edition of *Richard III*, John Jowett draws attention once again to the contribution that agents associated with the printing house made to early Shakespearean quartos. Jowett believes that the publisher Andrew Wise, although not solely responsible for all the changes introduced in Q2 and Q3, had access to the printer's copy for Q1 and that he introduced two extra lines in Q2, and new stage directions and other minor changes in Q3.[28]

Editors for the print medium have no other option but to use the textual apparatus to alert their readers to the presence of editorial variants introduced in early textual authorities. Conversely, my new Internet Shakespeare Edition of *The Reign of King Edward the Third* includes digital images and a diplomatic transcription not just of Q1, but also of the second quarto of 1599. Instead of highlighting editorial variants[29] between the early textual authorities of *Edward the Third* in the textual apparatus I can show the effect of such variants in their original context. More specifically, the inclusion of Q2 allows me to show how an early modern editor prepared the printer's copy for press.

Although many changes introduced in Q2 correct obvious mistakes and normalize missing, ambiguous, or misplaced speech headings, other changes represent sophisticated corrections and are worth considering in their dramatic context. An interesting cluster of variants occurs in 2.1.

Before King Edward confesses his love to the Countess of Salisbury, he makes her swear that she will pawn all that lies within a woman's power to give to satisfy his desires. The countess is therefore forced to use her remarkable rhetorical powers to prove that she is not breaking her oath by refusing to give in to the king's advances. She first points out that the king already has all the love that she can give him lawfully, and when the king retorts that it is her beauty which he demands, the following exchange ensues in Q1:

Count. O were it painted I would wipe it of,
And disposse my selfe to giue it thee,
But souereigne it is souldered to my life,
Take one and both for like an humble shaddow,
Yt hauntes the sunshine of my summers life,
But thou maist leue it me to sport with all,.
Count: As easie may my intellectual soule,
Be lent awaie and yet my bodie liue,
As lend my bodie pallace to my soule,
A waie from her and yet retaine my soule,.
My bodie is her bower her Court her abey,
And shee an Angell pure deuine vnspotted,
If I should leaue her house my Lord to thee,
I kill my poore soule and my poore soule me,
    (C3r 13–26; QLN 602–15)

Q2 introduces four changes. Two of these changes are straightforward corrections: Q2 rightly reassigns the line 'But thou maist leue it me to sport with all,.' to the king and restores 'dispossesse' from 'disposse'. The other two changes are more intriguing because they are not strictly necessary, given that the original readings in Q1 are dramatically weaker but viable alternatives.

In Q1, the countess explains that she would comply with the king's request, if her beauty could be severed from her life. In Q1 the king seems to ignore the subtle argument which the countess uses to justify her refusal, because he simply suggests that the countess 'leue' him her beauty 'to sport with all' (C3r 18; QLN 607). The countess's next move is to explain that she could as easily lend her intellectual soul and retain her body, as lend her body and retain her soul (C3r 19–22; QLN 608–11). In the lines that follow, the countess repeats this point, this time comparing her body to the house of her soul, stressing that she would kill her soul, were she to leave her body (C3r 23–6; QLN 612–15). In this last speech (C3r 19–26, QLN 608–15) the countess uses the verbs 'to lend' and 'to leave' indifferently.

The shift from print to electronic cultures 101

Q2 introduces two changes which make the logic of this exchange more stringent and persuasive. The king's line is altered to read 'lend' instead of 'leave' (C3r 18; QLN 607). By using the verb 'to lend' rather than 'to leave', the king refines his argument by suggesting that the countess does not need to part with her beauty *permanently* (dispossess) but only *temporarily* (lend), while the king enjoys it. The king, in other words, accepts that the countess cannot part with her beauty indefinitely and rephrases his request accordingly. The final change in Q2 transforms the countess's line 'If I should *leaue* her house' into 'If I should *lend* her house' (C3r 25; QLN 614). The advantage of this last change is that the countess is allowed to stress consistently that *lending* and *dispossessing* herself of her beauty would have the same dire consequences, thus invalidating the king's subtle distinction.

While editors of printed editions of *Edward the Third* can only signal Q2 variants in the textual apparatus, the electronic editor can take advantage of resources native to the medium of the Internet to visualize their effects within their immediate dramatic context. Editing *Edward the Third* for the electronic medium meant that I could include Q2 in its entirety and highlight the effects of specific clusters of Q2 variants by means of animated types. The new possibilities offered by the electronic medium to include the entire text of Q2 and to foreground the sophisticated level of editorial intervention that went into the preparation of the printer's copy have also far-reaching implications in terms of how editors view derivative editions. Giorgio Melchiori, for example, believes that 'there is no doubt that somebody undertook the task of going over a copy of Q1 in order to disentangle and clarify ... the confusions in stage directions and speech-headings ... and to detect and correct the original printers' most obvious misreadings of the manuscript'.[30] In other words, Q2 often intervenes where Q1 fails to reproduce the manuscript. However, although Melchiori's edition relies on Q2 more than 150 times, he urges editors to exercise 'extreme caution' when using it as a source of corrections or alternative readings, because, after all, Q2 is 'derivative'.

The stark distinction between 'substantive' editions and 'derivative' reprints is a useful tool because it helps editors establish the relative distance between early modern editions and their manuscript source(s). However, such a distinction is misleading because it implies that editors can confidently distinguish readings that belonged to an authorial or a theatrical manuscript from editorial or scribal interference. As Paul Werstine and William Long have argued, it is virtually impossible for editors to establish whether the printer's copy was the author's foul papers, a theatrical manuscript, an authorial fair copy, or a scribal transcription. In other words, although impossible to quantify, editorial or scribal interference in substantive editions cannot and should not be discounted. By the same token, because the printer's copy of early modern printed texts is almost invariably lost, editors cannot always establish whether sophisticated corrections in derivative editions reveal consultation of copy, editorial intervention which happens to restore a copy reading, or a sensible correction which, however, departs even further from copy. As Thomas L. Berger usefully points out, early Shakespearean quartos often require us to broaden the definition of what constitutes a 'substantive' edition. According to Berger, '[a]ny quarto text that may not be derived solely from an earlier quarto is substantive'.[31] Like Pollard's definition of 'good' and 'bad' quartos, the familiar distinction between 'substantive' editions and 'derivative' reprints may help editors make sense of the complex textual evidence provided by early modern printed play-texts, but inevitably oversimplifies it. Besides, the distinction between 'substantive' and 'derivative' editions implies that the only agency worth preserving is authorial. The possibility offered by the new medium to include multiple textual authorities allows editors finally to acknowledge the significant intervention of editorial agents who took an active role in establishing early modern dramatic texts.

By prompting fresh scrutiny of established assumptions about the relative authority of the extant editions of an early modern play-text, the electronic medium gives editors a chance to reflect on their current methods and practices. Animation and presentation of multiple variant textual authorities provide editors with powerful alternative ways of presenting textual evidence, which were simply not possible in codex form. The new presentational possibilities offered by the electronic medium in turn invite a comparison with the presentational options native to the medium of print. My edition of *Edward the Third*, for example, includes a diplomatic transcript of the 1596 quarto edition (Q1), digital images of the second quarto edition of 1599 (Q2), and of the major editions in the editorial tradition. Among these, Capell (1760), Warnke and Pröscholdt (1886), and C. F. Tucker Brooke (1905), are available in full. Recent editions (Riverside 1995; Sams 1996; Melchiori 1998; and Warren 2002, among others) are represented by digital images of short extracts in compliance with current copyright regulation. One of the most interesting consequences of being able to include such a wide range of editions is that they de-centre my own. Such diversity and dispersal of editorial authority is unimaginable in print editions, where the editorial tradition is carefully harnessed by the apparatus to document alternatives, but also to foreground the modern editor's decisions. The electronic editor who provides a modernized version of an

The shift from print to electronic cultures 103

early modern play-text is not exempt from decision-making, but the impact of his or her editorial decisions is not as far-reaching, because the user can compare the modern text with earlier editions, including the early textual authorities.

Another change brought about by the electronic medium is that the end result of an editor's labours is not a critical *edition* but a critical *archive*. A critical edition is structured hierarchically and privileges the modern text over other textual alternatives, which are cryptically and partially summarized in the textual apparatus. The critical archive provides accurate and searchable digital versions of the editions from which those textual alternatives derive. Besides, a critical edition gives an account of the theatrical/cinematic and critical reception of a play-text whereas a critical archive provides the very materials – scripts, reviews, press releases, photographs, interviews, extracts from published sources – which the critical edition interprets on behalf of the reader. Although not hierarchically structured, the archive is not simply a dauntingly large and acritically presented mass of information. The editor selects the material to be included in the archive and structures it by setting up a network of hyperlinks, which connect discrete items in the archive to other items in the same archive or on different Internet sites.

The nature of the electronic archive radically affects both the way in which editors envisage the editorial task and the way in which readers approach the materials which the editor provides. A printed critical edition helps the reader approach the text by establishing a clear hierarchy of meanings and interpretations. The electronic archive similarly provides predetermined searches, but the editor has no power to control how far the user is going to follow a sequence of links, which can lead to full versions of supporting materials, to critical assessments of the play, or even to sites outside the archive. The structure of the archive is open-ended and the virtually endless combinations of pathways which the user can follow utterly arbitrary. The user is thus encouraged to abandon linear reading in favour of dynamic interaction with texts and intertextual analysis. The electronic medium, in other words, not only widens access to rare texts but also transforms the *reader* into a *user*, or what can be described as a 'Barthesian' reader. The very nature of the provision offered by the electronic archive encourages users to constitute their own hierarchies of meanings and interpretations by choosing what other texts or supplementary materials should be allowed to signify alongside the main text. While critics of the possibilities offered by the electronic medium believe that users feel confused and overwhelmed by the amount of materials made available by electronic editors, supporters of the medium such as J. D. Bolter point out that hypertext 'explicates the powerful grasp of powerful readers for weaker readers'.[32]

Users of my edition of *Edward the Third* are encouraged to read the play intertextually by means of the wide range of materials available in the archive. The above-mentioned exchange between the king and the countess, for example, is linked not only to its sources in Froissart and Painter but also to other contemporary dramatic and non-dramatic texts. Given the disputed attribution of this play, users may be interested to find out whether a comparison with the sources reveals the same ability to construct eloquent arguments and exciting drama with which Shakespeare is traditionally associated. Similarly, users may be intrigued by the fact that the vocabulary used to describe children born out of adulterous affairs in *Edward the Third* is used again during the pleading scenes in *Measure for Measure*. The following passage in *Edward the Third*, for example,

> He that doth clip or counterfeit your stamp
> Shall die, my Lord; and will your sacred self
> Commit high treason against the King of heaven
> To stamp his image in forbidden metal
> Forgetting your allegiance and your oath?
> (QLN 629–33)

is famously echoed in *Measure for Measure*:

> It were as good
> To pardon him that hath from nature stolen
> A man already made, as to remit
> Their saucy sweetness, that do coin heaven's image
> In stamps that are forbid. 'Tis all as easy
> Falsely to take away a life true made
> As to put metal in restrainèd means
> To make a false one.
> (2.4.41–8)

Users considering the exchange between the king and the countess are also alerted to the fact that the countess's views on the relationship between the body and the soul are shared by many of Shakespeare's contemporaries. Users can access extracts from *Two Guides to a Good Life*, where the anonymous author explains that 'the soule is infused by God, [and] in that respect it is clean & without spot . . . for the bodie infectes not the soule, but the soule the body, whose instrument it is'.[33] According to this view, rape would not contaminate the countess's body, but connivance with the king's adulterous plans certainly would. Another contemporary of Shakespeare's reports the belief expressed by the countess that the body is the house of the soul, and that, should she leave the house to be ravaged by the king's lust, her soul would also die. In William Perkins's *The Whole Treatise of the Cases of Conscience*, 'the union of the bodie with the soule' is said to 'make one person', and that 'sinnes of uncleanness' are the most dangerous ones, because there are no others that leave 'a blot so deeply imprinted in [the soul]'.[34] Users of *Edward the Third* can therefore search and analyse a wider range of materials than an editor can ever hope to include in a printed edition. Hypertext editions seem almost to reproduce a Barthesian notion of the text as open and plural, except that the intertextual links made by the Barthesian reader are now materially visible as hyperlinks which fragment the text's pristine integrity on the printed page.

Many critics have noticed how hypertext embodies postmodern views of authorship and textuality as plural and unstable. As this essay has explained, the electronic medium can also be used to visualize several types of textual plurality and instability which were native to the medium of print in the early modern period. However, editors should be careful not to overlook the fact that early modern printers and publishers, far from advertising or celebrating the level of textual instability inherent to early modern print culture, invested time and effort in "perfecting" their texts. Elizabeth Eisenstein's investigation of the impact of the printing press on early modern Western European culture[35] has rightly been criticized for taking the claims to standardization, reliability, and fixity made by early modern printers and publishers too literally. The corrective hypothesis advanced by Adrian Johns has the advantage of overcoming the stark opposition between Eisenstein's idealization of stability as the defining value of early modern print culture and the emphasis recently placed by postmodern theorists on textual instability. According to Johns, although 'textual corruption ... actually increased with the advent of print, due to various combinations of piracy and careless printing ... printers and booksellers were manufacturers of credit'. 'The "printing revolution"', Johns adds, 'if there was one, consisted of changes in the conventions of handling and investing credit in textual materials.'[36] After all, it was from the publication of early modern play-texts that Shakespeare and his contemporaries started to emerge as singular, proprietary authors.[37]

The notions of Text, Author, and Canon are culturally- and medium-specific. Although the electronic medium has made these categories obsolete, electronic editors should not overlook the fact that the same categories acquired new cultural, ideological, and economic significance in the early modern period. In fact, another major benefit which editors can derive from the electronic medium is the possibility to include not only the full texts of earlier editions, but also digital images of the paratextual material which frames those texts. By including digital images of early title-pages, dedicatory epistles, printers' addresses, and lists of errata, the electronic editor encourages the user to regard each text as a complex cultural artefact. Rather than overlooking medium-specific ideological categories and the cultural and economic pressure from which printed drama emerged, the electronic archive encourages a cultural historical approach by making rare artefacts more widely accessible. Although digital images cannot replace consultation of the actual original textual authorities, the electronic archive can help future generations of students and textual scholars to consider the wider cultural implications of textual transmission of early modern printed drama. If the possibilities offered by the new medium represent a radical technological break from print culture, they can also lend powerful new insights into it.

NOTES

I would like to thank Michael Best (Internet Shakespeare Editions, general editor) and Eric Rasmussen (ISE, textual editor) for their support, and Richard Proudfoot for his useful suggestions. I would also like to thank the British Academy for an Overseas Conference Grant which I used to travel to the 31st Congress of the Shakespeare Association of America (Victoria, BC, April 2003), where I presented a paper on my Internet Shakespeare Edition of *The Reign of King Edward the Third*. The positive feedback to that paper prompted me to write this essay.

1. Jerome J. McGann, 'The Rationale of Hypertext', in *Electronic Text: Investigations in Method and Theory*, ed. Kathryn Sutherland (Oxford: Clarendon Press, 1997), p. 40.
2. John Jowett, 'After Oxford: Recent Developments in Textual Studies', in *The Shakespearean International Yearbook*, ed. W. R. Elton and J. M. Mucciolo (Aldershot: Ashgate, 1999), pp. 79–80.
3. Stephen Orgel, 'What is an Editor?', in *Shakespeare and the Editorial Tradition*, ed. Stephen Orgel and Sean Keilen (New York and London: Garland, 1999), pp. 117–18.
4. David Scott Kastan, 'The Mechanics of Culture: Editing Shakespeare Today', *Shakespeare Studies* 24 (1996), 35–6.
5. Michael Best, 'Standing in Rich Place: New Readings, New Interactions', in Internet Shakespeare Editions, http://web.uvic.ca/shakespeare/Annex/ticles/ArSAA2002/rich4.html. Visited 1 May 2003.
6. Margreta de Grazia and Peter Stallybrass, 'The Materiality of the Shakespearean Text', *Shakespeare Quarterly* 44 (1993), 263.

7. Sonia Massai (ed.), *The Reign of King Edward the Third*, Internet Shakespeare Editions, http://web.uvic.ca/shakespeare.
8. My collation of extant copies of Q1 is still in progress; the number of press-variants highlighted through animated type in my diplomatic transcript of Q1 is therefore bound to increase until my collation is completed.
9. Cf. Peter Donaldson, 'Digital Archive as Expanded Text: Shakespeare and Electronic Textuality', in *Electronic Text*, ed. Sutherland, pp. 173–97.
10. The site can be visited at http://web.uvic.ca/shakespeare.
11. Michael Warren (ed.), *The Complete King Lear* (Berkeley: University of California Press, 1989).
12. Bernice Kliman, 'The Enfolded *Hamlet*' in *The Shakespeare Newsletter*, extra issue (1996), 1–44, and Jesús Pérez Tronch (ed.), *A Synoptic Hamlet* (Valéncia: Sederi, Universitat de Valéncia, 2002).
13. Peter W. M. Blayney, *The Texts of 'King Lear' and Their Origins: Nicholas Okes and the First Quarto* (Cambridge University Press, 1982), p. 184.
14. Henry Woudhuysen, 'Early Play Texts: Forms and Formes', in *In Arden: Editing Shakespeare*, ed. Ann Thompson and Gordon McMullan (London: Thomson Learning, 2003), pp. 48–61. Although Woudhuysen concludes that 'there is conflicting evidence in [the] printing [of plays] about the need to be sparing in the use of paper, . . . the presence of [blank leaves] . . . might be taken to challenge received ideas about the relative value placed on printed plays' (pp. 59, 55).
15. See, for example, Barbara Mowat, 'The Theatre and Literary Culture', in *A New History of Early English Drama*, ed. J. D. Cox and D. S. Kastan (New York: Columbia University Press, 1997), pp. 213–30, and Julie Stone Peters, *The Theatre of the Book: Print, Text and Performance, 1480–1880* (Oxford University Press, 2000).
16. David Bevington and Eric Rasmussen (eds.), *Christopher Marlowe: 'Doctor Faustus' and Other Plays* (Oxford: Clarendon Press, 1985), p. xxvi.
17. Albrecht Wagner (ed.), *Marlowes Werke. I. 'Tamburlaine'* (Heilbronn, 1885), pp. xxii–xxxi, and Una Ellis-Fermor (ed.), *Tamburlaine the Great* (London: Methuen, 1930), pp. 281–2.
18. Ethel Seaton, 'Review of *The Works and Life of Christopher Marlowe. . . .* Volume II. *Tamburlaine the Great*, in two parts. Edited by U. M. Ellis-Fermor . . .', *Review of English Studies* 8 (1932), 467–8.
19. David Fuller (ed.), *Tamburlaine the Great, Parts 1 and 2* and Edward J. Esche (ed.), *The Massacre at Paris with the Death of the Duke of Guise*, in *The Complete Works of Christopher Marlowe*, gen. ed. Roma Gill, 5 vols. (Oxford: Clarendon Press, 1987–98), vol. v, pp. xlvii–xlviii.
20. For more details, see John S. Farmer (ed.), *The Dramatic Writings of Richard Edwards, Thomas Norton and Thomas Sackville* (London: Early English Drama Society, 1906), pp. 163–6.
21. Seaton, 'Review', 469, and Fuller (ed.), *Tamburlaine*, p. xlix.
22. See, for example, Lukas Erne, *Shakespeare as Literary Dramatist* (Cambridge University Press, 2003).

23. Henry Woudhuysen, 'The Foundations of Shakespeare's Text', the Shakespeare Lecture, delivered at the British Academy on 23 April 2003.
24. See, for example, Erne, *Shakespeare*, pp. 97–8.
25. John Jowett, 'Henry Chettle and the First Quarto of *Romeo and Juliet*', *Publications of the Bibliographical Society of America* 92 (1998), 57.
26. *Ibid.*, 67.
27. Lynette Hunter, 'Why has Q4 *Romeo and Juliet* such an Intelligent Editor?', in *Re-Constructing the Text: Literary Texts in Transmission*, ed. Maureen Bell *et al.* (Aldershot: Ashgate, 2001), p. 20.
28. John Jowett (ed.), *Richard III* (Oxford University Press, 2000), pp. 115–16.
29. Editors of *Edward the Third* agree that variants between Q1 and Q2 are editorial rather than authorial because Q2 normalizes speech prefixes and other features of the text fairly systematically but fails to correct obvious mistakes, such as 'a hellie spout of bloud' [a Hellespont of blood] at QLN 1010.
30. Giorgio Melchiori (ed.), *King Edward III* (Cambridge University Press, 1998), p. 175.
31. Thomas Berger, 'Press Variants in Substantive Shakespearian Quartos', *The Library* 6th series, 10 (1988), 232.
32. J. D. Bolter, 'Authors and Readers in an Age of Electronic Texts', in *Literary Texts in an Electronic Age: Scholarly Implications and Library Services*, ed. Brett Sutton (University of Illinois at Urbana-Champaign, 1994), p. 7.
33. *Two Guides to a Good Life: Or, The Genealogy of Vertue and the Nathomy of Sinne* (London, 1604; *STC* 12466), C1r.
34. William Perkins, *The Whole Treatise of the Cases of Conscience, Distinguished into Three Bookes* (London, 1604; *STC* 19669), pp. 189–90.
35. Elizabeth Eisenstein, *The Printing Press as an Agent of Change*, 2 vols. (Cambridge University Press, 1979).
36. Adrian Johns, *The Nature of the Book: Print and Knowledge in the Making* (University of Chicago Press, 1998), pp. 31, 33.
37. Title-pages of early modern play-texts often advertised not only the name of the author, but also a link with the author's 'true and perfect copy' and even with the author's intentions. See, for example, the second quarto of *Hamlet* (1604), which is advertised as being 'newly imprinted and enlarged to almost as much againe as it was, according to the true and perfect Coppie'. The title-page of *The Duchess of Malfi* (1623) similarly informs its readers that the text derives from the 'perfect and exact Coppy, with diuerse things Printed, that the length of the Play would not beare in the Presentment'. The title-pages of *Microcosmus* (1637) and *The Unfortunate Mother* (1640) make the connection with the author even more explicit by claiming that these plays were 'Set down according to the intention of the Authour Thomas Nabbes'.

PART II
Presenting the play

CHAPTER 7

'Your sum of parts': doubling in 'Hamlet'
Ann Thompson and Neil Taylor

This essay explores how what we think we know about the historical practice of doubling on Shakespeare's stage informs or might inform the editing of his plays. We are currently editing *Hamlet* for the Arden Shakespeare (third series) and we start from the 'Guidelines' issued to all editors (and partly written by Ann Thompson as one of the general editors). Guideline 13d5 in the version of this document revised in June 2000 is headed 'Staging and casting demands' and states that the Introduction 'should include a graphic representation of the latter, and some comment on doubling possibilities, cross-referenced to the List of Roles'. Editors are referred to various published examples of casting charts, such as those supplied by David Bradley and T. J. King,[1] though they are warned that some assumptions about doubling are 'rigid and questionable' so they should, as always, think for themselves. In practice, only seven out of seventeen plays published so far in Arden3 provide a casting chart, and of these only three provide much discussion of the issues involved (though it is true that some editors who do not provide a chart nevertheless discuss some specific casting issues, as we shall specify below). We propose to explore why the inclusion of a casting chart for each play might be thought desirable in an edition, and why the assumptions that underpin them might be thought 'questionable'. We shall illustrate our argument with examples from *Hamlet*.

Guideline 13d5 arose partly from discussions Ann had had with some theatre directors who were apparently unaware that doubling was a routine practice on the Elizabethan and Jacobean stage and who had assumed that they could not afford to put on Shakespeare because they would need too many actors. It has to be said, of course, that doubling as a practice dates back to medieval and Tudor drama, when itinerant acting companies were very small, and all the actors probably had to double. Itinerant companies grew larger – there were fourteen in Lord Derby's company, for example, when it visited Chatsworth in 1611[2] – and, while the professional acting companies that made their bases in London after 1576 continued with doubling, there increasingly emerged 'specialist' actors, who took up the main parts and doubled less than those playing the more minor parts. But modern directors and audiences are so used to a 'star-conscious' style of casting whereby actors playing large or even medium-sized parts are not expected to double, that they are surprised, sometimes baffled, but often excited by the notion of a more egalitarian sharing of work among a relatively small company. Recent London productions of some of Shakespeare's plays with very small casts indeed such as Red Shift's 1999 Q1 *Hamlet* (with eight) and Shakespeare's Globe's 2001 *Cymbeline* (with six) have proved that pushing doubling to extreme limits can be enjoyable and exhilarating.

Scholars and students gain new perspectives on the plays and especially on Shakespeare's methods of dramatic construction when they take into account the fact that for most of his career he was writing for a stable company of around ten men and three or four boys. The need to keep complex doubling patterns in mind while dramatizing material from the multi-character chronicle histories, for example, draws our attention to the basic 'engineering' of the plays in a way that might be compared to the requirements of the 'law of re-entry', that is the necessary convention whereby Shakespeare almost always avoids having a character enter at the beginning of a scene if he or she had been on stage at the end of the preceding one.[3] While modern actors may complain about the lack of parts for women, doubling conventions remind us that the boys who played the women may also have been kept busy with other roles as young men, pages, servants, etc. Some scholars have argued that the convention of doubling required the audience to overlook the individual identities of the actors whose virtuoso skills made them unrecognizable in their different roles, while others have argued that doubling could create a significant relationship between the roles doubled.

Evidence of the practice of doubling on the English stage can be traced back to the fifteenth century with the Croxton *Play of the Blessed Sacrament*.[4] The original incentive was probably economic: an acting company, be it itinerant or resident, needed to be kept as small as possible, so actors would often be required to play more than one part. However, there is a limit to the number of parts that can be played in a particular performance. Russell Thorndike claimed that last minute emergencies once obliged him to play ten parts in *Macbeth*, but that at one point this meant he met himself on stage.[5] Actors have to have time to change costume between an exit and an entrance (though productions of *A Midsummer Night's Dream* since Peter Brook's in 1970 have allowed minimal or no time for the actors of Oberon and Titania to transform themselves into Theseus and Hippolyta in 4.1). One would also assume that, normally, a character is only played by one actor, though this 'rule' has been broken in productions of *The Comedy of Errors*, for example, by the Royal Shakespeare Company in 1990 and Shakespeare's Globe in 1999, where one actor played each pair of twins and a 'double' was provided in the final scene, and in the RSC 1969 production of *The Winter's Tale* where Judi Dench played both Hermione and Perdita, with a 'double' standing in at the end. This particular doubling goes back to Mary Anderson at the London Lyceum in 1887.[6] Female parts on Shakespeare's stage were of course played by boys, so scholars who have attempted to calculate the minimum numbers of actors required for productions of his plays have usually divided the company into two groups, men and boys. Some have gone further and assumed that the core company was supplemented by 'hired men' for non-speaking and very small parts, thus introducing a third group.

In addition to doubling for practical purposes (what Sprague calls 'deficiency' doubling), several scholars have argued for the practice of 'conceptual doubling' whereby the audience is assumed to be aware of the practice and to make connections between the roles doubled. Thomas L. Berger, for example, speculates that in *Henry V* the three traitors, Cambridge, Scroop, and Grey, are replaced 'not only thematically but literally' by the three honest soldiers, Bates, Court, and Williams, and that the actors of Bardolph and Nym, 'sworn brothers in filching', have previously appeared as the Bishops of Canterbury and Ely. In such cases the audience's 'quasi-recognition' of the actors adds another layer to the meaning.[7] Alan Dessen finds 'limited evidence' for conceptual doubling in the moral plays of the 1560s and 1570s which were printed with casting assignments, but he notes that these were very differently constructed plays, with four or five actors playing as many as twenty roles.[8] In 1966 Homer Swander argued for the doubling of Posthumus and Cloten in *Cymbeline*.[9] Ralph Berry proposed the doubling of Edward IV and Richmond in *Richard III*, and, on a larger scale, the Roman crowd at the beginning of *Coriolanus* and the Volscian crowd at the end.[10] William A. Ringler suggested another 'group doubling', which would certainly carry significance – that of the four 'rude mechanicals' (Flute, Starveling, Snout, and Snug) with Titania's four fairies (Pease-blossom, Cobweb, Moth, and Mustard-seed) in *A Midsummer Night's Dream*.[11] But, looking back in 1991 the actor and director Tony Church expressed a lack of enthusiasm for conceptual doubling when it becomes the means by which a director attempts to 'explain' Shakespeare.[12]

All but one of the Arden3 editors who have supplied casting charts are editors of the history plays; they are, in order of publication, T. W. Craik for

Henry V (1995), Ronald Knowles for *2 Henry VI* (1999), Edward Burns for *1 Henry VI* (2000), Gordon McMullan for *Henry VIII* (2000), John D. Cox and Eric Rasmussen for *3 Henry VI* (2001), Charles R. Forker for *Richard II* (2002), and David Scott Kastan for *1 Henry IV* (2002). The exception is Giorgio Melchiori who supplied a casting chart for *The Merry Wives of Windsor* (2000), a play that has obvious close links with the Histories. This generic concentration is perhaps not surprising as these plays tend to have large numbers of speaking roles and hence require considerable ingenuity in casting. Cox and Rasmussen, for example, argue that in *3 Henry VI* 'sixty-seven roles require twenty-one adult actors, all of whom are on stage at once in a tense confrontation between York and Lancaster in 1.1, while four other scenes require fifteen or more actors to be on stage at the same time'.[13] They manage to cast the play with eight adult actors, five hired men, and four boys, coming out with a chart quite similar but not identical to that compiled by King. Edward Burns, on the other hand, casts *1 Henry VI* for fourteen adult actors and two boys, as compared with King's argument for a cast of thirty for this play at the Rose: fifteen 'major' players, two boys, and thirteen 'minor' players. David Scott Kastan is equally economical with his actors, casting *1 Henry IV* for thirteen, as against King's twenty-two and Bradley's sixteen. T. W. Craik notes that the forty-nine roles of Folio *Henry V* are reduced to forty in the 1600 quarto but apparently does not go so far as Gary Taylor who assumes that many of the alterations in the quarto text can be explained by the assumption that the play had to be recast for a company of no more than eleven actors.[14]

Most of these editors provide casting information in a separate Appendix (Melchiori incorporates it into the Introduction), or, as is suggested in the 'Guidelines', they discuss it in the notes to their List of Roles. For the most part, they are concerned with practical or 'deficiency' doubling, though a few do speculate about conceptual doubling. Ronald Knowles, for example, refers in his Introduction to *2 Henry VI* to the 'subtle doubling' in the BBC version of that play,[15] and, going beyond the History plays, R. A. Foakes discusses the often-mooted doubling of Cordelia and the Fool in *King Lear*.[16] Henry Woudhuysen refers to Stephen Booth's suggestion that the same boy actor might have doubled Rosaline and Jacquenetta in *Love's Labour's Lost*,[17] and he is one of the Arden editors whose play requires him to posit an unusual sort of company, in this case one consisting of nine adults and six boys. Jonathan Bate discusses the heavy demands on casting made by the opening scene of *Titus Andronicus* which requires at least twenty-five actors, and he suggests some 'dramatically striking doubling possibilities' such as Bassianus with 1 Goth, Mutius with Young Lucius, Quintus and

Martius with Caius and Sempronius.[18] David Bevington agrees with King that a large cast of fourteen adults and four boys is needed for *Troilus and Cressida* and relates this to the arguments for a private performance.[19] Finally, Lois Potter notes the need for a high number of boy actors at the very end of Shakespeare's career, in the collaborative *The Two Noble Kinsmen*.[20]

Unusually for the Arden3 series, which has already published conflated texts of *King Lear*, *Othello*, and *Troilus and Cressida*, we are publishing all three texts of *Hamlet*, so we will be providing separate casting charts for each text. In 1992, three scholars (Bradley, King, and Scott McMillin) all went into print with doubling analyses of all three texts, and each reached a different set of conclusions. This was largely because each was using a different set of 'rules'. The rules are not always articulated in such exercises, but variations include whether actors double both male and female roles, whether speaking actors double non-speaking roles, whether actors double parts where there are few or even no intervening lines to cover a costume-change, and so forth. There does not seem to be any agreement that there is a direct correlation between the length of a text and the minimum size of the company needed to perform it. In the case of *Hamlet*, the second quarto (Q2) of 1604/5 is the longest text and the first quarto (Q1) of 1603 by far the shortest. While Bradley and King seem influenced by the traditional assumption that 'bad' or 'short' quartos are abridged texts designed for performance by touring (and therefore smaller) companies, McMillin argues that the longer the text, the easier doubling becomes. He had previously calculated that Q1 needed thirteen actors but Q2 needed only twelve, but he now revised these figures downward.[21] Acknowledging Albert Weiner's 1962 edition of Q1, which calculated that the text would actually have needed only twelve actors,[22] McMillin questioned Weiner's methodology, which unnecessarily precluded doubling within the same scene, even when an actor had time to exit and then re-enter in a new role. By allowing such in-scene doubling, McMillin had now found a way of doing both Q1 and Q2 with only eleven actors.

The charts in tables 7.1, 7.2, and 7.3 are those we are using in the Arden3 *Hamlet*. We have a chart for each text – each listing all the speaking parts and all the scenes in that text as we are printing it, and each indicating in which scene each character appears, whether or not they are on stage at the beginning or at the end of the scene in question, and what kind of role it is (male or female character; adult or boy actor). Finally, each chart speculatively proposes a pattern of doubling for that text, which, for the purposes of comparison, is as similar as we can make it to the pattern we are entertaining for the other two texts.

Table 7.1 *Casting chart for Q1 'Hamlet' from Arden3, ed. Thompson and Taylor*

Actor	Scene 1	2	3	4	5	6	7	8	9	10	11	12	13	14	15	16	17	Actor
1	1S -	Ba -				Mo -	Ro -	Ro -	- Ro -		- Ro -	Fo				2M -	- Ge	1
2	Ba	- Ho -					- Dk -		Dk -							- Pr	- Fo	2
3	- Ho	- Ho -		Ho	- Ho				- Ho -					Ho		- Ho -	Ho -	3
4	- Ma	Vo-Ma-		Ma	- Ma		- Vo-PP-		PP-Lu								- Vo	4
5	- Gh -	Ki -		- Gh -	Gh -		Ki -	Ki	- Ki -	Ki	- Gh-Ki		Ki		Ki	- Ki	- Ki	5
6		Ha		Ha -	Ha		Ha		Ha	- Ha -	- Ha -					- Ha -	Ha	6
7		Co -	- Co			Co	- Co -	Co -	- Co -		Co -					Gr		7
8		Le -	Le -				Gi -	Gi -	- Gi -		- Gi -		- Le -		Le	- Le	- Le	8
9+		Qu -					Qu -	Qu	- Qu -		Qu -		Qu -	Qu	- Qu	- Qu	- Qu	9+
10+			Of			- Of	- Of -		- Of -				- Of -					10+
11+		Cn -					- Cn-Dc -		Dc -								- Am	11+

Key

-    -   enters after beginning of scene
          -    exits before end of scene

italic   female
bold   male
+   boy actor

Speaking roles in order of entry

1S	1 Sentinel	Co	Corambis	PP	Player Prologue
Ba	Barnardo	Vo	Voltemar	Lu	Player Lucianus
Ho	Horatio	Cn	Cornelia	Lo	Lord
Ma	Marcellus	Of	Ofelia	Fo	Fortenbrasse
Gh	Ghost	Mo	Montano	Gr	Gravedigger
Ki	King	Gi	Gilderstone	2M	Second man
Qu	Queen	Ro	Rossencraft	Pr	Priest
Ha	Hamlet	Dk	Player Duke	Ge	Braggart Gentleman
Le	Leartes	Dc	Player Duchess	Am	Ambassador

The charts assume that acting companies in Shakespeare's day wished to restrict the number of actors they employed. But they also assume that some non-speaking parts might be played by people who were not necessarily regular members of the company. The charts therefore attempt to cast all the speaking roles in each of the three texts of *Hamlet* with as few actors as possible. Of course, our attempt to be as economical of the company's workforce as is logically possible produces results which may rarely if ever have been put into practice.

For the purpose of the exercise our charts obey six 'rules'. They are that (1) every line in the relevant text is performed; (2) no role is played by more than one actor, but (3) one actor can play any number of roles – so long as (4) he or 'she' has time to leave the stage for at least a few minutes before returning in a new role; (5) female roles are played by boys; (6) boys can nevertheless also occasionally play adult male roles.

We have set ourselves these rules. The first is a function of the artifice of any such exercise and is rarely, if ever, obeyed in practice. The other rules are either supported by some evidence or else seem highly probable. Thus we believe it would have been exceptional for more than one actor to play a particular role during a particular performance (but, of course, it can happen). We have evidence that 'doubling' happened in the Elizabethan theatre, just as it still happens in the modern theatre. Suspension of disbelief is probably easier if time elapses between appearances of an actor who is doubling parts, and any change in costume or hand-held stage properties takes time, but time is also in the hands of the actors so there can be no rule about the amount of dialogue which needs to be delivered before a re-entry in another role. There is evidence that Elizabethan professional actors were always, or almost always, male and that boys normally played female roles, but, of course, there may have been exceptions. Finally, there is no reason to believe that boys could never have played adult male roles. Of course, they played both women and adult males in the plays put on by the children's companies, a topic that is discussed in the Induction to John Marston's *Antonio and Mellida*. We also need to acknowledge, firstly that the principle behind our casting charts – the attempt to be as economical of the company's workforce as is logically possible – represents a theoretical extreme (once again, rarely if ever put into practice), and secondly that there are alternative doubling patterns which follow the same principle and keep to our rules.

The minimum number of actors needed for speaking roles is bound to be at least the number of actors on stage at that point in the play when the largest number of speaking roles is present. In many plays the last scene

Table 7.2 Casting chart for Q2 'Hamlet' from Arden3, ed. Thompson and Taylor

Actor	1.1	1.2	1.3	1.4	1.5	2.1	2.2	3.1	3.2	3.3	3.4	4.1	4.2	4.3	4.4	4.5	4.6	4.7	5.1	5.2
1	Fr -						Ro -	Ro -	-Ro -	Ro -		Ro -	Ro -	-Ro -	-Ro -				2M -	-Os
2	Ba	-Ba -				Re -	-PK -		PK -						Fo -	-Ge -	-Sa		-Pr	-Fo
3	-Ho	-Ho -		Ho -	-Ho				-Ho -							-Ho -	Ge -		-Ho -	Ho
4	-Ma	Vo-Ma-		Ma -	-Ma		-Vo-PP-		PP-Lu-								Ho -			
5	-Gh -	Ki -		-Gh -	Gh -		Ki -	Ki	-Ki -	Ki	-Gh -	Ki		Ki		-Ki		Ki	-Ki -	-Ki
6		Ha		Ha -	Ha		-Ha	-Ha -	Ha	-Ha -	-Ha		Ha	-Ha -	-Ha				-Ha -	Ha
7		Po -	-Po	Ha -		Po	-Po -	Po	-Po -	-Po -	Po				Ca -				Gr	-Lo -
8		La -	La -				Gu -	Gu -	-Gu -	Gu -		Gu -	-Gu -	-Gu -	-Gu	-La		La -	-La	-La
9+		Qu -					Qu -	Qu -	-Qu -	Qu	Qu	Qu				Qu -		-Qu	-Qu	-Qu
10+			Op			-Op		Op	-Op -							-Op -				
11+		Cn -					-Cn-PQ -		PQ -							-Me -		-Me -		-Am

Key

- -   enters after beginning of scene
         exits before end of scene

italic   female
bold   male
+   boy actor

Speaking roles in order of entry

Ba	Barnardo	Vo	Voltemand	Fo	Fortinbras
Fr	Francisco	Cn	Cornelius	Ca	Captain
Ho	Horatio	Op	Ophelia	Ge	Gentleman
Ma	Marcellus	Re	Reynaldo	Me	Messenger
Gh	Ghost	Gu	Guildenstern	Sa	Sailor
Ki	King	Ro	Rosencrantz	Pr	Priest
Qu	Queen	PP	Player Prologue	Gr	Gravedigger
Po	Polonius	PK	Player King	2M	Second man
La	Laertes	PQ	Player Queen	Os	Osric
Ha	Hamlet	Lu	Player Lucianus	Lo	Lord
				Am	Ambassador

requires the largest cast of speaking characters, so that is the starting-point for a doubling calculation, but in *Hamlet* it is the performance of 'The Murder of Gonzago'. In Shakespeare's comedies the final scene is one in which all, or at least most, of the characters assemble for the resolution of their difficulties in reconciliation and marriage. In the tragedies, the final scene is also the opportunity to resolve the plot, but usually some characters have by this time gone missing. In *Hamlet*, the players never return after their play has been stopped, the Ghost makes his last appearance in the closet scene, and Hamlet himself has a hand in the premature removal of those characters which Q2 calls Polonius, Ophelia, Rosencrantz, and Guildenstern.

What emerges from the exercise is that, even though Q1 has twenty-five speaking roles, Q2 thirty-one, and F thirty, all three texts could, at a pinch, be acted by a company made up of eight adults and three boys. This is McMillin's conclusion in his 1992 essay, and it is ours, too. There are other ways of achieving the same result, but the particular distribution of roles in these charts doubles the King with the Ghost (after all, Hamlet himself plays with the idea, both in 'The Murder of Gonzago' and in his own coinage, 'uncle–father'), and Polonius–Corambis with the Gravedigger.

It also doubles Marcellus with Voltemand–Voltemar. This is in order to accommodate (while not necessarily committing us to) a popular theory about the origins of Q1. Q2 and F are close to the wording of the first five scenes of Q1 but only occasionally close thereafter. Paul Werstine, who has explored (and largely exploded) the theory that Q1 is a memorial reconstruction of Q2/F, traces the theory back to 1880–1, when both Grant White and W. H. Widgery independently argued that the text of Q1 derives from the attempts of the actor who played Voltemand to reconstruct the play from his memory of having performed in it.[23] But Voltemand alone does not account for all the passages of closeness between the texts, so the hunt began for an actor who would have been on stage at all the points where the texts coincide. Since no one character fits that bill, this has obliged the theorists to posit an actor playing more than one part.

Widgery favoured someone doubling Voltemand and the Player King; W. W. Greg (1910) preferred Voltemand and Marcellus; Henry David Gray (1915) rejected Voltemand and went for Marcellus and the Player (or Players) acting the Prologue and Lucianus; Dover Wilson (1918) reinstated Voltemand but extended the list to include a trio of the Second Gravedigger, the Priest, and the English Ambassador.[24] Unfortunately for Wilson, Voltemand and the English Ambassador are both on stage at the same moment. Unfortunately for all the theorists, as Werstine points out,

Table 7.3 Casting chart for F 'Hamlet' from Arden3, ed. Thompson and Taylor

Actor	Scene 1.1	1.2	1.3	1.4	1.5	2.1	2.2	3.1	3.2	3.3	3.4	3.5	3.6	3.7	4.1	4.2	4.3	5.1	5.2
1	Fr -						Ro -	Ro -	**Ro** -	Ro -		- Ro -	- Ro -	Fo		- Sa		2M -	- Os
2	Ba	- Ba -					- PK -		PK -									- Pr	- Fo
3	- Ho	- Ho -		Ho	- Ho	Re -			- Ho -						Ho -	Ho		-Ho -	Ho
4	- Ma	-Vo-Ma-		Ma	- Ma		-Vo-PP-		PP-Lu-										
5	- Gh -	Ki-		- Gh -	Gh -		Ki -	Ki	Ki -	Ki	- Gh -		Ki		- Ki		Ki	- Ki	- Ki
6		Ha		Ha-	Ha		- Ha	-Ha -	Ha	- Ha -	- Ha	Ha	- Ha -				- Ha -	- Ha -	Ha
7		*Po* -	- *Po*			*Po*	- *Po* -	*Po* -	- *Po* -	- *Po* -	*Po*							Gr	
8		*La* -	*La* -				*Gu* -	*Gu* -	- *Gu* -	*Gu* -		- *Gu* -	- *Gu* -		- *La* -	At -	*La* -	- *La* -	- *La*
9+		*Qu* -					*Qu* -	*Qu* -	- *Qu* -		*Qu*				*Qu* -		- *Qu* -	- *Qu* -	- *Qu*
10+		*Op* -	*Op*			- *Op*		*Op*	- *Op* -						- *Op* -				
11+		- Cn -					- Cn - *PQ* -		*PQ* -						- Me -		- Me -	- Ge	- Am

Key
-   enters after beginning of scene
-   exits before end of scene

italic female
bold male
+   boy actor

Speaking roles in order of entry

Ba	Barnardo	Op	Ophelia	Fo	Fortinbras
Fr	Francisco	Vo	Voltemand	Ca	Captain
Ho	Horatio	Cn	Cornelius	Me	Messenger
Ma	Marcellus	Re	Reynoldo	At	Attendant
Gh	Ghost	Gu	Guildensterne	Sa	Sailor
Ki	King	Ro	Rosincrance	Gr	Gravedigger
Qu	Queen	PP	Player Prologue	2M	Second Man
Ha	Hamlet	PK	Player King	Pr	Priest
Po	Polonius	PQ	Player Queen	Ge	Gentleman
La	Laertes	Lu	Player Lucianus	Os	Osricke
				Am	Ambassador

none of the doubling scenarios to date really 'fits'. When these characters are present, the texts are sometimes close, but they are also sometimes not close at all. And sometimes, the texts are close when these characters are not on stage. However, in the accompanying charts, we have entertained Irace's theory, first mooted in 1992, that the same actor playing Marcellus might have doubled Voltemand, the Prologue, and Lucianus.[25] The charts reveal that, while such an actor would have been quite busy in the early scenes, he would thereafter have been unemployed for the bulk of the play. (This could, of course, be 'corrected' if we were to adopt some of Dover Wilson's theory and also attribute to him such parts as the Second Gravedigger and the Priest.) As it stands, then, the memorial reconstruction theory seems uneconomical, and yet we assume that doubling arose out of a need to save on man- and boy-power.

Yet four hundred years on, and even when the original conditions no longer demand it, doubling persists. In 1986, after surveying over 100 productions of *Hamlet*, Ralph Berry came to the conclusion that, even though there is no natural pattern of doubling required by the play, certain permutations of doubling have become traditional.[26] Some scholars committed to a belief in memorial reconstruction have assumed the doubling of Marcellus and Voltemand, and some of them have even added the Prologue and Lucianus from 'The Murder of Gonzago', but Berry found no recorded example of any of this actually happening on stage. Some companies have doubled Polonius and the First Gravedigger since at least 1730, but the practice of doubling the Ghost and the King is a relatively recent one, beginning with Gielgud's production in 1939. The Ghost has also doubled with the First Gravedigger, and even with Laertes.[27]

For all the ignorance of doubling exhibited by some modern directors, an acting company as large and, seemingly, as well-funded, as London's Royal National Theatre was still doubling parts in 2000, when John Caird's widely acclaimed production of *Hamlet*, starring Simon Russell Beale, not only doubled the Ghost with the Player King, but Polonius with the Gravedigger, Reynaldo with Francisco, Osric with a Player, and Barnardo with the Priest. A year later, Steven Pimlott's RSC production, starring Sam West, again doubled Polonius with the Gravedigger, but more unusually employed what Michael Dobson called 'cunning thematic casting' by doubling two landowners (the Ghost with Osric), and two proxies for Hamlet (Lucianus with Fortinbras).[28]

On Shakespeare's stage, the actor playing Ophelia may have doubled Osric, which would have been unthinkable for long stretches of the play's history.[29] In recent years gender has again become less of a determinant in casting: in Peter Zadek's 1999 production at the Vienna Festival, Ophelia doubled Fortinbras and in the same year Red Shift's Ophelia doubled the Second Gravedigger. Cinema, with its greater emphasis on more naturalistic casting and its commitment to close-up photography, might seem to offer little scope for actors to double parts, but film technology makes it very easy for one actor to play twins, as in A. Edward Sutherland's *The Boys from Syracuse* (1940) or James Cellan Jones's BBC Television *Comedy of Errors* (1983) – or indeed for twins to play one character, as in Celestino Coronado's 1976 *Hamlet*. Perhaps it even offers the ultimate actor's dream (indeed Bottom's dream) in Peter Greenaway's *Prospero's Books* (1991), which begins with one actor, John Gielgud, speaking all the parts.

It could be argued that a special kind of 'doubling' occurs when the same actor plays different parts in different plays, or different parts in the same play on different nights, and the audience is likely to recognize this fact. Ian McKellen played both Richard II and Edward II in a Prospect Players season in 1968, and Michael Pennington played Richard II, Suffolk, Buckingham, and Hal in the English Shakespeare Company's *The Wars of the Roses* in 1989, while in 1973 John Barton directed an RSC production in which Richard Pasco and Ian Richardson interchanged the parts of Richard and Bolingbroke on successive nights. In *Hamlet*, Polonius recalls playing Julius Caesar in a play at university (3.2.102): many readers have read this as a joking allusion on Shakespeare's part to his own play of that name, performed in 1599. In his 1982 Arden edition, Harold Jenkins glossed Polonius's statement, 'Brutus killed me', 'It is likely enough that the roles of Caesar and Brutus... were taken by the same actors as now played Polonius and Hamlet; so that "Hamlet" would already have killed Polonius in a previous play, and, ironically, is to do the same "brute part" in this.'[30] The Hollywood star system, and its equivalents in the theatre dating back to Garrick and beyond, have always assumed that audiences, in this sense, 'double' when they 'recognize' a particular actor, and directors cast either according to type, or even against type.

How, then, does an appreciation of doubling inform an editor's work? For editors of eclectic editions, single-text editions, or multiple-text editions of *Hamlet*, doubling has been an essential element in the discussion of the relationship between the three texts, since the theory that Q1 was a memorial reconstruction usually assumes that the reconstructors were actors. While the creation of doubling charts can be a harmless editorial pastime, it can also have its dangers: a colleague tells us that editors have been known to delay a messenger's entrance or accelerate a courtier's exit

'Your sum of parts': doubling in 'Hamlet'

where such a move would open up a new doubling opportunity! But an editor's responsibilities go beyond the preparation of the text, and include the interpretation of that text. The charts are intended to stimulate thinking about the original conditions of performance, and the conditions of performance in subsequent ages including our own. They can also illuminate not just the play's mechanical structure but its thematic organization, and its implicit treatment of such things as age, gender, and even sexuality.

Our own experience of analysing and speculating on the casting structure of the three *Hamlet*s has led us to ponder some interesting characteristics of the plays' anatomies. For all their differences in length and in language, Q1 and the other two texts of *Hamlet* are extraordinarily similar in their casting patterns. They provide virtually the same doubling possibilities and they need exactly the same number of actors to cover all the parts. Read according to this methodology at least, the three texts of *Hamlet* share essentially the same structure, deploying as they do a similar distribution of parts across a similar pattern of scenes.

The long tradition of doubling certain parts reinforces the play's self-conscious concern with the theatre and with theatricality. It also seems to call attention to Hamlet's 'crisis of identity' and his own mental habit of seeing the portraiture of one person, or one role, in another. Carole Corbeil took advantage of these resonances, as well as the fact that doubling in *Hamlet* is such a long-established tradition, when she used doubling as a conceit in her 1997 novel, *In the Wings*. Describing a production of the play in Toronto, she introduces us to

> Reg, who plays Barnardo and messengers and the Player Queen; Ben, in leather and chains, who plays the Ghost, the Player King, the gravedigger, and Fortinbras; Josh, who plays Horatio and Guildenstern, and Reid who plays Laertes and Rosencrantz – all of them ready to change into other beings... all of them swimming in this stew.[31]

Allan, the actor playing Hamlet, 'envies Ben, who has developed a perfect turn for each of his characters'. He envies him for the opportunity for versatility and for transformation which doubling affords him. Meanwhile 'Ben thinks he should be playing Hamlet.'[32] It is pretty clear that the novelist's allocation of parts in this stew is deliberately chaotic, which allows us to speculate about the kind of production her *Hamlet* is, and the kind of universe both it and her novel inhabit. What is less clear, however, is whether or not Corbeil has deliberately created a universe which is not just a stew, but an impossible object. She is asking a lot of Josh when she requires him to double Horatio and Guildenstern. For it cannot be done. They are both required to be on stage during the performance of Hamlet's play.

Indeed, as the charts make clear, one thing which all three texts of *Hamlet* have in common is the fact that the actors playing Hamlet, the Queen, and Horatio are very unlikely to be doubling any other parts. The actor playing Hamlet could play Francisco in the opening scene or Reynaldo/Montano or the Captain in F or a Sailor in Q2/F. For that matter, so could the boy playing the Queen. The least able to double is the actor playing Horatio (who cannot really play any other part in any of the three texts). This 'marking' of these three roles seems to call for an explanation. That the actor playing Hamlet should be a special case is unsurprising. The centrality and dominance of the role within the play, and for us the modern cultural significance of the role of Hamlet and those who play it, seem to have prepared us for it. The Queen's marking could be read as the marking, not of her individuality but of her relationship with Hamlet, and therefore reinforce conventional interpretations of the centrality of that relationship to the play's meanings. But that the actor playing Horatio should be someone who can never be anyone else – is a striking thought. Does his marking, like the Queen's, call attention to his relationship with Hamlet (and, in Q1, because of the unique scene 14, with the Queen in relation to Hamlet)? Does it reinforce our sense that he is to a remarkable degree unengaged with the action of the play? Or does it reinforce Hamlet's own view of Horatio as an ever-fixed mark, who must be encouraged to go on being himself to the end of the play?

The charts show us that the King and the Ghost never meet on stage. They can therefore be doubled, and they often are. But in 'The Murder of Gonzago', Hamlet confronts Claudius with his double – or rather, his doubles, and others' doubles too. Hamlet's play is one in which every actor has to be read as doubling roles in Hamlet's life – the Player King suggests his father but also his uncle, the Player Queen his mother but also his aunt, and Lucianus a villain and, thereby, his uncle, but also a nephew and, thereby, himself.

On the other hand, the charts show us that Hamlet and Fortinbras do meet on stage. What they don't show us – or, at least, what these crude over-simplified charts don't show us – is that the two princes never get the opportunity to be introduced. Like the twins in *The Comedy of Errors* and *Twelfth Night*, they just 'miss' each other throughout the complexities of the action until the last scene. But unlike the twins, their eventual meeting is too late, for Fortinbras enters as Hamlet expires. By a doubling of accidental judgements, Hamlet comes within a whisker, not just of becoming the King but of becoming eligible to double Fortinbras too.

NOTES

1. See David Bradley, *From Text to Performance in the Elizabethan Theatre: Preparing the Play for the Stage* (Cambridge University Press, 1992), and T. J. King, *Casting Shakespeare's Plays: London Actors and Their Roles, 1590–1642* (Cambridge University Press, 1992).
2. See Siobhan Keenan, *Travelling Players in Shakespeare's England* (London: Palgrave, 2002), p. 11.
3. Irwin Smith, 'Their Exits and Re-entrances', *Shakespeare Quarterly* 18 (1967), 7–16.
4. See E. K. Chambers, *The Medieval Stage*, 2 vols. (Oxford University Press, 1903), vol. 1, p. 427.
5. A. C. Sprague, *The Doubling of Parts in Shakespeare's Plays* (London: The Society for Theatre Research, 1966), p. 13.
6. Denis Bartholomeusz, *'The Winter's Tale' in Performance in England and America 1611–1976* (Cambridge University Press, 1982), pp. 116–22.
7. Thomas L. Berger, 'Casting *Henry V*', *Shakespeare Studies* 20 (1988), 89–104.
8. Alan C. Dessen, 'Conceptual Casting in the Age of Shakespeare: Evidence from *Mucedorus*', *Shakespeare Quarterly* 43 (1992), 67–70.
9. Homer D. Swander, '*Cymbeline*: Religious Idea and Dramatic Design', in *Pacific Coast Studies in Shakespeare*, ed. Waldo F. McNeir and Thelma N. Greenfield (Eugene: University of Oregon Press, 1966), pp. 248–62. See also Stephen Booth, 'Speculations on Doubling in Shakespeare's Plays', in *Shakespeare: The Theatrical Dimension*, ed. Philip C. McGuire and David A. Samuelson (New York: AMS Press, 1979), pp. 103–31, rpt in Booth's *'King Lear', 'Macbeth', Indefinition, and Tragedy* (New Haven and London: Yale University Press, 1983), pp. 127–55, who mentions this among other speculations about conceptual doubling.
10. Ralph Berry, *Shakespeare in Performance: Castings and Metamorphoses* (New York: Macmillan, 1993), pp. 15–16, 41–55.
11. William Ringler, Jr, 'The Number of Actors in Shakespeare's Early Plays', in *The Seventeenth-Century Stage*, ed. G. E. Bentley (University of Chicago Press, 1968), pp. 110–34.
12. Tony Church, '"Jack and Jill": A Consideration of *Love's Labour's Lost* and *A Midsummer Night's Dream* from the Point of View of Actor and Director', in *The Arts of Performance in Elizabethan and Early Stuart Drama*, ed. Murray Biggs *et al.* (Edinburgh University Press, 1991), p. 141.
13. John D. Cox and Eric Rasmussen (eds.), *King Henry VI Part 3* (London: Thomson Learning, 2001), p. 410.
14. Gary Taylor, 'We Happy Few: the 1600 Abridgement', in Stanley Wells and Gary Taylor, *Modernizing Shakespeare's Spelling, with Three Studies in the Text of 'Henry V'* (Oxford University Press, 1979), pp. 72–119.

15. Ronald Knowles (ed.), *King Henry VI Part II* (London: Thomson Learning, 1999), p. 24.
16. R. A. Foakes (ed.), *King Lear* (Walton-on-Thames: Thomas Nelson, 1997), pp. 146–8.
17. Henry Woudhuysen (ed.), *Love's Labour's Lost* (London: Thomson Learning, 1998), p. 59.
18. Jonathan Bate (ed.), *Titus Andronicus* (London: Routledge, 1995), pp. 93–5.
19. David Bevington (ed.), *Troilus and Cressida* (Walton-on-Thames: Thomas Nelson, 1998), p. 127.
20. Lois Potter (ed.), *The Two Noble Kinsmen* (Walton-on-Thames: Thomas Nelson, 1997), pp. 64–6.
21. See Scott McMillin, *The Elizabethan Theatre and 'The Book of Sir Thomas More'* (Ithaca and London: Cornell University Press, 1987), p. 88, and McMillin, 'Casting the *Hamlet* Quartos: the Limit of Eleven', in *The 'Hamlet' First Published (Q1, 1603): Origins, Form, Intertextualities*, ed. Thomas Clayton (Newark: University of Delaware Press, 1992), p. 190.
22. See Albert B. Weiner (ed.), *'Hamlet': The First Quarto* (Great Neck: Barron's Educational Series, 1962), pp. 48–50.
23. Paul Werstine, 'A Century of "Bad" Shakespeare Quartos', *Shakespeare Quarterly* 50 (1999), 317, n. 17.
24. See W. W. Greg, 'The *Hamlet* Quartos, 1603, 1604', *Modern Language Review* 5 (1910), 196–7, Henry David Gray, 'The First Quarto "Hamlet"', *Modern Language Review* 10 (1915), 171–80, and John Dover Wilson, 'The "Hamlet" Transcript, 1593', *The Library* 3rd series, 9 (1918), 153–85 and 217–47.
25. See Kathleen O. Irace, 'Origins and Agents of Q1 *Hamlet*', in *The 'Hamlet' First Published*, ed. Clayton, pp. 95–6, and Irace, *Reforming the Bad Quartos: Performance and Provenance of Six Shakespearean First Editions* (Newark: University of Delaware Press, 1994), pp. 118–19. Later, in her edition of Q1 (Cambridge University Press, 1998), she excluded the Prologue from this list (p. 7).
26. Ralph Berry, 'Hamlet's Doubles', *Shakespeare Quarterly* 37 (1986), 204–12.
27. See Berry, *Shakespeare in Performance*, p. 15.
28. Michael Dobson, 'Shakespeare Performances in England, 2001', *Shakespeare Survey* 55 (2002), 297.
29. See Andrew Gurr and Mariko Ichikawa, *Staging in Shakespeare's Theatres* (Oxford University Press, 2000), p. 152.
30. Harold Jenkins (ed.), *Hamlet* (London: Methuen, 1982), pp. 103, 294.
31. Carole Corbeil, *In the Wings* (Toronto: Stoddart, 1997), p. 219.
32. *Ibid.*

CHAPTER 8

The perception of error: the editing and the performance of the opening of 'Coriolanus'

Michael Warren

There are many obstacles to the lively performance of our classics. The worst are the theatrical hacks with their reluctance to think or feel. There is a traditional style of performance which is automatically counted as part of our cultural heritage, although it only harms the true heritage, the work itself; it is really a tradition of damaging the classics. The old masterpieces become as it were dustier and dustier with neglect, and the copyists more or less conscientiously include the dust in their replica. What gets lost above all is the classics' original freshness, the element of surprise (in terms of their period), of newness, of productive stimulus that is the hallmark of such works. The traditional way of playing them suits the convenience of producers, actors and audience alike... Before undertaking to produce one of the classics we must be aware of all this. We have to see the work afresh... We must bring out the ideas originally contained in it...[1]

I would like to take the opportunity of revisiting a textual crux about which I first wrote many years ago.[2] My discussion then was a relatively brief part of a larger argument; in reopening the subject I wish to explore it more thoroughly, to broaden the conception of the interpretative issues, to reflect on certain patterns in the behaviour of editors, and to speculate about cultural prejudices that influence the editing and consequently the construction of Shakespeare's texts for the actor, the scholar, and the common reader.

I

Coriolanus survives solely in the text printed in the First Folio of 1623, where it appears as the first of the tragedies; there is no alternative textual authority. The play opens with '*a Company of Mutinous Citizens, with Staues, Clubs, and other weapons*' (TLN 2–3; 1.1.0) discussing the motives and the objectives of their protest. This conversation involves three speech prefixes only: '1.*Cit*'; '2.*Cit*'; and '*All*'. Menenius enters to them; both the numbered citizens make a single brief comment upon his character, and then the Second Citizen ('2.*Cit*') alone engages in debate with Menenius. At TLN 172 (1.1.146) Caius Martius himself enters: he abuses the citizens immediately, and after one reply from '2.*Cit*' ('We haue euer your good word', TLN 177; 1.1.149) the citizens have no more speech cues before their exit ('*Citizens steale away*', TLN 289; 1.1.235).

This is the raw material that provides the foundation for studying and performing the opening of *Coriolanus*, but it is not what is customarily played, nor is it what is customarily read, studied, and interpreted. In the process of preparing texts for reading and acting, editors have traditionally made a number of alterations. They are of two kinds: first, editors customarily reassign at least one of the speeches assigned to '*All*'; second, almost all editors reassign some of the speeches of '2.*Cit*' to '1.*Cit*'.

Speeches assigned to '*All*' present problems for theatrical presentation. E. A. J. Honigmann has argued for a varied interpretation of such speech prefixes, separating those which serve 'an obvious choric or ritual function' and can be delivered in unison from those 'that are individualised, not ritualistic, and [that] always sound wrong in the theatre if uttered by more than a single voice'.[3] In the case of the opening of *Coriolanus*, editors usually retain the first four '*All*' speech prefixes: 'Speake, speake' (TLN 6; 1.1.2); 'Resolu'd, resolu'd' (TLN 9; 1.1.4); 'We know't, we know't' (TLN 12; 1.1.7); and 'No more talking on't; Let it be done, away, away' (TLN 15; 1.1.10). Although the last of those four may well seem 'individualised' in Honigmann's sense, he does not include it with the next two when he cites them as his first examples of his second category: 'Against him first: He's a very dog to the Commonalty' (TLN 29–30; 1.1.21) and 'Nay, but speak not maliciously' (TLN 36; 1.1.26). The editorial treatment of these speech prefixes varies. The first, 'Against him first... Commonalty', is retained for '*All*' by Philip Brockbank (Arden2, 1976), David Bevington (HarperCollins, 1992), R. B. Parker (Oxford, 1994), John F. Andrews (Everyman, 1998), Jonathan Crewe (Pelican, 1999), and Lee Bliss (New Cambridge, 2000); it is given to the First Citizen by George Hibbard (New Penguin, 1967), and G. Blakemore Evans and J. J. M. Tobin (Riverside, 2nd edn 1997); the Oxford *Complete Works* (1986) divides it into two parts, assigning them to Third and Fourth Citizen respectively. The second, 'Nay, but speak not maliciously', is frequently reassigned to the Second Citizen. Of the nine editions mentioned above, seven make that change; the Oxford *Complete Works* assigns it to a Fifth Citizen, and John F. Andrews retains the Folio ascription to '*All*'. The last speech of '*All*', the command 'Come, come' (TLN 50; 1.1.37) as the Citizens respond to the First Citizen's cry 'To th'Capitoll' (TLN 49; 1.1.36), remains unchanged in all editions.

The reassignment of the two longer speeches indicates a response on the part of the editors to the issue of performance, but the choice of speakers is obviously not self-evident, even though in practice there is a high level of agreement. However, that choice is just part of a more extensive series of changes that follows. In response to the First Citizen's query, 'Soft, who comes heere?' the Second Citizen answers 'Worthy *Menenius Agrippa*, one that hath always lou'd the people', to which the First Citizen rejoins 'He's one honest enough, wold al the rest wer so' (TLN 51–5; 1.1.38–41). From this point in the Folio text the First Citizen becomes silent, and all the succeeding thirteen speeches of engagement with Menenius and Martius on behalf of the citizens are given by the Second Citizen. Seven of the nine modern editions, however, alter the text and reassign the speeches to the First Citizen; in so doing they continue an editorial tradition that begins over two hundred years ago with the work of Capell. The two exceptions are the editions of John F. Andrews and Lee Bliss.

This traditional sequence of emendations of the text has been regularly justified. For instance, R. B. Parker explains his rationale for the thirteen changes in a brief note: 'Up to this point First Citizen has been belligerently hostile to the patricians, while Second Citizen has demurred and acted as peacemaker; Capell's alterations maintain this consistency of character.'[4] This is a condensed version of Philip Brockbank's note in the Arden2 edition: 'Up to this point seven of the First Citizen's eight contributions to the dialogue (in F) have been hostile to authority and to Martius, while the Second Citizen's four interventions have been sympathetic or cautionary. Apparent consistency of character requires that the critical or watchful exchanges with Menenius in the rest of the scene be offered by the citizens' leader.'[5] George Hibbard's dismissal of the F readings is more perfunctory: 'The Folio assigns this speech and the rest of the dialogue with Menenius to the Second Citizen. This must be wrong, since the Second Citizen is kindly disposed towards Menenius and Martius. It is the First Citizen who is the leader of the crowd and its mouthpiece.'[6] The editors of the Oxford *Complete Works* assume the wisdom of the change without comment, although they mention two dissenting voices; however, unlike all the other editors except Parker they attend to the bibliographical problem of explaining the origin of the supposed error. Having argued earlier that the printer's copy was probably scribal rather than authorial in origin, they write briefly: 'F has been defended by [Charles] Knight and [Wilbur] Sanders, but might arise from misinterpretation of unparticularized or absent prefixes in Shakespeare's manuscript – probably by an annotator or scribe.'[7] Parker suggests similarly that 'problems with the designation of speeches for numbered but unnamed citizens in 1.1 ... probably derive from confusions in the copy-text itself'.[8]

Whereas most editors simply move swiftly from their local dissatisfaction with the Folio readings to their emendations, Parker and the Oxford editors are distinctive in their recognition of the obligation to propose how the error that they perceive originated. In the course of a review of the Arden edition Richard Proudfoot questioned Brockbank's judgement on these very grounds: 'Thus, in 1,1, Capell's reassignment to *1 Citizen* of speeches given in F to *2. Cit* is accepted in aid of "apparent consistency of character", without direct comment on the fact that the F error, if indeed it is one, must presumably go back to copy.'[9] Proudfoot thus presents two major challenges to the conventional behaviour. First, he draws attention to the need for some explanation why the ascription to '2.*Cit*' should be regarded as an error and, if an error, how it was made thirteen times; and second, he highlights the implications of 'apparent' in Brockbank's phrase 'apparent consistency of character', suggesting that some other conception of a consistent character might provide a satisfactory explanation. What if, denying the editorial impulse to detect and manage error, one were to assume that the text is correct? And what if one were to interpret the behaviour of the First and Second Citizens in ways less reductive than those advanced by Parker, Brockbank, and Hibbard?

It is these possibilities that inform the work of Knight and Sanders, to which the Oxford *Complete Works* editors refer, and of Andrews and Bliss. Brockbank summarizes and rejects the position of the nineteenth-century editor Knight:

Knight retains the F assignment with the comment, "The *first* Citizen is a hater of public *men* – the *second*, of public *measures*; the first would kill Coriolanus – the second would repeal the laws relating to corn and usury"; he adds that the "low brawler" could not argue so well with Menenius. The First Citizen is not without wit, however, and it is hard to imagine him a mute audience to Menenius and the Second Citizen.[10]

Knight's apt and useful distinction pushes Brockbank to introduce a dimension of theatrical imagination into a debate that is otherwise carried out at a level of static characterological observation.

Sanders, however, expands the terms of understanding still further. In the first pages of a chapter on *Coriolanus*, Sanders develops an elaborate narrative of the opening of the play in which he addresses the stage action in a way that others do not. In place of a dialogue between Hostility and Moderation exemplified by the two citizens, he conceives a complex stage action in which their roles are not opposed in a merely diagrammatic fashion. Rather than presenting a First Citizen who is just a confident 'low brawler', he draws attention to the First Citizen's stopping of the advance on the Capitol in the first line of the play ('Before we proceed any further, heare me speake', TLN 5; 1.1.1), interpreting it as evidence of his 'vacillating extremism' and of his losing his nerve just before the crisis.[11] Sanders constructs a version of the succeeding stage action: the First Citizen 'gradually talks himself back into courage by resisting Second Citizen's unacceptable version of moderation; is newly galvanised by reassuring sounds from the other side of the city; and then, at the very moment he has got his insurrectionary juggernaut into motion, blows the whistle on it yet again – "Soft, who comes here?"'[12] Sanders conceives of the scene dynamically with shifts in the action and complexity of behaviour. The crowd is not reduced to a 'stage-mob' of 'the picturesquely choreographed kind', a simple unified force impelled by a leader: he conceives of the mixture of temerity and fear in the crowd, and as factors in the action the 'precariousness of group solidarity' and the 'desire for self-preservation'.[13]

Sanders's approaches to these opening lines, though brief, reveal an attention to theatrical possibility which is largely absent from other commentators; he invests speeches with significant potential beyond the simple limiting opposition that others have espoused. Although the relations between the characters are based in a binary opposition, here, as in so many other places in Shakespeare's works, the opposition is not static; rather it is a foundation on which more complex variations are played. In justifying his interpretation of a particular passage Sanders argues that 'Shakespeare's conception is finer' than the editors perceive,[14] but the issue is not the perception of the skill of the playwright but the readiness to respond to the text as a document related to performance and as such open to multiple performance choices.

Andrews does not discuss either question in his edition; he merely includes the speech prefixes in a list of passages in which he 'retains First Folio readings, spelling forms, or punctuation practices' commonly altered in other modern editions (pp. xl–xlvii). Bliss, however, addresses the two questions directly in a single paragraph of her 'Textual Analysis' where she justifies her retention of the F assignments to '2.*Cit*'. Reviewing past scholarship and the presumption of error, she concludes that 'This seems to be a case in which F is at least as likely to be correct as not, and this edition chooses to follow it.'[15] In interpreting the behaviour of the First and Second Citizens, she proposes that the distribution of speeches in F 'suggests not only that this "Company" [of Mutinous Citizens] includes a hot-head who thinks killing Coriolanus will solve their problems, but also a more reasonable Second Citizen who becomes their natural spokesman, a man who can see the complexity both of their situation and of Coriolanus (as can other commoners, like the three groups of citizens in 2.3, or the soldiers laying cushions in 2.2)'.[16] Bliss's rejection of the editorial tradition is admirably succinct, and leads one to hope that future editors may follow her and Andrews's example.

It is in this context of thought about text and performance that I wish to build on the work of Sanders and Bliss and on my own earlier work[17] to make further arguments for the retention of the speech prefix '2.*Cit*' for the speeches after the entrance of Menenius. In so doing I shall challenge some customary habits of thought in the editorial tradition; I shall also advocate the adoption of a more theatrically informed and more politically reflective imagination than has usually been employed in the past.

II

An editor, like a critic or a director, has a conception of the nature of the '*Company of Mutinous Citizens*', and that conception, among many things, will influence the interpretation of the entrance of Menenius and the subsequent stage actions. It should be obvious that the distribution of the two speeches of '*All*' at TLN 29–30 and 36 (1.1.21, 26) has small but crucial effects: if the first is assigned to the First Citizen and the second to the Second Citizen (Hibbard, Evans, Bevington) the crowd of citizens is reduced to a homogeneous group that utters confirmatory shouts, and the argument of the scene is focused entirely on the First and Second Citizens; if the first speech is not reassigned to the First Citizen and yet the second is given to the Second Citizen (Brockbank, Parker, Crewe, Bliss), a situation is created in which the Second Citizen nevertheless remains the sole voice of dissent. If, however, those speeches are given to other voices in the crowd (as in the Oxford *Complete Works*), various forms of interrelation, attitude, and possibility of action are introduced. The entrance of Menenius is an important transition in the action – a 'beat' in theatrical parlance – and how it is conceived (consciously or unconsciously) then informs all discussion of the succeeding scene; but little critical attention is given to the moment.

Unlike the editors, however, Sanders discloses his imagined scenario for the action:

It is only a solitary old man who 'comes'. But the ancient habits of subservience in First Citizen are too strong. For this is a patrician! And with one last muttered

Perception of error and the opening of 'Coriolanus' 133

'He's one honest enough, would all the rest were so,' he melts into the crowd, to be heard no more.

As a result Menenius finds himself searching in vain for the ringleader: 'What work's my countrymen in hand?' he asks mildly. 'Where go you with bats and clubs?' (No one stirs.) 'The matter?' (Still no response.) 'Speak, I pray you.'

The editors apparently feel so keenly for Menenius's bewilderment here, that they have provided him with the ringleader he is unable to detect.[18]

Sanders presents a performable interpretation of this brief sequence, and he continues by describing the emergence of the Second Citizen as the spokesperson. Although Sanders initially imagines the First Citizen's melting into the crowd before Menenius speaks, he conceives him otherwise in his next paragraph as 'unmanned by the new atmosphere of chastened deference'.[19] And in keeping with his mode of dramatic recreation, Sanders then poses and answers a rhetorical question:

Who then [is to speak]? The same man who was quirky enough to question the majority view before, who seems to welcome the patrician's arrival as likely to break up the entrenched battle-lines of ignorant confrontation, and who is about to emerge as grasping, better than any, the one unanswerable sanction of oppressed misery (his reply to the benignant query, 'Mine honest neighbours, will you undo yourselves?' is 'We cannot sir, we are undone already'). So finally it is Second Citizen's stolidly matter-of-fact voice that breaks the silence, at once disowning his primacy in the matter, and accepting with a shrug his necessary implication.[20]

Sanders's interpretation of the transition presents a sequence of stage actions, visual and oral, that show the coming to prominence of the Second Citizen: he founds his reading on a series of constructions of the behaviour of Menenius and his reception, specifically the tone of Menenius' inquiry and the presumed behaviour of the First Citizen. While his conception of the scene is plausible, what matters in its relation to the editorial tradition is that it is merely one of many approaches that may be taken to the interpretation, theatrical or literary, of this sequence. Although he is attentive to the motives of the citizens, Sanders reads the scene in terms of the experience of Menenius, the predicament in which he finds himself, a 'solitary old man' encountering a restless and agitated 'mob' and unable to discern a 'ringleader'. Implicit in these statements is Sanders's undisclosed agenda for Menenius. I suspect that Sanders considers that Menenius has not happened here by chance but that he has come alone to negotiate in risky circumstances while similar negotiations are taking place on the other side of the city, and that he expects to deal honestly and sympathetically with the citizens' 'ringleader' after establishing an 'atmosphere of chastened deference' in the citizens. But such a reading of the scene does not exclude others. Even though the First and Second Citizens speak of Menenius in terms of honesty and love respectively, there is no reason to deny to him political craft and strategic objectives in this encounter; after all, it is a major political crisis, and he is a notable patrician. It is equally plausible to conceive of Menenius as encountering a group of citizens more threatening than he anticipated, with the First Citizen prominent as their leader; that, attending to or ignoring the First Citizen, he enters into a bantering speech with them, in which ironic mockery is notable in the apparent naïveté of the reference to 'work' and of the innocent question 'Where go you with Bats and Clubs?'; and that his inquiry into 'The matter' produces a silence not because no one knows who is to speak but because every citizen knows that Menenius knows well what the 'matter' is. Their lack of response may be a deliberate aggressive silence in the face of perceived craftiness. Such a Menenius is not the friend of the common people that the Second Citizen describes but a politician on a crucial mission, alone in a dangerous part of the city; his command, 'Speake I pray you', which Sanders reads as an open invitation to the assembled company and which all the editors presumably read as addressed to the First Citizen, may instead be directed to the Second Citizen as the person with whom Menenius chooses to negotiate.

As it appears in the Folio, this sequence is rich in possibilities. Sanders articulates a good process by which a modest and moderate Second Citizen fulfils his public duty by emerging reluctantly to become the spokesperson for the common people when the First Citizen 'melts into the crowd'. I wish to alter the balance further and suggest two other ways in which the Second Citizen may come to prominence. Why should not prominence be thrust upon him through Menenius' agency, as the latter takes command of the situation under a guise of sweet reasonableness? Editors appear to read the command 'Speake I pray you' as addressed to the First Citizen. Sanders reads it as addressed to the assembled company. But there are alternative possibilities. Menenius may be taking the initiative in the crisis rather than (as he wishes to appear) discussing their predicament on their terms; he may select the Second Citizen in full view of the First Citizen, forestalling the latter's response by addressing another whom he has been able to perceive as more tractable. Sanders imagines the speech delivered with pauses for responses as Menenius searches in vain for the 'ringleader'. However, the speech may also be delivered with brisk command and assumed authority, with sardonic humour as a defensive strategy in a situation of considerable menace, a situation in which Menenius is all too aware of the identity of the 'ringleader'; the apparently courteous conclusion 'I pray you' may be interpreted as showing genuine respect or barely concealed condescension.

Alternatively, if the First Citizen melts into the crowd, it may be that the crowd itself pushes forward the articulate, perhaps reluctant, perhaps eager Second Citizen to speak on their behalf, recognizing his capacity for expressing himself in opposition to a powerful speaker. It is also possible that Menenius addresses a third citizen, some other person whom the Second Citizen does not wish to speak. Nothing in the text specifically warrants any of my readings over Sanders's or any other; each gives variety and vitality to the text and to the stage; each merely asserts implicitly that the form of Menenius' speech cannot be advanced as a solid justification for the alteration of the speech prefixes that follow. Moreover, each enables the development of further thought about the continuing action of the scene in the light of performance.

If the speech prefixes are changed, the succeeding conversation is largely a fulfilment of expectations: as Menenius presents the patrician point of view the First Citizen opposes him in the hostile terms that he has rehearsed. This is not to say that such a performance may not contain nuances and subtleties of interpretation – there is always opportunity for the actors' enrichment of the individual moments. However, the theatrical situation is potentially less complex (although, admittedly, also potentially more explosive) if there are two primary figures in opposition than if Menenius engages a new, less predictable spokesperson. The editorial tradition ignores and simultaneously pre-empts such further discussion of the events of the scene between Menenius and the First Citizen since the justification of the change is based on the prior prediction of the First Citizen's behaviour. An editor who makes this change does so as a consequence of knowing 'what the scene is about', rather than considering how variously the scene as printed in the Folio may be played.

If, however, the Folio speech prefixes are retained and the Second Citizen becomes the spokesperson either of his own volition or by the imposition of Menenius' will, are there dimensions to his character that go beyond the social-psychological elements that so far have been the foundations for the discussion? Successful theatrical performance depends greatly on differentiation: a homogeneous crowd is less interesting than a various crowd. Although no evidence is present in the text to require such an interpretation, the parts of the First and Second Citizens may be played with significant difference in social rank, evident in clothing, deportment, or voice; if the Second Citizen is conceived as a person of different rank or educational background from the First, both the shared concerns and the conflicts between them may be read more sharply and the crowd appear more complex; if Menenius chooses in the Second Citizen a person whom he discerns as in some way closer to himself, more responsive to his position and so more to his advantage in negotiation, the situation of social conflict is intensified and complicated.

Sanders presents one interpretation of how the Second Citizen may conduct himself after finding himself in the unexpected position of prominence. He conceives of a Second Citizen who in response to Menenius' invitation to speak 'disown[s] his primacy in the matter, and accept[s] with a shrug his necessary implication', becoming under the pressure of Menenius' rhetoric and his own conspicuousness 'the hostage of his own eloquence'.[21] Sanders offers a sympathetic reading of the Second Citizen's predicament, but he uses it to a more imaginative end than the exploration of that character's mind and motives. In Sanders's view the crucial element of the scene is Menenius' misunderstanding of the man with whom he is dealing: the patrician mistakes the Second Citizen's 'percipiently mistrustful' responses to his speeches as a sign that the Second Citizen is a 'trouble-maker ... And thus with sublime unconsciousness and with acute irony, Menenius turns this man, potentially his most valuable ally, into the seditious agitator we have watched him refusing to be'.[22] By the time that he calls him 'the great Toe of this Assembly' (TLN 163; 1.1.138) he has converted a reluctant and thoughtful participant into the leader he earlier had no desire to be. Sanders uses this reading to stress the complexity of the political and personal relations in the scene, Menenius' 'genial expediency' and limited vision, the Second Citizen's sense of justice and his capacity for confusion of response; he proposes that in this scene 'Shakespeare is mobilising the self-defeating energies of political contradiction.'[23]

As with Sanders's interpretation of the entrance of Menenius, this scenario is sound: it provides for the development of the Second Citizen in his role, for the perception of a misjudgement on the part of Menenius (not the last that he will make in the play), and for a conception of a many-headed multitude that does not disallow the seriousness and good sense of the citizens. But again it is not the only possible reading of the scene; every detail of the delivery of each speech depends on the one before, and all depend on whether in the grossest terms the Second Citizen chooses to speak or is chosen by Menenius. If the latter, and if the Second Citizen has been conceived as more educated and of higher social rank than the First, then his response to Menenius, 'Our busines is not vnknowne to th'Senat, they haue had inkling this fortnight what we intend to do, w[hich] now wee'l shew em in deeds ... ' (TLN 59–61; 1.1.44–6), may be performed so that the strength of the assertion shows either the ease with which the Second Citizen adjusts to the new role, or else a discomfort in the confrontational role that he finds that his position and Menenius' challenge impose on him; if the latter, he may either continue to manifest some insecurity throughout the speech, or else he may start to gain confidence with the threat of 'deeds' and close in the confident threat of their 'strong arms'.

The range of possible interpretation may be illustrated from a second passage. Menenius is interrupted twice during his 'Belly' speech; the second interruption is an anticipatory development of Menenius' conceit that Menenius himself then cuts off:

> Your Bellies answer: What
> The Kingly crown'd head, the vigilant eye,
> The Counsailor Heart, the Arme our Souldier,
> Our Steed the Legge, the Tongue our Trumpeter,
> With other Muniments and petty helpes
> In this our Fabricke, if that they ———
> (TLN 117–22; 1.1.97–102)

The speech is presumably read by the editors who ascribe it to the First Citizen as either an example of his imitative rhetoric or as evidence that he too has some education or at least an intelligence apt for this kind of debate; such interpretations are legitimate. But the speech may also be considered as revealing attributes specific to the Second Citizen and used thus in the development of that role. If the Second Citizen is as intelligent and learned as Menenius (though less privileged in social rank), this statement may alert Menenius to what he has not appreciated fully before; his perception may provoke him to the derisive strategy of mocking interruption as a way of trying to maintain control of a perilous situation in which much is at stake for him: 'What then? Fore me, this Fellow speakes. / What then? What then?' (TLN 123–4; 1.1.102–3). Sanders considers this response part of a process in which Menenius 'enlist[s] the laughter of his fellows, by deriding his unplebeian fluency, by flaunting a superior patrician good humour',[24] but in so doing he appears to deny the possibility that it may be not fluency but equal intelligence, learning, and dignity that the Second Citizen displays, and that such qualities threaten Menenius and provoke him to treat him with explicit disrespect later ('the great Toe of this Assembly').

Nothing of Sanders's or my own thinking that I have presented as available interpretation of the action of this scene is conclusive evidence that the speeches under discussion must belong to the Second Citizen. Similarly, everything in this discussion makes clear that there is no necessity for perceiving the speech attributions to be in error and so reassigning them to the First Citizen. Error is a risky concept; the idea of others' error is a temptation.

However, this argument should not be closed without some attention to a speech that strongly challenges its hypothesis, the last line of the Second Citizen. Martius' initial speech abuses the citizens:

> Thanks. What's the matter you dissentious rogues
> That rubbing the poore Itch of your Opinion,
> Make your selues Scabs.
>
> (TLN 174–6; 1.1.147–9)

The Second Citizen responds with 'We haue euer your good word' (TLN 177; 1.1.149). The customary reassignment to the First Citizen relates this remark to his personal attack on Martius in his third and fourth speeches, in which he urges the citizens to kill him as 'chiefe enemy to the people' (TLN 10–11, 13–14; 1.1.5–6, 8–9), and contrasts it to the Second Citizen's readiness earlier in the same scene to defend Martius: in three speeches there the Second Citizen questions the wisdom of focusing their aggression on Martius, raises the issue of his 'Seruices' to Rome, defends his pride as a fault in his nature for which he is not responsible, and argues against accusations of covetousness in him (TLN 27–8, 31–2, 42–4; 1.1.20, 22–3, 31–2). Reclaiming this last speech for the Second Citizen, Sanders describes the 'muttered disgust' of this speech in his mouth, associating it in an odd phrase with 'a potentiality of contemptuous affection'.[25] Sanders appears to be straining here, trying to reconcile this line with the positions adopted in the earlier dialogue. But if, as both Sanders and I maintain in our interpretations, the Second Citizen has undergone a transformation of role under pressure of events, though perhaps not of identity, it would be hardly surprising if he were to utter such a defence of the citizens against such an undiplomatic and unprovoked attack. Instead of static character playing itself out predictably, one would have dynamic interpersonal activity and transformation in a moment of political crisis.

III

The act of arguing for the restoration of original readings in Shakespeare texts after centuries of acceptance of emendation usually occasions resistance characterized by charges of excessive ingenuity in interpretation. The familiar and customary reading, the immediately clear and intelligible reading, is sanctioned by prior acts of scholarship and prior performances; and doubtless the emended text always makes good sense in its own terms, and in its good sense appears to be 'right'. However, it is important to acknowledge how difficult yet intelligible and interpretable so much of the Shakespeare text is, and that another difficulty should not immediately be discerned and dismissed as an error; moreover, experience of performance often reveals that what presents problems in reading may present few upon the stage. Such reasoning usually leads to the charge that some interpretation can be found for anything, especially by actors, and that in detecting error the textual critic or the editor restores some kind of objective judgement to a highly subjective activity. However, although objective measures may grant a certain degree of probability in some cases, they are not in themselves absolutely reliable in all circumstances. Moreover, in this case the initial perception of error has nothing to do with objective observation and is itself a matter of judgement. It is not as if this crux were an instance of a single word form that is unintelligible or unpronounceable; rather it is a series of recognizable and superficially unexceptional speech prefixes that nevertheless challenge the interpretative sensibility of the reader and the actor. It is worth remembering that no editor before Capell detected this error. Perhaps the emendation has a relation to Capell's historical period, when a significant body of the King's overseas subjects were expressing vigorous dissatisfaction with their government, and dissent was not unknown at home.

When an emendation has persisted for two hundred years one may well ask what purpose it satisfies, if simple intelligibility is not at issue. In this instance the desire for simplicity may be a prime concern; the shift in speaking roles is unexpected and demands a more complex response to the events than is required when there is continuity of focus of activity. Again, tradition is itself powerfully formative in intellectual activity, and the weight of two hundred years of tradition in a context where other errors are perceptible is significant. However, while accepting that the genuine desire to clarify that which is perceived as error plays a considerable part in this process, I wish to point out certain features of these particular emendations that merit contemplation.

In the context of a theatrical approach to the text which concedes that no interpretation can be regarded as a sufficient, exclusive, or definitive explanation of the text, I would like to suggest a possible interpretation of the consequences of the transfer in almost all editions of the thirteen speech prefixes to the First Citizen, especially in the context of the almost universal assignment of 'Nay, but speak not maliciously' to the Second Citizen. With the questioning of the First Citizen's view of events marginalized in a Second Citizen who is silent after Menenius enters, the diversity of the

'*Company of Mutinous Citizens*' is reduced; the threat of violence that they pose is maintained strongly by the continuing leadership in the succeeding debate of the intransigent and murderous First Citizen, a figure whom Brockbank calls 'hostile to authority' and Parker 'belligerently hostile'.[26] I would argue that in suppressing the more moderate voice of the Second Citizen, editors not only alter the potential theatrical shape of the scene but they modify its theatrical politics also. They increase the potential for the interpretation of the scene as an archetypal conservative image of the angry, imminently lethal crowd of aggrieved citizens menacing a figure of authority (Coriolanus) and finally controlled by the paternalist reasoning of another (Menenius); they diminish the opportunity to interpret the crowd as various in its opinions and led in debate by a person who has opposed the killing of Coriolanus, stressing his military record and his lack of covetousness. I would argue that the emendations inflect the text towards greater respect for the patricians' position and less for the citizens'. In this regard the language of Sanders's argument is ironically revealing, for, despite his espousal of the Folio's assignment of speeches, in his reading of the scene he describes Menenius as entering to confront a 'mob', a pejorative term not used in the play, and seeking a 'ringleader', an equally pejorative term that suggests the reprehensibility of the person and the cause;[27] he implies that Menenius is right to assume that such a 'mob' of citizens will be led by such an individual.

I wish to suggest that the tradition of editing this scene manifests a conservative cultural bias, revealing a limited respect for the cause of the citizens and a far more sympathetic attitude towards Menenius; it encourages an interpretation of the citizens as a solid group, a 'mob', and of Menenius as a benign and honest patrician. Of course, some of this may be the unintended consequence of the difference in perception of named and unnamed characters, but it can be reasonably ascribed to the casual perpetuation by scholars of habitual conservative forms of thought about the nature of the political life of the common people – the assumption of a model of protest against perceived injustice that involves an angry 'mob' with a single 'ringleader' that can be restrained from its purpose by a diplomatic authority figure. I would not wish to leave unnoticed the fact that the text itself in the Folio displays negative attitudes towards the citizens in the language of the stage directions: they are '*Mutinous Citizens*' (TLN 2; 1.1.0), they '*steale away*' (TLN 279; 1.1.235), they enter as '*a rabble of Plebeians*' (TLN 1886; 3.1.181), their attack on Martius is '*this Mutinie*' and, after being '*beat in*' (TLN 1949–50; 3.1.231), they return as '*the rabble againe*' (TLN 1992; 3.1.265). Nevertheless, there is no reason why these stage directions should be allowed to influence the issue of the ascription of speech prefixes. There are no grounds, bibliographical or interpretative, to require the emendations, and in this crux scholars should be ready to break with tradition.

NOTES

1. Bertolt Brecht, 'Classical Status as an Inhibiting Factor', in *Brecht on Theatre*, ed. and trans. John Willett (New York: Hill and Wang, 1964), p. 272.
2. 'Textual Problems, Editorial Assertions in Editions of Shakespeare', in *Textual Criticism and Literary Interpretation*, ed. Jerome J. McGann (University of Chicago Press, 1985), pp. 23–37. I wish to express my gratitude to the many colleagues with whom I have explored this scene and from whose advice I have benefited: Alan Dessen, Audrey Stanley, and the members of their Folger Institute, 'Shakespeare Examined through Performance' (April 1996); Alan Armstrong and the members of his National Endowment for the Humanities institute at Southern Oregon University, 'Shakespeare in Ashland' (July 1996); Barry Kraft, dramaturg of the Oregon Shakespeare Festival in Ashland, who discussed with me the decisions made in the 1996 production of *Coriolanus*, in which he played the Second Citizen; and lastly the members of the company of the Shakespeare Santa Cruz 2002 production of *Coriolanus*, for which I served as dramaturge.
3. E. A. J. Honigmann, 'Re-enter the Stage Direction: Shakespeare and Some Contemporaries', *Shakespeare Survey* 29 (1976), 121.
4. R. B. Parker (ed.), *Coriolanus* (Oxford University Press, 1994), p. 162n.
5. Philip Brockbank (ed.), *Coriolanus* (London: Methuen, 1976), p. 98n.
6. George Hibbard (ed.), *Coriolanus* (Harmondsworth: Penguin, 1967), p. 191.
7. Stanley Wells and Gary Taylor with John Jowett and William Montgomery, *William Shakespeare: A Textual Companion* (Oxford University Press, 1987), p. 594.
8. Parker (ed.), *Coriolanus*, p. 137. He continues: 'About a dozen speeches are wrongly assigned in F, probably because the compositors misread abbreviated speech-headings which either closely resembled each other in the manuscript or were unclearly aligned along its margins'; see also Thomas Clayton, 'Today We Have Parting of Names: a Preliminary Enquiry into Some Editorial Speech-(Be)headings in *Coriolanus*' in *Shakespeare's Speech Headings*, ed. George Walton Williams (Newark: University of Delaware Press, 1997), pp. 61–99.
9. Richard Proudfoot, 'The Year's Contributions to Shakespearian Study: 3. Textual Studies', *Shakespeare Survey* 30 (1977), 204.
10. Brockbank (ed.), *Coriolanus*, p. 98n.
11. Wilbur Sanders and Howard Jacobson, *Shakespeare's Magnanimity: Four Tragic Heroes, Their Friends and Families* (New York: Oxford University Press, 1978), p. 138.
12. *Ibid.*

13. *Ibid.*, pp. 138–9.
14. *Ibid.*, p. 139.
15. Lee Bliss (ed.), *Coriolanus* (Cambridge University Press, 2000), p. 280.
16. *Ibid.*, p. 279.
17. In the article cited in footnote 2 (above), I challenged the reassignment of any of the speeches of '*All*' to either the First or Second Citizens and proposed that the thirteen contested speech prefixes of the Second Citizen not be emended (p. 32).
18. Sanders, *Shakespeare's Magnanimity*, p. 139.
19. *Ibid.*
20. *Ibid.*
21. *Ibid.*, pp. 139–40.
22. *Ibid.*, p. 140.
23. *Ibid.*, pp. 140–1.
24. *Ibid.*, p. 140.
25. *Ibid.*, p. 141.
26. Brockbank (ed.), *Coriolanus*, p. 98n.; Parker (ed.), *Coriolanus*, p. 162n.
27. Sanders, *Shakespeare's Magnanimity*, pp. 138–9.

CHAPTER 9

Modern spelling: the hard choices

David Bevington

Whether to edit in modern spelling or old spelling, or to adopt some compromise between the two, is still an unresolved issue in the academy. Both in critical editions and in texts intended chiefly for classroom use, editors sometimes choose old spelling, especially for certain authors like John Donne. The Riverside Shakespeare carries forward into its second edition (1997) the practice of retaining certain archaic spellings, such as 'strook twelf' for 'struck twelve' (*Hamlet*, 1.1.7), as suggestive of Renaissance pronunciation, in the face of the impossibility of doing so with linguistic consistency; some words are retained in their archaic form, most are modernized. Theatrically minded editors sometimes succumb to the siren call of regarding original punctuation as indicative of speech rhythms in the theatre, despite the textual evidence that a great deal of such pointing is the work of scribes and compositors rather than the authors.[1] The result is that when critics quote from Renaissance texts in scholarly essays and monographs, one finds a variety of practices side by side. Jonson is often quoted from the reliable critical edition of Herford and Simpson in old spelling, whereas Shakespeare is almost always in modern spelling.

Can one edit a critical edition in scholarly fashion without old spelling? The textual generation of Fredson Bowers was convinced that one could not; modern spelling was for dumbed-down college texts or popular consumption only, whereas the 'definitive' critical edition undertook to record all the textual variants involved in the process of printing and re-editing old texts. The results have not been uniformly happy. Thomas Marc Parrott's animated editing of George Chapman's comedies,[2] for example, was replaced by a 'definitive' critical edition issued by the University of Illinois Press[3] that replaced Parrott's engaging critical commentary with page after page of textual apparatus. These volumes gather dust on the library shelves of even the most august research libraries, along with Bowers's editions of Marlowe, and Beaumont and Fletcher.[4]

The case for modern spelling has been addressed by Stanley Wells in two short studies, one a chapter on 'Old and Modern Spellings' in his book on *Re-Editing Shakespeare for the Modern Reader* and the other a monograph on *Modernizing Shakespeare's Spelling*.[5] My present purpose is to revisit the topic with added examples, from Shakespeare and also from his contemporaries in Renaissance drama, in order to fill out our perspective on the difficulties involved and to ask what our criteria ought to be in making choices. How extensive is the problem? We need to know just how often the issue comes up, and in what various forms, in order to move towards a consensus on a general policy but also on the level of detail. The problem is eminently pragmatic; it comes down to case histories, and it continually involves a consideration of consistency.

We should not expect to be entirely consistent. Edmund Spenser demands special handling because of his choice to write in an archaic language. Can one partly modernize Spenser while retaining the visibly archaic forms? Can these procedures be applied to texts by other early modern writers? In outline, one can proceed to do this, first by using modern equivalents of 'i' for 'j' and 'u' for 'v' as in 'iudge' ('judge') and 'loue' ('love'). One can modernize by deleting the final 'e' in 'overwhelme' or 'poore' or 'goodnesse', especially when, as in most cases, the final 'e' appears to have no metrical significance. One may then proceed to regularize the spellings of words that look to be eminently alike one another in old and modern spelling: 'country' for 'Countrey', 'virtue' for 'vertue', 'liberal' for 'liberall', 'precious' for 'pretious'. Surely the distortion in such choices is minimal, and early modern spelling affords us variants in the rendition of such words that often include the more modern form; 'precious', 'country', etc., are by no means hard to find in early modern texts. Plenty of books of the period choose to print 'love' rather than 'loue'; this is more a matter of typeface than of spelling. To that extent what we are doing is more a regularization than a rigorous modernization.

Changes in the English language complicate the issue. Chaucer resists modernization, though editors do regularize his texts to an extent (and run the risk of creating an idealized scheme of sounded or unsounded vowels that may give us greater regularity than is warranted). The Corpus Christi cycles do not modernize well, or the Scottish Chaucerians. What about the lyrics of Thomas Wyatt, or early sixteenth-century plays like John Heywood's *Four PP* or *The Play of the Weather*? We have difficulty determining a fixed chronological point at which we can modernize texts, especially when authors like Spenser make consciously archaic choices. Nonetheless, *Euphues* and the prose plays of John Lyly modernize well in the 1580s, as does *Gorboduc* or Peele's *The Arraignment of Paris* or Greene's *Friar Bacon and Friar Bungay*. By the time of the high Renaissance in English drama, we have reached a point in pragmatic terms when, arguably, modernization creates notably fewer problems than before. Hard and fast rules about this are inherently out of the question; it is a matter of pragmatics at the very local level of individual word choice.

One consideration that gives one pause is that a number of words in early modern English are spelled with remarkable consistency in ways that we have abandoned. The word we recognize as 'precedent' is almost always 'president' in early modern dramatic texts. So too with 'bason' for our word 'basin' and 'alablaster' for 'alabaster', 'sent' for 'scent', and 'accompt' for 'account'. 'Whither' is very apt to appear as 'whether', 'thither' as 'thether'. I have lost count of how many times I have found 'whose' instead of the form 'who's', as in 'Whose that?' 'Gilt' is much more likely to be 'guilt'; 'lose' is apt to be 'loose'; 'too' is often 'to'; 'vile' is more often 'vild' or 'vilde'. 'Wrestle' is 'wrastle', 'strew' is 'strow', 'show' is 'shew'.

A modern spelling edition will want to choose the more modern form in all these cases, no doubt, arguing implicitly that we are dealing with 'the same word', the spelling of which has shifted according to rules of vocalic change and the like. The argument is practical as well: it is confusing for today's readers to encounter 'whether' when the context seems plainly to call for 'whither' in our spelling, and 'president', as colourful as it may look in its original form, invites distracting resonances that presumably do not inhere in the intended meaning of 'precedent'. A modernized text can be very helpful in substituting 'Ay' for 'I' when the meaning appears to be one of affirmation, though the chances for editorial error or arbitrary choice in converting 'I' to 'Ay' are not always small. In *The Roaring Girl* (3.3.159–60), for example, when Sir Davy Dapper inquires of an arresting sergeant if the latter is acquainted with Sir Davy's prodigal son ('You know the unthrift Jack Dapper?'), the sergeant replies, in the quarto text of 1611, 'I, I sir, that gull?', leaving the editor to decide if this should be modernized as 'I? I, sir? That gull?' or 'Ay, ay, sir. That gull?' or 'I? Ay, sir, that gull?' (I prefer the latter, but you see what I mean.)

Similarly, the phrase 'to blame' is fraught with hazard. What does one do, for example, with De Flores's complaining to Beatrice of ingratitude in *The Changeling* (3.4.96): 'y'are too blame in't'? This spelling of the first quarto (1653) is a common way of rendering this phrase, and is often modernized to 'You're to blame in it', as indeed perhaps it should be. Yet one worries that it may mean 'You're too blameworthy' and that one is effacing a resonance of meaning that early modern English usage would have supported. The

Oxford English Dictionary (*OED*) supports the modernization; it insists that the dative infinitive form 'to blame' was misunderstood in the sixteenth and seventeenth centuries as 'too' with 'blame' taken as the adjective, 'blameworthy, culpable' (*OED* Blame v. 6). Yet this assertive conclusion overlooks the persistent use of the spelling 'too' in such constructions, and the very instances cited in the *OED* from Shakespeare arouse doubt. In *Richard III* (2.2.13), the young son of Clarence laments of his father's death that 'The King mine Vnckle [King Edward IV] is too blame for it' (Folio text), and in *1 Henry IV* (3.1.177) we find Worcester upbraiding Hotspur for his hotheadedness with 'In faith my Lord you are too wilfull blame' (1598 quarto). Especially in this last example, in its position after 'wilfull' the word 'blame' must surely take on some sense of blameworthiness. Perhaps 'wilfull blame' should be hyphenated in a modern spelling edition, in the sense of 'blameworthy for too much self-will', or as the Norton Shakespeare glosses it more simply, 'stubborn'. I find no modern spelling edition that prints 'you are to willful blame'; that would make no sense. Even if the reading of 'too blame' as 'too blameworthy' was a misunderstanding, then, it seems to have been persistent, and to give up the original reading is to mask that resonance. On the whole, the best plan is probably to print 'to blame' in most instances though not in that from *1 Henry IV*, and then explain in a note and collate with a textual note so that the inquisitive reader can follow one's choices. But it's a compromise.

Modern spelling obscures other sorts of misinformation that is culturally and linguistically revealing. One such kind of homogenizing of language occurs when we conceal false etymologies. 'Abhominable' is a case in point. The common Elizabethan spelling 'abhominable' points to a supposed but fallacious derivation from *ab* + *homine*, away from mankind, inhuman, beastly, whereas 'abominable' is more historically explained (as in the *OED*) as derived from the Latin '*abominari*', to deprecate as an ill omen, or '*abominabilis*', deserving imprecation or abhorrence, ultimately from *ab*, off or away from, + *omen*. In Shakespeare, the form occurs in the First Folio eighteen times according to the *OED*, always as 'abhominable' (sixteen instances) along with 'abhominably' and 'abhominations' (one instance each). In addition, not tallied by the *OED*, there is one quarto-only instance in *Pericles* and, from *The Rape of Lucrece*, two instances of 'abhomination' and one of 'abhominations'. To this list, the *OED* might have added that the word appears as 'abhominable' or 'abhominably' in all the related quartos: *Love's Labour's Lost* (1598), *1 Henry IV* (1598), *2 Henry IV* (1600), *Troilus and Cressida* (1609), *Titus Andronicus* (1594), *King Lear* (1608), and *Hamlet* (1604–5). The only significant variation to this pattern is in *Love's Labour's Lost*, when Holofernes, in a virtuoso display of pedantry, inveighs against 'rackers of orthography' who say 'dout' when they should say 'doubt', 'det' for 'debt', 'cauf' for 'calf', 'ne' for 'neigh', and so on, concluding (in the quarto reading) that 'This is abhominible, which we would call abbominable' (5.1.23–4). The Folio here regularizes 'abbominable' to 'abhominable', surely erroneously, for it obliterates the joke. Should an editor keep 'abbominable' in *Love's Labour's Lost*, as the Riverside Shakespeare does? Most editors, including the Oxford Shakespeare editors, change that one instance to 'abominable' to make clearer the contrast between 'abhominable' and 'abominable'.

As one might expect, Ben Jonson gets it right from the linguists' point of view. We find forms of 'abominable' in *The Alchemist*, 1.1.117 ('"Sdeath, you abominable paire of stinkards') and 5.3.45–6 ('abomination / Is in the house'). *Bartholomew Fair*, not surprisingly, has a feast of 'abominable' words, often in the mouth of Busy or attributed to him, but also by Wasp and Knockem: 1.2.77, 1.4.32, 1.6.79, 4.1.93, 4.5.52, 5.5.99 and 101. Middleton's *A Chaste Maid in Cheapside*, on the other hand, prints 'ahbominable' (4.1.231), a metathesized form that presumably represents 'abhominable'.

The variation between 'necromancy' and 'negromancy' similarly reveals an uncertainty and perhaps a debate as to etymological origins. The preferred form linguistically is 'necromancy', from *necro*, a dead body or person, + *mantia*, divination or prophecy, hence an asserted power of revealing future events by means of communication with the dead (*OED*). 'Negromancy' is, like 'abhominable', a misunderstood derivation, in this case from *nigro*, black, + *mantia*, divination, hence black magic and prognostication. Shakespeare never uses either form, but it turns up thrice towards the beginning of Marlowe's *Doctor Faustus*, where in the A-text of 1604 it is varied as 'Negromancy' or 'Negromantike' and 'Negromantique' but always choosing the black magic derivation, whereas the B-text of 1616 shows a mixed response to the question of spelling: in the first instance (Prologue 25), the B-text prints 'Necromancie', whereas in the second (1.1.52) it is close to the A-text reading with 'Negromantick'. The third instance (1.1.107) is in a passage that is cut from the B-text. Modern editions tend to modernize all these to 'necromancy' and 'necromantic', but at the expense of information about an interesting word and what the Elizabethans thought it meant. Since the play is all about black magic, the issue is significant. Commentary notes help, of course, but there is still an admitted impoverishment. Robert Greene's *Friar Bacon and Friar Bungay*, probably in exploitation of the popularity of *Doctor Faustus*, frequently introduces the word in various forms and with apparent indifference as to the implied etymological origin: Nigromancer, nigromanticke, Necromantia, Nigromancie, nigromansie, Nicromanticke, necromantick. The 'nig-' forms predominate (I count eight instances, at 1.94 and 122, 2.54, 6.147, 11.15, 12.26, and 13.84 and 90), but 'nec-' forms appear also (2.3, 9.47), and, as though by way of perfect compromise, the 'nic' form in 'Nicromanticke' turns up at 2.144 and 9.86. Such variation in spelling may suggest a source in the author's papers, though the first quarto also bears the imprint of theatrical use.[6] Webster's *The White Devil* prefers 'Nigromancer' in its single use of the term (2.2.8). Jonson, ever the purist, chooses *'necromancie'* in *The Alchemist*, 1.3.11. No modern spelling edition would choose to preserve all the chaotic variety represented in these samples, and yet important linguistic information is being obscured.

Etymological derivation is similarly confused in the choice of 'ancient' and 'ensign'. Examples from the *OED* indicate how 'ancient' is used in an adjectival sense of 'senior, superior in age', or as a title of dignity, an elder; compare the French *'l'officier le plus ancien'*, the senior officer. As a substantive, the word can mean ensign, standard, flag, or the standard-bearer, the 'ensign' in military rank; here the term applies to 'ancient Pistol' in *2 Henry IV* and *Henry V*, and to Iago in *Othello*, 'his moorship's ancient' (1.1.33). The *OED*'s explanation is that 'ancient' in this sense is a corruption of 'ensign', 'which, like *ensyne, enseygne*, were confounded with ... *ancient*, with which they thus became formally identified from 16th to 18th c.'. In the 1622 quarto and the 1623 Folio texts of *Othello*, the word is variously spelled 'Ancient', 'Auncient', 'Auntient', 'Aunciant'. Rafe uses 'Ancient' as a term of military rank in *The Knight of the Burning Pestle*, 5.2.2 and 4, along with 'Lieuetenant', 'Captaine', and 'Sergeant'. The meaning is clear. Should an editor simply modernize to 'Ensign'? That is the straightforward policy of the Oxford Shakespeare, and it is entirely defensible. At the same time, one loses a resonance of something venerable and senior, as when Albany in *King Lear* resolves to 'determine / With th'ancient of war on our proceeding' (5.2.33–4), that is, consult with veteran officers on how to proceed. 'Ancient' here has the connotation both of military rank and seniority. The historical semantic confusion of 'ancient' and 'ensign' surrounds the word 'ancient' with an aura of military experience and seniority that is lost in modernization.

The history of the word 'engineer' is no less interesting in terms of the problem it poses for an editor. The forms usually encountered in the early modern drama include 'ingener' and 'enginer'. *The Harvard Concordance* is caught between stools: it lists one example under 'ingener' ('And in th'essential vesture of creation / Does tire the ingener', *Othello*, 2.1.66–7) and two others under 'enginer' ('then there's Achilles, a rare enginer!', *Troilus and Cressida*, 2.3.8, and 'For 'tis the sport to have the enginer / Hoist with his own petard', *Hamlet*, 3.4.213). The abitrariness of such a division is made manifest in the fact that the quarto *Troilus* reading is 'inginer' while the Folio reading is 'Enginer'. (In *Hamlet*, the word is part of a passage cut from the Folio text.) For a modernizing editor, the problem is compounded by the fact that 'engineer' today has taken on a professional and technical meaning to the virtual exclusion of all others, even though originally it meant, more broadly, one who contrives, designs, or invents. As the *OED* explains, the word derives from the Latin *ingenium* and the medieval Latin *ingeniare* and *ingeniarotem*; then, in the sixteenth century, the word assumed the prefix 'en-', as though derived from 'engine', to contrive, + 'er'. The '-eer' ending, appearing early in the seventeenth century, may owe something to the French *ingénieur*.

All this helps explain why we encounter 'enginer', 'ingener', and 'engineer' more or less interchangeably. Jonson, in *Bartholomew Fair*, predictably prefers the Latinate form, 'Ingener', as at 2.2.17, where he uses it to mean a deviser of entertainments. Shakespeare's usages, cited above, are variously applied: in *Othello* it means a poet, one who devises, as in Jonson; in *Troilus*, it means either one who digs countermines and tunnels or one who devises such strategies; in *Hamlet*, it means a designer or maker of military contrivances, such as explosives used to blow in the door or wall of a fortification. One could conceivably use 'engineer' as a spelling to convey something like the military meanings, but as a word for 'poet' it is very apt to lead the inexperienced reader astray. Should one resort to preserving some older form of the word in *Othello* and *Bartholomew Fair* as a way of putting the reader on notice that the usage is archaic? No easy answers here.

In the case of 'travel' and 'travail', we are dealing with words that were originally identical but have come to acquire separate meanings. One encounters the forms 'trauell', 'trauail', 'trauaile', etc., in early modern texts, meaning, from at least the thirteenth century, either to journey or to labour. The *OED* regards the latter as the earlier meaning, but not by much. The conflation of meanings no doubt arises from the manifest difficulties and dangers of travel. Here the problem for the modernizing editor appears in its classic form: what to do when a word indifferently can mean one or the other in early modern usage, or both, whereas modern spelling differentiates. One is almost sure to lose resonances here by whatever choice is made. Presumably the thing to do is to choose what the editor regards as the dominant meaning in context and then explain in a note what is lost by that choice.

Thus, in Webster's *The White Devil*, Bracciano, appearing unbidden at the trial of Vittoria and afforded no chair, lays a gown under him as he sits on the floor, saying, 'An unbidden guest / Should trauaile as dutch-women go to church: / Beare their stooles with them' (3.2.5–7). The uninvited guest is imagined as travelling to church and also labouring in this endeavour, carrying his own stool. Justice Overdo, in *Bartholomew Fair*, speaks of 'this daies trauell'; he appears to mean both his laboursome endeavour to rid the fair of iniquity and the journey that such an undertaking requires of him (2.4.63). Old Merrythought in *The Knight of the Burning Pestle* speaks of a woman that will 'sing a cath [catch] in her Trauell', that is, will be merry even in her labour of childbirth; here the word predominantly means 'travail,' 'pain and labour', even though it is spelled 'Trauell' in the 1613 quarto. Examples abound in Shakespeare. 'Metal' and 'mettle' present a similar difficulty and linguistic history. Here the older term is 'metal', passing directly from Latin *metallum* (mine, quarry, and the metal obtained by mining, from Greek μέταλλον, mine) into all the Romance and Teutonic languages of Europe (*OED* metal n.) By the sixteenth century the word was in use figuratively to mean the 'stuff' of which a person is made. The word 'mettle', which we now use specifically in this sense, was originally a variant spelling used indiscriminately in all senses. *The Harvard Concordance* provides two discrete lists, one for 'metal' and one for 'mettle', and one can see the overall difference, but the original spellings will not support a number of the individual distinctions. What is one to make of Wolsey's saying, in *Henry VIII* to Suffolk, 'Now I feele / Of what course [coarse] Mettle ye are molded, Enuy' (3.2.240–1), which the *Concordance* lists under 'metal'? The senses of 'metal' and 'mettle' blend imperceptibly, and indeed one could argue that 'mettle' is predominant. Whoever heard of a metal called Envy? Similarly, in the Folio text of *King Lear*, we hear Regan proclaiming 'I am made of that self-mettle as my Sister' (1.1.69; the quarto reads 'I am made of the selfe same mettall that my sister is'), whereas the *Concordance*, though following the Folio reading, lists the instance under 'metal'. The quarto–Folio variation suggests an indifferent meaning of both metal and mettle. Conversely, when in *Much Ado about Nothing* Beatrice vows never to take a husband 'til God make men of some other mettal then earth' (the 1600 quarto, 2.1.55–6; the Folio text reads 'mettall'), the *Concordance* lists the instance under 'mettle', even though the association of 'metal' with 'earth' is strong, and the original spellings are arguably closer to 'metal' than to 'mettle'. I say this not to pick on the *Concordance*, which runs into problems of this sort because it is tied to the Riverside text, but because the phenomenon illustrates how ambiguities of this sort can lead to what appear to be inconsistent editorial choices. With 'metal' and 'mettle' one is faced with Hobson's choice – also in other authors, of course, besides Shakespeare. See, for example, *The Revenger's Tragedy*, where Vindice accuses his mother thus: 'I sent from the Dukes sonne, / Tryed you, and found you base mettell' (4.4.31). The overlap of meaning of 'metal' and 'mettle' arises from the metaphor of alchemical testing as applied to a person to see what 'stuff' she is made of.

With 'antic' and 'antique' we confront a similar difficulty. 'Antic', 'antike', anticke', and 'antique' are reasonably interchangeable in early modern English. 'Antic', apparently from the Italian *antico* but used more as an equivalent of the Italian *grottesco*, from 'a cauerne or hole vnder grounde' (*OED* citing Florio), was originally applied to 'fantastic representations of human, animal, and floral forms, incongruously running into one another' and hence signifying that which is incongruous, bizarre, or grotesque. Antique goes back to the Latin *antiquus, anticus*, meaning former, earlier, ancient. 'The modern ANTIC is a parallel form', reports the *OED*, 'which has always been distinct in sense in English, though both were spelt *antik(e, antick(e* in 16th c.' *The Harvard Concordance* accordingly supplies two lists, which are by and large comprehensible in their distinctions, though the original spellings do not support the distinction and some instances challenge the separation. When, for instance, Theseus says, in *A Midsummer Night's Dream*, 'I neuer may beleeue / These antique fables, nor these Fairy toyes' (5.2.2–3 in the 1600 quarto; the Folio spells the word 'anticke'), one wonders why the *Concordance* lists it as an instance of 'antic'. The reading of 'bizarre, grotesque' is of course possible, but so is 'ancient, hoary'. The editor gets to choose, scarcely comforted by the fact that the quarto opts for 'antique' while the Folio prefers 'anticke', a variant perhaps of 'antic', though ambivalently so. When the First Witch in *Macbeth* bids her sister witches 'performe your Antique round' (Folio text, 4.1.130), one sees the argument for modernizing it to 'antic', as does the Riverside text and hence the *Concordance*, but the sense of an ancient ritual is invitingly present. The 'antique pen' in Sonnet 19.10 is, arguably, both ancient and antic, capricious, fantastic. Jonson demonstrates the complete interchangeability of 'antic' and 'antique', even for a learned scholar like himself, when he has Volpone tempt Celia by saying, 'my dwarfe shall dance, / My eunuch sing, my foole make vp the antique', where he clearly means by 'antique' a grotesque dance or pageant, and where he intends the word to be pronounced 'ANT-ic' (*Volpone*, 1616 Folio text, 3.7.219).

'Mask' and 'masque', 'maskers' and 'masquers' blend into each other in ways that challenge the editor's ideas of consistency. A good instance is in *Love's Labour's Lost*, where Boyet announces to the French Princess and her ladies, 'The Trompet soundes, be maskt, the maskers come' (5.2.157). Are they not masquers? *The Harvard Concordance* makes an attempt to differentiate 'masker' and 'maskers' (one instance each) from 'masquers', but it is hard to see in what sense the 'maskers' just cited above (listed under 'maskers') differ from the 'masquers' (or 'Maskers') sent over by King Lewis of France to 'revel it' with King Edward IV and his new bride, the former Lady Grey (*3 Henry VI*, 3.3.224). (Lewis speaks with biting irony; he proposes to send soldiers.) The line is repeated at 4.1.94 to King Edward himself by a messenger. In both instances the word in the Folio text is 'Maskers', though the *Concordance* lists these instances under 'masquers'.

In several instances, the context gives virtually no guidance as to choice. 'Our masking mates by this time for us stay', urges Lorenzo to Jessica in *The Merchant of Venice* (2.6.60). This is listed in the *Concordance* under 'masquing', but why? Is not 'masking' as suitable a reading? At the start of this same scene, the quarto states, 'Enter the maskers.' Does this signify maskers or masquers? There is no effective difference, and yet an editor must choose, and try to choose in a way that is consistent with other choices. The problem is common in other dramatists as well. Beaumont and Fletcher's *The Maid's Tragedy*, which features a masque-within-the play in 1.2, calls it a 'Maske' in the early quartos, both as a title (1.2.116.1) and in the dialogue: 'Begin the Maske' (1.2.111). Here at least the choice is easy: however it is spelled, an elaborate evening's entertainment with aristocratic participants in masks is a 'masque' by conventional definition. Other examples given here are maddeningly undetermined.

One instance of divergent meanings that I particularly enjoy is that of 'moth' and 'mote'. I expect that this is because, when I had chosen as editor of the Bantam Shakespeare to call Don Armado's petite squire in *Love's Labour's Lost* 'Mote' rather than 'Moth', as it appears in the 1598 quarto, Joe Papp, who had agreed to write a series of introductions to the plays for the Bantam Shakespeare back in 1979, was heard to complain to an interviewer about some hair-brained editor (meaning me) who had got it into his head to call this character 'Mote' instead of by his right name. Well, Joe (now in heaven or wherever), may I ask that you consider the following: the word is indeed consistently spelled 'Moth' in the 1598 quarto of *Love's Labour's Lost* in naming the character in 1.2 and 3.1. So too with the brief naming of one of the four fairies ('*Pease-blossome, Cobweb, Moth*, and

Mustard-seede') bidden to attend on Bottom the Weaver in the 1600 quarto of *A Midsummer Night's Dream*. However, that word was interchangeable with 'mote' in early Modern English; it would have sounded identical on stage, without sounding the 'h'.

The spellings of the word in other Shakespearean passages plainly demonstrates this interchangeability, though you will have surmised by now that *The Harvard Concordance* obfuscates the difference. It has two lists: 'moth', including the above examples, and 'mote'. The latter list includes the following: 'You found his Moth, the King your Moth did see', where clearly we would say 'mote', since the speaker (Berowne) is talking about small specks and defects like a 'beam' in the eye (*Love's Labour's Lost*, 4.3.157); 'A moth will turne the ballance; which *Pyramus*, which *Thisbe*', plainly in reference to a tiny amount (*A Midsummer Night's Dream*, 5.1.315); 'O heauen: that there were but a moth in yours, / A grain, a dust, a gnat', where young Arthur asks Hubert to consider what it would be like to have even a minute particle in his eye as a distant token of what it would be like to be blinded (*King John*, 4.1.91–2); and, perhaps most vividly and even comically illustrating the point, 'A moth it is to trouble the mindes eye', said by Horatio as he thinks of a metaphorical speck of dust (1604 quarto of *Hamlet*; not included in the 1603 quarto or the First Folio). Only in *The Rape of Lucrece* does the spelling with which we are familiar appear: 'Through cristall wals ech little mote will peepe' (1251). A brief reference by Gower in *Pericles* to 'moates and shadows' (4.4.21) illustrates another spelling possibility in the plural.

Plainly, then, the spelling 'moth' gives no guidance as to whether it means 'moth' or 'mote' other than by way of context, and the instances in Shakespeare in which the context is clear are heavily weighted towards 'mote'. The usages all point to the word as signifying something tiny. That meaning certainly applies to the young lad in *Love's Labour's Lost* and to the fairy in *A Midsummer Night's Dream*. In the latter, a 'mote' is a speck much like a mustard-seed or pease-blossom and is gossamer and insubstantial like a cobweb. I would not want to deny the reader the pleasure of thinking of moths also, flittering about, but moths are not particularly like pease-blossoms. I would not want to deny the real likelihood that Shakespeare appreciated the implicit wordplay. I am ready to defend my choice of printing 'mote' in a modern spelling edition as arguably conveying a central meaning too easily overlooked.

In most of the foregoing examples – ancient–ensign, travel–travail, inginer–engineer, metal–mettle, antic–antique – what was originally a single word has diverged into two separate words with separate linguistic history. ('Mote' and 'moth' have separate histories.) The editor's choice is not always easier when the choice is simply between spelling variations of the same word. More often, the modernizing editor has to face an array of choices between two or more spellings of what is historically the same word, but in which the early modern form or forms are so appealingly unlike their modern counterpart that one wonders if one is not giving up something substantial by modernizing. In some instances, what is lost is a more visible manifestation of the word's etymological history.

Our word 'porpoise', for example, is, if you like, a debased and flattened rendition of the Latinate form we find in Jonson's *Epicene*, where Truewit torments Morose by assuring him that his new bride, Epicene, 'snores like a *porcpisce*' (1616 Folio, 4.4.140). Similarly, in *Volpone*, Peregrine mockingly astonishes Sir Politic Would-be by telling him news of 'three porcpisces seen aboue the bridge' in London (Folio, 2.1.40). Here we see plainly the etymology from the Latin *porcus* + *pisces*, a hogfish or 'seaswine'; compare the German *Meerschwein* and modern French *marsouin* that is derived from the German, or the Italian *porco marino* and Spanish *puerco marino*. One would expect classical purity of Jonson. Shakespeare may have known a more colloquial pronunciation; in the one instance of this word in the Shakespeare corpus, from the textually shaky *Pericles*, the Third Mariner describes how 'I saw the Porpas how he bounst and tumbled', 2.1.24–5). Webster's *The Duchess of Malfi* reflects a similar slippage when Silvio says of the Cardinal's threatening faces: 'He lifts vp 's nose, like a fowle Por-pisse before a storme' (3.3.53). Certainly the modernizing editor will feel a strong obligation to modernize the word, especially in the light of these tendencies in pronunciation, but one does so at the expense of losing sight of a Holofernes-like debate during the period between classical purists like Jonson and more 'popular' writers like Webster and Shakespeare.

More difficult is the choice, perhaps, when an author prefers one antique spelling throughout, such as 'porpentine'. Shakespeare's printed texts invariably choose this form, in *The Comedy of Errors* (five instances), *2 Henry VI*, *Troilus and Cressida*, and, best known of all, *Hamlet*, in which the ghost of Hamlet's father speaks of horrors able to make 'each particular haire to stand an end, / Like quils vpon the fearfull Porpentine' (1604 quarto, 1.5.20–1; the Folio spelling of 'Porpentine' is the same). The spelling in the 1609 quarto *Troilus* is 'Porpentin', in the Folio it is 'Porpentine' (2.1.26). Here editors are apt to part ways: the Riverside chooses 'porpentine', the Oxford 'porcupine', and so on.

Is the issue complicated by the fact that the word's main use in Shakespeare is to identify the Courtesan's establishment in *The Comedy of Errors*? Should one be conservative about place names? The word is spelled the same whether applied to this establishment or to the animal, as in *Hamlet*, *Troilus*, and in *2 Henry VI* ('the sharpe-quill'd Porpentine', 3.1.363), suggesting of course that the Courtesan's place is named after the animal, like 'the Phoenix' in the same play. Thus one should stick with one spelling. The logic of modern spelling urges 'porcupine', admittedly at the loss of linguistic flavour and probably some indication of pronunciation (though a modern spelling edition moves in this direction only at the cost of inconsistency). In this instance, etymology favours 'porcupine' as giving visible evidence of the Latin *porcus spinus*, from *spina* (thorn), variously represented in Romances languages as *puerco espin* (Spanish), *porco espinho* (Portuguese), and *porc-épic* (French). Presumably for that reason the *OED* regards 'porpentine' as simply a variant spelling. Earlier instances in English of similar spellings – portpen, portepyne, porpyn, pork poynt, porpoynt, etc. – suggest how such a phonetic variant came about. The fact remains that Shakespeare preferred 'porpentine', and that by modernizing one obscures another instance in which he chose not to follow that etymologically 'correct' choice.

The case of ostrich vs. estrich provides a similar instance. Modernizing editors generally fall into two camps, one cautiously preserving what appears to be an 'authentic' archaic spelling and the other boldly accepting the modern form of the word. A third, straddling position is, predictably, that of the Riverside Shakespeare and hence of *The Harvard Concordance*, in which we find two separate lists, for 'ostridge' and 'estridge'. ('Ostrich' does not appear, despite the fact that the Riverside purports to be a modern spelling edition.) True enough, in the Folio *2 Henry VI* we find 'Ostridge' (4.10.28), but it is surely worth noting that the word is spelled 'Astridge' in the comparable speech in *The First Part of the Contention*. There are only two instances of the 'es–' spelling in the Folio, 'Estridges' in *1 Henry IV* (4.1.98, also in the 1598 quarto) and 'Estridge' in *Antony and Cleopatra* (3.13.200). Given such a small sample, and the difference between quarto and Folio in the example from *2 Henry IV*, one could certainly argue for a choice of one consistent spelling in these three instances. Etymological history suggests how plausible both the 'es–' and 'os–' spellings must have been: to the Greek στρουθόσ (sparrow, hence μέγασ στρουθόσ, ostrich) is appended a prefix perhaps derived from 'avis', bird. Jonson votes in favour of 'estrich' as the more correct form (not 'estridge', as in Shakespeare); see, for example, *Epicene*, 4.1.49, and *The Alchemist*, 2.2.69.

'Bankrout' is another archaic spelling that attracts conservative modernizers; it is a very common form of 'bankrupt' in early modern speech. Florio cites the Italian *banca rotta*, literally 'the bank broken' or insolvent (so explained also in Samuel Johnson's *Dictionary*); Cotgrave cites a French adaptation *banqueroute*. As thus derived, the word seems also to have been influenced by the Latin–*ruptus*, as in 'abrupt', resulting in a single lexical item with two divergent forms. *The Harvard Concordance* once again provides us with two lists, as though Shakespeare distinguished the two forms for different meanings or shades of meaning. True it is that the three instances listed under 'bankrupt' spell the word thus in the Folio (in *As You Like It*, *Two Gentlemen*, and *Timon of Athens*), but the record is more confused in the more numerous listing for 'bankrout'. We find 'bankerout' in *Comedy of Errors* (4.2.58) and *Love's Labour's Lost*, Folio text 1.1.27 ('bancrout' in the 1598 quarto). It is 'banckrout' in the 1599 quarto and 'Banckrout' in the Folio text of *Romeo and Juliet* (3.2.57). 'Bankrout' does appear in *A Midsummer Night's Dream* (1600 quarto and Folio texts, 3.2.85), *The Merchant of Venice* (1600 quarto and Folio, 3.1.41 and 4.1.122), *Venus and Adonis*, 466, *The Rape of Lucrece*, 140 and 711, and *Sonnets*, 67.9. Yet in *Richard II* the Folio text at 2.1.151 reads 'bankrupt' while the 1597 quarto reads 'bankrout', and at 2.1.257 we find the same division: 'bankrupt' in the Folio and 'bankrout' in the quarto. *The Concordance*'s dual list can be defended technically if one privileges the quarto of *Richard II* over the Folio (it is the better copy-text) and allows for variances between 'bankerout' and 'banckrout' and 'bankrout', but surely the disparities of spelling in the case of *Richard II* prove that the distinctions are arbitrary at best. What idea of usage could possibly distinguish 'that poore and broken bankrupt' (*As You Like It*, 2.1.57) from 'poore banckrout break at once?' (*Romeo and Juliet*, 1599 quarto, 3.2.57)? Whatever choice an editor makes, it should not be that of the Riverside Shakespeare and *The Harvard Concordance*, which merely preserves the vagaries of scribes, printers, or authors willing to spell a word various ways. Then why not choose the modern 'bankrupt' in a modernized edition? The fact is that variations on 'bankrout' are common spelling elsewhere in the early modern period, as in *The Revenger's Tragedy* ('banqrout', 1607/8 quarto, 3.4.12) and *A Chaste Maid in Cheapside* ('bankrout', 1630 quarto, 3.3.10). The history sketched here suggests that trying to see something worth preserving in the older form is delusory.

Many other examples could be adduced – shamefast–shamefaced, beholding–beholden, mushrump–mushroom, apricocks–apricots, hartechocke–artichoke, concumbers–cucumbers, handkercher–handkerchief, loose–lose, chirurgeon–surgeon, sound–swoon, inprimis–imprimis, vild–vile, lanthorn–lantern, throughly–thoroughly – to demonstrate further that modernizing of spelling exacts a measurable cost in terms of verbal resonances, multiple plays of meaning, metre, characterization of speaker, dialectal speech, and still more. Yet the benefits outweigh the costs by making early modern texts more available to readers in terms of today's idioms. What I hope this essay will have suggested is that an editor must spend a great deal of time with historical dictionaries in order to be fully aware of etymological histories. Well-informed commentary can explain what has been lost by modernization. A middle ground, of attempting to hold on to archaic spellings on a selective basis, is almost sure to produce inconsistencies and misrepresentations. One needs to embrace modernization in all its implications, most of all when problems arise. In Spenser's famous dictum, 'Be bold, be bold, but not too bold.'

NOTES

1. See, for example, John Russell Brown (ed.), *The Duchess of Malfi* (Manchester University Press, 1974), p. lxxii, and *The White Devil* (Manchester University Press, 1960), p. lxxi. Except as otherwise noted, quotations from Renaissance plays are from *English Renaissance Drama: A Norton Anthology*, ed. David Bevington, Lars Engle, Katharine Eisaman Maus, and Eric Rasmussen (New York: Norton, 2002).
2. Thomas Marc Parrott (ed.), *The Plays and Poems of George Chapman: The Comedies* (London: Routledge and Sons, New York: E. P. Dutton, 1914).
3. Alan Holaday (ed.), *Chapman, George: The Comedies: A Critical Edition* (Urbana: University of Illinois Press, 1970).
4. Fredson Bowers (ed.), *The Complete Works of Christopher Marlowe*, 2 vols. (Cambridge University Press, 1973, 2nd edn 1981); Bowers (gen. ed.), *The Dramatic Works in the Beaumont and Fletcher Canon*, 10 vols. (Cambridge University Press, 1966–96).
5. Stanley Wells, *Re-Editing Shakespeare for the Modern Reader* (Oxford: Clarendon Press, 1984); Stanley Wells and Gary Taylor, *Modernizing Shakespeare's Spelling, with Three Studies in the Text of 'Henry V'* (Oxford: Clarendon Press, 1979).
6. Daniel Seltzer (ed.), *Friar Bacon and Friar Bungay* (Lincoln: University of Nebraska Press, 1963), p. xi.

CHAPTER 10

The staging of Shakespeare's drama in print editions

Margaret Jane Kidnie

When do we consider the stage directions of a play complete? Which stage directions *must* be provided for the script not to be regarded as either unfinished or corrupted? If one does not, or cannot, assume the controlling and legitimating influence of an author, these questions, which in essence concern the ontology of play-texts, are less easy to resolve than one might think. They cannot be resolved through reference to actual performance. Scripts exist as texts — as words on a page — and so rely entirely on printed or written conventions to convey meaning to a reader. Some readers, certainly, will bring to their encounter with the script an awareness of theatrical conventions — the customs and practices that shape performance at particular historical moments. As Gary Taylor memorably and suggestively explains this dynamic in relation to Shakespeare's drama, 'The *written* text . . . depended upon an *unwritten* para-text . . . an invisible life-support system of stage directions, which Shakespeare could either expect his first readers to supply, or which those first readers would expect Shakespeare to supply orally.'[1] The actors in Shakespeare's theatre, in other words, read these scripts through the lens of the prevailing theatrical conventions of their day. We should be clear, however, that this 'unwritten para-text', whether in the form it took in Shakespeare's theatre or the form it takes in our own, is, by definition, non-textual. It is something a reader brings to, rather than finds in, a script; it is part of the bridge that allows theatrical personnel to move from text to performance, yet equally forcefully separates text from performance as distinct media. To adopt a slightly different emphasis, there is no necessary or transparent link between scripted text and staged performance. Scripts are not comparable to performance, nor can they encode it.

Umberto Eco's ideas about the open work are helpful as a theoretical framework within which to grasp this point about the relation of text to performance. He notes that some works that exist in a print medium, more than others, open themselves to 'the free response of the addressee', and he writes that 'Blank space surrounding a word, typographical adjustments, and spatial composition in the page setting of the poetic text – all contribute to create a halo of indefiniteness and to make the text pregnant with infinite suggestive possibilities.'[2] But as he goes on to explain, these interpretations remain within a 'field of possibility' suggested by the author.[3] The author may not have anticipated them, but they are not unlimited. To apply to theatre Eco's insights into poetry and musical composition, what we find is that whereas the script offers copious, but not infinite, possibility, a theatrical performance offers a singular reading, or instantiation, of the script. The perceived meaning of that singular reading will undoubtedly vary among spectators. However, the activity of interpreting actors' bodies and gestures, costumes, sets and lighting, theatrical space, all the elements, in short, that inform one's experience of performance, is of a different creative order than the activities either of transforming a script into performance, with the sorts of choices that involves, or of reading dramatic literature.

A playwright cannot tell the reader every detail of the theatrical and fictional spaces, every actor's tone of voice and gestures, the build and costuming of each character (although some turn-of-the-twentieth-century dramatists such as George Bernard Shaw certainly attempted it). There will always be elements that are left undescribed, that a reader may choose to fix in a particular way in his or her imagination – or indeed, may choose to leave unfixed, open. Comprehensiveness of direction is impossible, and so we are cast back to what, as readers, we might consider an acceptable 'bare minimum' of direction in a play-text. Perhaps this 'bare minimum' might be understood as entrance and exit cues to tell the reader which characters are in the scene at any given point, and speech prefixes to tell the reader which characters speak which lines. Exceptions in our own time, however, even to this seemingly narrow definition are readily available: the script of Michael Frayn's *Copenhagen*, for instance, includes no entrance or exit cues, and Sarah Kane's *4.48 Psychosis*, a three-hand play, includes no speech prefixes, as well as no entrance or exit cues.[4]

When we turn to Shakespeare's time, we find that rarely, if ever, do early modern scripts achieve the 'bare minimum' posited above: speech prefixes can be ambiguous, and entrances and especially exits are frequently not included, or seem misplaced. Scholarly and editorial opinion has tended to characterize the printed staging of these texts as flawed or deficient. E. A. J. Honigmann suggests that his practical suggestions for the editorial treatment of printed directions

build on assumptions which are not, I believe, controversial. First, Shakespeare was careless about stage directions. He often omitted them, or left them incomplete, or inserted them in approximately but not precisely the correct place. Secondly, some stage directions in the good Quartos, and many more in the Folio, were added or misplaced by scriveners, prompters, Folio editors or compositors.[5]

Leslie Thomson argues that 'every Shakespeare play requires the addition of some basic stage directions and the correction of others to bring them into conformity with implications in the dialogue', and in an earlier article, I myself described the play-texts as surviving only as 'textual fragments'.[6]

Yet the striking diversity exhibited by play-texts of our own time, and the difficulties implicit in defining a notion of completeness when it comes to the stage directions even of modern print editions, might lead us to a contrary conclusion – namely, that early modern writers, book-keepers, printers, and readers had different expectations of a script. This conclusion is supported by the work of William B. Long on the manuscript drama of the Elizabethan–Jacobean–Caroline period. Long argues that study of the extant theatrical playbooks demonstrates that they were by no means the 'clean, complete, and well-ordered'[7] documents that editors have often imagined them to be:

> These manuscript plays are by no means invariably neat and orderly; authorial stage directions are very seldom changed in the theater; speech-heads are not regularized; copious markings do not appear to handle properties, entrances, and music. Regularization and completeness simply were not factors in theatrical marking of an author's papers. Theatrical personnel seem to have marked the book only in response to problems.

The players, Long concludes, 'did not possess or desire to possess books in which all problems had been solved and all ambiguities worked out'.[8] The uniform consistency with which the directions of early modern printed and manuscript drama embody what we tend to think of as error suggests that it may not be the texts, but our conception of 'completeness,' which is faulty, or at least anachronistic. Shakespeare's stage directions seem to have conformed, as far as we can tell, to early modern theatrical standards of textual completeness and correctness. These scripts, in other words, are not deficient in any absolute or transhistorical sense. They just seem deficient to us.

A couple of potential responses to this interpretation of the textual condition of early modern drama immediately present themselves. We could treat these documents, as Stephen Orgel has suggested, as 'artifacts, and ... preserve as much as [we] can of their archeology'.[9] John Cox, elsewhere in this volume, presents a similar view, strongly arguing in favour of cautious editorial intervention and the use of commentary as a way to guide the reader

Staging Shakespeare's drama in print editions 161

to staging possibilities. A second possible response is to acknowledge that modern readers have different expectations of a script from their early modern counterparts, and to accommodate those expectations in order to make a first-time encounter with Shakespeare's drama in the print medium less alienating. This is not to imply, necessarily, that the extant directions are faulty or incomplete, but simply to modify the stage directions found in those written and printed documents to conform better to modern notions of completeness. As assumptions about 'completeness' change, so will the editions we prepare. Not too long ago characters would be directed by editors to enter reading letters, now they tend to read papers; characters at one time entered anterooms in Scottish castles, now they simply enter the scene. Both of these adjustments indicate an increased sensitivity on the parts both of readers and editors to theatrical space, and are evidence of ever-changing fashions in the way stage directions are adapted to modern sensibilities and conventions: 'As editors, we stage the plays we contemplate, and in the process they become our own.'[10]

Thus editorial treatment of stage directions is a provisional and conventionalized process. Moreover, the level of interpretation implicit in this activity will increase proportionately, the more thoroughly an editor sets out to *translate*, in effect, early modern stage directions into a form more readily recognized by modern readers. There are good and compelling reasons, mostly associated with the perceived needs of the first-time reader, why we might attempt this translation, and it seems overly dogmatic to insist that *no* edition or series should try to make the textual staging of early modern drama more accessible to the modern user. However, we should be clear what such translation, as currently – and often silently – practised by editors of early modern drama, involves: extant stage directions are rephrased, supplemented, and moved either to an earlier or later moment in a scene; extant directions are omitted (usually because they are thought overly 'literary' or untheatrical), while new directions are created; speech prefixes are altered in order to reassign speeches from one character to another; characters are removed from, or added to, entrance and exit directions. I rehearse these common editorial procedures simply to dispel any illusions that modernized editions, as traditionally constructed, are somehow 'authentic', something more than an interpretative performance. As Stanley Wells has explained the situation,

every editor since Rowe's time who has claimed to be doing anything more than supervising the preparation of a diplomatic reprint or of a typographical or photographic facsimile has, however conservative he may have been in his treatment of dialogue, been willing to add directions which have no claim to explicit authenticity, and to adjust the original directions in the interests of clarity and consistency of presentation.[11]

The notion of authenticity, a problematic claim even in relation to the earliest quartos and Folio of Shakespeare's drama (should we define 'the authentic' as what was printed? what Shakespeare may have written? what we think the players performed?), sits particularly uneasily with a desire to render staging in the print medium accessible to a modern reader.[12]

Editorial practice in matters of print staging has traditionally been informed by the contradictory beliefs that early modern play-texts are radically unstable and indeterminate, and that there are better, or even demonstrably accurate, directions that might be inserted into the text to guide the reader. This is particularly a problem when editors come to consider where precisely to introduce a direction. In a recent article, George Walton Williams points out that the moment when Romeo and Juliet first kiss during their shared sonnet in 1.5 is ambiguous: there is no stage direction in any of the texts to cue a kiss, and the question is not resolved through analysis of the dialogue.[13] Clearly the lovers kiss, but where? A kiss might reasonably fall after either, 'Then moue not while my prayers effect I take:' or the line that follows, 'Thus from my lips, by thine my sin is purg'd' (TLN 685–6). Taking issue with the view that Romeo's two-line speech should not be interrupted with a kiss, to argue instead that 'the kiss is the punctuation of the sonnet', Williams concludes that 'Fortunately, most modern editions have recognized that the *proper* location for the direction is as the Arden has it [after TLN 685].'[14] And thus a subjective preference in an indeterminate case is transformed into correct editorial procedure. But even if editors avoid arguing the necessary placement of a particular direction, they necessarily have to place it. Antony Hammond, discussing the entrance of Ferdinand into his sister's closet in *The Duchess of Malfi*, captures both the problem and the frustration it can entail for the editor:

If I were staging this, I would have Ferdinand enter unseen. (It does not much matter where; one of the curses of editing is that you have to *choose*, when choice is impossible: our note reads, 'the timing of this entry is not self-evident, nor does it need to be precisely determined . . .' Still, you have to print it somewhere!)[15]

Alan C. Dessen provides numerous examples where editorial directions in print editions offer not the only, nor even arguably the best, staging available. He shows how stage directions, and their placement, in Shakespeare's early quartos and Folio are more workable than editors have imagined, and he provides a keen sense of the options closed down by editorial intervention. Such interpretative treatment of the early documents is characterized as an inappropriate 'rescripting' of the texts. The burden of Dessen's chapter is that 'Choices must be made. But on what basis and by whom?'[16]

As a theatre historian, Dessen is most concerned to recover, as far as possible, what might have happened on the stage in the early modern period. Perhaps for this reason, he is less concerned to shape extant stage directions for a modern reader than he is to explore the potential of the texts by 'field-testing' them in the theatre.[17] '[D]ecisions *must* be made', and errors and inconsistencies should be cleared up by the editor for the reader, but 'If it ain't broke, don't fix it.'[18] But how can an editor tell when a text is broken? More crucially, if we agree with Honigmann and Long that playwrights, theatre personnel, and copyists did not seem to take much care with – or to put that differently, did not feel the need to specify with precision, consistently, or in great detail – the staging of a play in its written form, then how much significance should we attribute to the particular placement of a printed direction? Surely the upshot of Dessen's analysis is not that early modern editions of Shakespeare's drama are 'unbroken', but that modernized editions necessarily efface a plurality of staging options that readers of the drama might do well to consider.

So the real question is perhaps not which single staging option editors should or might present to their readers, but how we might translate the stage directions of early modern scripts in such a way as to make readers aware of textual indeterminacy. Dessen implies that users would engage with issues of staging more freely and creatively if editors simply adopted a more hands-off attitude:

Given the range of options in the Quarto, the *user* of these modern editions should ask: is making such a choice ... the function of the editor? ... [D]o students, critics, actors, and directors want from their editions (that are to serve as playscripts) a plausible but iffy decision that may in turn close down equally valid or theatrically interesting options of which the reader is no longer aware?[19]

However, as already discussed, the reason why editors attempt at all to translate the conventions governing directions in early modern play-texts into a form more easily recognized by, and therefore accessible to, a modern user is because we assume at least some readers lack the skills required to interpret for themselves what Dessen characterizes elsewhere as a foreign vocabulary.[20] The stage directions found in early modern scripts are not incomplete in any transhistorical sense, but they can feel alienating to a modern first-time user. Rather than insist that all users should become experts in the 'grammar' of early modern theatrical conventions (the drama's 'unwritten para-text') – conventions that even editors and theatre historians are still seeking to understand fully – we make what is unfamiliar seem familiar. That process *necessarily* requires editors to interpret, or 'rescript', Shakespeare's drama. Not to make those choices, and yet to assume that readers are unable to infer a range of choices for themselves, would be an inconsistent editorial rationale.

Intervention thus seems inevitable in these types of editions, but perhaps less inevitable is the form it might take. Editorial models, after all, come into being over time, and many of the print conventions we take for granted derive not from the Elizabethan, Jacobean, or even Caroline periods, but were shaped in the first decade of the eighteenth century when 'Shakespeare's first named editor, the practising playwright Nicholas Rowe . . . laid the foundations of modern texts.'[21] In 'Modernizing Shakespeare: Nicholas Rowe and *The Tempest*', Peter Holland discusses a trial sheet dated 1708 which is currently lodged at the British Library. It consists of eight pages of text, and seems to show how Rowe tried out possible ideas for the presentation of his edition of Shakespeare's *Complete Works*, published in 1709. As Holland explains, 'it seems to be an experiment in setting, establishing both the format for the page and significant elements of the house style that would be used for the full edition'.[22]

This trial sheet makes one aware, in a very concrete way, of the constructedness of an editorial tradition that can otherwise seem transparent, or 'natural'. Rowe *experimented with* possible formats. That form of creative endeavour is required of very few of us today, mostly because editors are asked to adopt the series conventions of the publishing house for whom they prepare their texts. Looking at some of the series currently available on the market, it seems even general editors are reluctant to play around too much with presentation. There is the clear-page format espoused by Penguin and the Oxford *Complete Works*, there is the facing-page commentary found in the New Folger and Cambridge Schools series, and there are the various hierarchical arrangements of text, collation, and commentary which are typical of the Oxford, Arden3, and New Cambridge single-volume series. What varies in these series is the arrangement of the editorial apparatus: the visual presentation of the dialogue and stage directions is remarkably consistent.

Perhaps it is time for editors, in the spirit of Rowe, to begin experimenting more freely with the layout of the edited page, particularly in relation to stage directions, and to develop conventions with which we might guide users, not to a 'proper' choice, but rather to an awareness of choice and an imaginative interaction with the drama. What kind of editorial format can draw to the reader's attention what Eco calls the 'infinite suggestive possibilities' of the script?[23] How might we prompt readers' creativity in such a way as to allow for independent responses that might well exceed the editor's expectations? One innovation is suggested by a characteristic feature of the manuscript plays and playbooks of the early modern period – the marginal stage direction. Playwrights and scribes not infrequently located directions in the right margin of the page, while bookholders typically introduced them into the left margin for added visibility.[24] Mariko Ichikawa attends specifically to manuscript cues for getting on and off the stage, noting that 'mid-scene entrances are often marked in the right or left margin without any break in the dialogue, and exits are almost always marked on the right'.[25] Manuscript directions, whether in the left or right margins, are sometimes underlined, boxed, or bracketed to set them apart from the rest of the page, and rarely can they be aligned visually with a precise moment in the dialogue. Figure 2 photoquotes a passage from the scribal manuscript of *The Second Maiden's Tragedy* in which one finds three directions in the left margin; the first two cues are evidently scribal ('Enter Nobles', 'Enter Heluetius'), and the third added by the playhouse book-keeper ('florish').[26] Figure 3 photoquotes a direction ('Enter A messenger') ranged in the right margin of the manuscript of *The Book of Sir Thomas Moore*. Occasionally a similar sort of spatial display can be detected in the printed texts. The stage directions in Figure 4 ('It spreads his armes', 'The cocke crowes'), for example, reproduced from Q2 *Hamlet*, preserve the textual ambiguity typical of the manuscript drama. If we agree with Honigmann, Orgel, Wells, and others that relocating, rewriting, and newly inventing stage directions for the interpretative benefit of the reader is acceptable, or at least accepted, editorial practice, then relocating extant and editorially devised directions into the margin of the page is intervention of exactly the same order, but to a different effect. Instead of trying to accomplish the impossible, to fix (in both senses of the word) an unstable print document, this strategy builds into the spatial presentation of the page the textual indeterminacy typical of directions found in early modern printed and manuscript drama. Such a page design begins to transfer the interpretative activity from the editor to the reader, and yet signals to the reader that there are options to consider.

This essay will turn now to consider the potential merits and limitations of such a presentation of early modern scripts through close analysis of 'kissing scenes' found in *Troilus and Cressida* (TLN 2549–626), and *Romeo and Juliet* (TLN 666–94). The passages have been mocked up and included as

2 *The Second Maiden's Tragedy*, MS. Lansdowne 807, f. 55b.

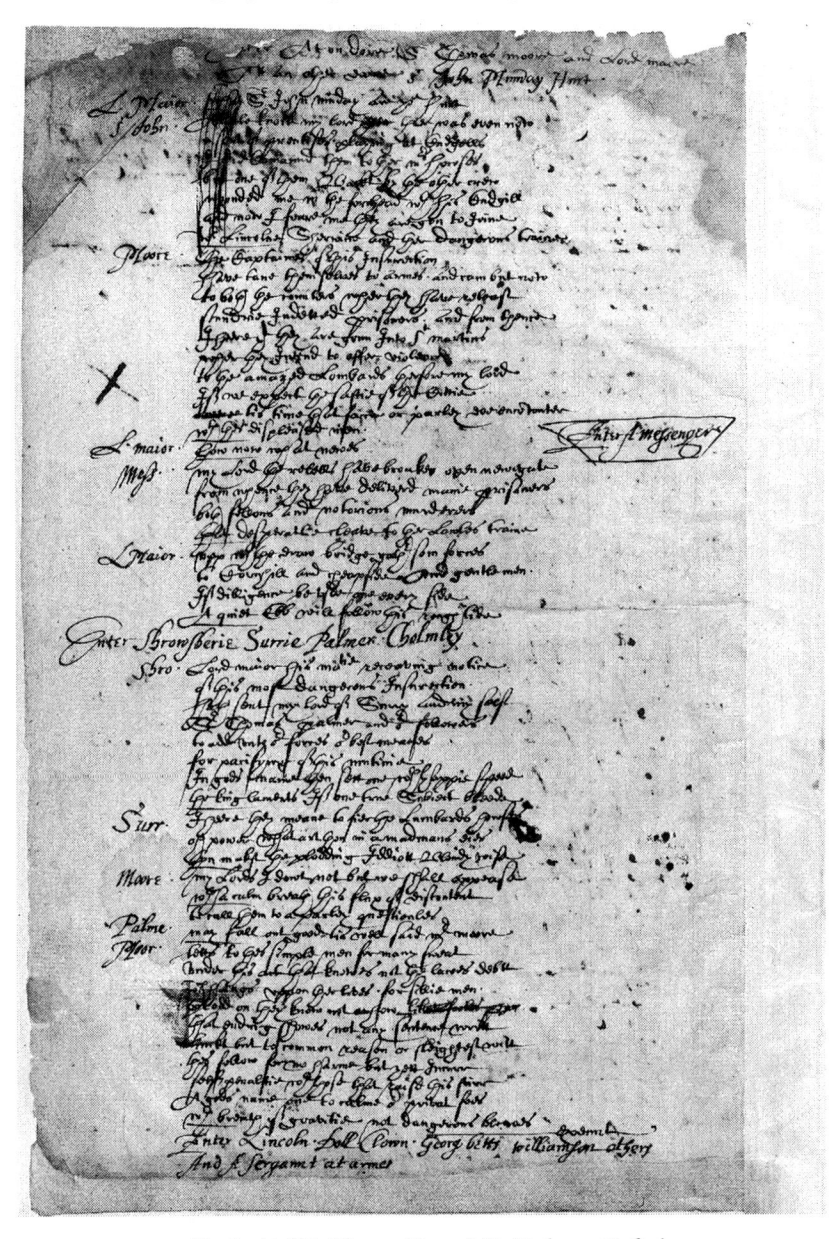

3 *The Book of Sir Thomas Moore*, MS. Harley 7368, f. 7b.

Prince of Denmarke.

But soft, behold, loe where it comes againe
Ile crosse it though it blast mee : stay illusion, *It spreads*
If thou hast any sound or vse of voyce, *his armes.*
Speake to me, if there be any good thing to be done
That may to thee doe ease, and grace to mee,
Speake to me.
If thou art priuie to thy countries fate
Which happily foreknowing may auoyd
O speake :
Or if thou hast vphoorded in thy life
Extorted treasure in the wombe of earth
For which they say your spirits oft walke in death. *The cocke*
Speake of it, stay and speake, stop it *Marcellus*. *crowes.*
  Mar. Shall I strike it with my partizan?
  Hor. Doe if it will not stand.
  Bar. Tis heere.
  Hor. Tis heere.
  Mar. Tis gone.
We doe it wrong being so Maiesticall
To offer it the showe of violence,
For it is as the ayre, invulnerable,
And our vaine blowes malicious mockery.
  Bar. It was about to speake when the cock crewe.
  Hor. And then it started like a guilty thing,
Vpon a fearefull summons; I haue heard,
The Cock that is the trumpet to the morne,
Doth with his lofty and shrill sounding throat
Awake the God of day, and at his warning
Whether in sea or fire, in earth or ayre
Th'extrauagant and erring spirit hies
To his confine, and of the truth heerein
This present obiect made probation.
  Mar. It faded on the crowing of the Cock.
Some say that euer gainst that season comes
Wherein our Sauiours birth is celebrated
This bird of dawning singeth all night long,
And then they say no spirit dare sturre abraode
The nights are wholsome, then no plannets strike,
No fairy takes, nor witch hath power to charme

4 The second quarto of *Hamlet* (1604), sig. B3r.

Figures 5 and 6 as a starting-point for discussion (all line references that follow are to these extracts). What I am experimenting with in these samples is how typographical features such as contrasting fonts and arrows might be combined with spatial arrangements to impact on the dynamics of the reading experience. While the edited passages assume annotations off the page, either in a single-volume or complete works edition, they could easily be adapted to accommodate collation and annotations at the bottom of the page. The pragmatic decisions underlying these mock-ups are informed by the realization, underscored years ago by Jerome J. McGann in relation to Romantic and Modernist literature, that 'the reading eye is a scanning mechanism as well as a linear decoder'.[27] In other words, the visual design of a page encodes information in a manner quite apart from the linguistic meaning of the words printed on that page, or to put that yet a different way, readers construct meaning, not just by *reading* a page, but by *looking at* a page.

The most immediately apparent design feature of the extracts is the way the page is dominated by two boxes that share a vertical wall, the narrower box to the left enclosing most of the stage directions, and the other enclosing the dialogue and speech prefixes. A consequence of this display is that, visually, each box tends to some extent to operate independently of the other; one's eye is drawn *down* each box, rather than relentlessly *across* the page. Conceptual links are therefore suggested not just between the stage directions and the dialogue, but from one stage direction to another, a two-axis reading dynamic that requires, for purposes of clarity, the use of character names in place of personal pronouns in the left column. In the *Troilus and Cressida* sample, this spatial arrangement allows one to visualize as a grouping the kisses that occur early in the scene. The lack of open white space left by these multiple directions creates an impression of activity in the margin of the page that can be clearly associated with, but operates at a distance from, the main text.

This distance is an important interpretative feature of the page design, and it is an effect which is visually emphasized on the page with the black line that separates the two boxes. The reader's eye is forced to flit back and forth across that line in a manner that disrupts the smooth flow of the reading experience. Moreover, there is nobody to control what one looks at, or when. Those boxes implicitly give readers permission to choose themselves when to dip into the stage directions – or when, indeed, to ignore them. Ideologically, such a format demystifies the editorial function, displaying the relation between stage direction and dialogue as a particular, rather than inevitable, print construction. Methodologically, it asks readers to contribute imaginatively to that performance, to construct for

Enter Ajax armed, Agamemnon, Achilles, Ulysses, Menelaus, Nestor, Patroclus, Calchas, and others.	AGAMEMNON
	  Here art thou in appointment fresh and fair,
	  Anticipating time with starting courage.
	  Give with thy trumpet a loud note to Troy,
	  Thou dreadful Ajax, that the appalled air
	  May pierce the head of the great combatant 5
	  And hale him hither.

[Ajax passes money to trumpeter]	AJAX Thou trumpet, there's my purse.
	  Now crack thy lungs and split thy brazen pipe.
	  Blow, villain, till thy sphered bias cheek
	  Outswell the colic of puffed Aquilon.
	  Come, stretch thy chest and let thy eyes spout blood; 10
	  Thou blow'st for Hector.

[Trumpet sounds]	ULYSSES No trumpet answers.

[Enter Diomedes and Cressida▼]	ACHILLES 'Tis but early days.
	AGAMEMNON
	  Is not yond Diomed with Calchas' daughter?
	ULYSSES
	  'Tis he. I ken the manner of his gait.
	  He rises on the toe: that spirit of his 15
	  In aspiration lifts him from the ground.

[Enter Diomedes and Cressida▲]	AGAMEMNON Is this the lady Cressid? DIOMEDES Even she.

[Agamemnon kisses Cressida]	AGAMEMNON
	  Most dearly welcome to the Greeks, sweet lady.
	NESTOR
	  Our General doth salute you with a kiss.
	ULYSSES
	  Yet is the kindness but particular; 20
	  'Twere better she were kissed in general.
	NESTOR

[Nestor kisses Cressida]	And very courtly counsel. I'll begin. So much for Nestor. ACHILLES

[Achilles kisses Cressida]	I'll take that winter from your lips, fair lady.
	  Achilles bids you welcome. 25
	MENELAUS
	  I had good argument for kissing once.
	PATROCLUS

[Patroclus kisses Cressida]	But that's no argument for kissing now;
	  For thus popped Paris in his hardiment,
	  And parted thus you and your argument.
	ULYSSES
	  O deadly gall, and theme of all our scorns! 30
	  For which we lose our heads to gild his horns.
	PATROCLUS

[Patroclus kisses Cressida]	The first was Menelaus' kiss; this, mine.
	  Patroclus kisses you.
	MENELAUS O this is trim.
	PATROCLUS
	  Paris and I kiss evermore for him.
	MENELAUS
	  I'll have my kiss, sir. – Lady, by your leave. 35

5 *Troilus and Cressida*, TLN 2549–626 (Act 4.6), layout design prepared by Margaret Jane Kidnie.

	CRESSIDA	
	In kissing do you render or receive?	
	MENELAUS	
	Both take and give.	
	CRESSIDA I'll make my match to live,	
	The kiss you take is better than you give.	
	Therefore no kiss.	
	MENELAUS	
	I'll give you boot: I'll give you three for one.	40
	CRESSIDA	
	You are an odd man: give even or give none.	
	MENELAUS	
	An odd man, lady? Every man is odd.	
	CRESSIDA	
	No, Paris is not – for you know 'tis true	
	That you are odd, and he is even with you.	
	MENELAUS	
	You fillip me o' th' head.	
	CRESSIDA No, I'll be sworn.	45
	ULYSSES	
	It were no match, your nail against his horn.	
	May I, sweet lady, beg a kiss of you?	
	CRESSIDA	
	You may.	
	ULYSSES I do desire it.	
	CRESSIDA Why, beg too.	
	ULYSSES	
	Why then, for Venus' sake, give me a kiss,	
	When Helen is a maid again, and his –	50
	CRESSIDA	
	I am your debtor; claim it when 'tis due.	
	ULYSSES	
	Never's my day, and then a kiss of you.	
	DIOMEDES	
[Diomedes and	Lady, a word. I'll bring you to your father.	
Cressida move to	NESTOR	
join Calchas]	A woman of quick sense.	
	ULYSSES Fie, fie upon her!	
[Exit Cressida and	There's language in her eye, her cheek, her lip;	55
Calchas▼]	Nay, her foot speaks. Her wanton spirits look out	
	At every joint and motive of her body.	
	O these encounterers so glib of tongue,	
	That give accosting welcome ere it comes,	
	And wide unclasp the tables of their thoughts	60
	To every ticklish reader, set them down	
[Exit Cressida and	For sluttish spoils of opportunity	
Calchas▲]	And daughters of the game.	
Flourish. Enter all of	ALL The Trojans' trumpet.	
Troy: Hector	AGAMEMNON	
[armed], Paris,	Yonder comes the troop.	
Aeneas, Helenus,	AENEAS	
[Troilus], and	Hail, all you state of Greece! What shall be done	65
attendants.	To him that victory commands? …	

5 *(cont.)*

themselves (in various possible ways) the precise relation between the dialogue and stage directions. The use of a different font and type size between the two boxes means that the directions cueing the male characters to kiss Cressida, for instance, fail to map precisely onto any one moment, or even any single line of dialogue. Turning to *Romeo and Juliet*, this format sidesteps entirely editorial debates about where exactly in the printed text the lovers should kiss for the first time (see lines 18–19). This is no derogation of editorial responsibility; instead, it is to recognize that there can be no 'right' choice, and to locate the interpretative decision firmly with the reader.

In this format, mid-scene entrances and exits, like cues to kiss, sound trumpets, or pass money, are 'open', insofar as they cannot be graphically fixed to a specific moment in the dialogue. The entrance of the Trojans to the Greeks, for example, visually occurs somewhere between the Greeks hearing the Trojan trumpet sound and Aeneas' opening lines, 'Hail, all you state of Greece! What shall be done / To him that victory commands?' (lines 63–6). This example creates as an effect in the print medium the sense one has when watching a theatrical performance of action occurring in time and space. The Trojans' entrance into the text, in other words – as the marginal display literally suggests – might be read as diachronic, rather than synchronic, taking place over three or more lines of dialogue. Yet while this presentation in some ways imitates the effect of theatrical performance, there is no pretence that live theatre might in any way be captured on the page. The 'performance' that this display effects is specifically a *textual* performance.

The uncertainties surrounding Cressida's entrance and exit raise slightly different issues of editorial tact. She might begin to enter as early as the sounding of the trumpet to summon Hector to field, or merely in time for Agamemnon to confirm her identity with the line 'Is this the lady Cressid?' (line 17). She might then exit immediately after Diomedes says he will bring her to her father, or not until after Ulysses has given an account of her as one of the 'sluttish spoils of opportunity / And daughters of the game' (lines 62–3). An ambiguous 'Exeunt' after Ulysses' speech in the Folio gives some support to a late exit for Cressida, but by no means conclusively resolves the question. In both of these instances, the edited sample experiments with unobtrusive arrows in the left margin to guide the reader by delimiting a probable range within which the entrance and exit might occur. Instead of presenting the reader with what can only be an arbitrary editorial decision, new print conventions are developed to suggest a field of possibility, thus turning the interpretative process back to the reader.

Staging Shakespeare's drama in print editions 173

However, this treatment of staging in the print medium is in some respects as rigid as the more conventional format. Calchas, for example, is cued to enter at the top of the scene. This merely reproduces the direction provided in both the quarto and Folio, but editors often argue that the inclusion of Calchas is an error since he never speaks, despite being reunited with his daughter, and so they erase his presence. If Calchas does not enter with the others, then Diomedes' offer to bring Cressida to her father at line 53 would seem to prompt editors to add an exit for Diomedes and Cressida; if Calchas is included in that opening direction, Diomedes' offer might instead prompt a cue for Diomedes and Cressida to cross to Calchas, and then the 'Exeunt' printed in the Folio might be interpreted to refer to Cressida and Calchas, not Cressida and Diomedes. This latter arrangement is particularly convenient as Diomedes speaks again later in the scene.[28] A decision has to be made, and at the moment that decision remains with the editor.

Is Cressida's father part of the 'textual performance' of this scene, or not? More to the point, is it possible to create a page design that can provide guidance to the reader by signalling, rather than simply closing down, interpretative options? Perhaps editors might rephrase their stage directions: Calchas 'may' enter. While such a solution presents advantages, the particular problem the conditional tense presents is that of knowing when to stop: Cressida might exit with Calchas; she might exit with Diomedes; she might exit with an unnamed attendant. Why cite on the page some, but not all, of the possibilities that 'might' occur? The marginalia not only become unwieldy, but also, paradoxically, prescriptive all over again as the scope of the reader's imagination becomes limited to choosing among the options set out by the editor.

A slightly different situation in which one is tempted to use the 'might' construction is found in the *Romeo and Juliet* extract – do the lovers kiss a second time at the Capulet ball? If they did, it would probably occur somewhere in the shared line in which Romeo says 'Give me my sin again', to which Juliet responds 'You kiss by th'book' (line 22). A kiss here seems far less certain than that the lovers might take, or touch, hands at Romeo's lines, 'If I profane with my unworthiest hand / This holy shrine' (lines 5–6). An inexperienced reader might easily fail to infer physical contact at lines 5–6, and yet, oddly enough, it is rarely cued by editors. To return to the kiss, it seems as likely as not that the Nurse interrupts a second kiss before it can be effected. The only conclusion we can draw about this textual moment is that one might *imagine* the lovers kissing again. The editorial dilemma is aptly summarized by Williams: 'The absence of a direction here

	TYBALT
	Patience perforce with wilful choler meeting
	Makes my flesh tremble in their different greeting.
	I will withdraw, but this intrusion shall,
Exit [Tybalt]	Now seeming sweet, convert to bitt'rest gall.
	ROMEO
[Romeo takes	If I profane with my unworthiest hand 5
Juliet by the hand]	This holy shrine, the gentler sin is this:
	My lips, two blushing pilgrims, ready stand
	To smooth that rough touch with a tender kiss.
	JULIET
	Good pilgrim, you do wrong your hand too much,
	Which mannerly devotion shows in this. 10
	For saints have hands that pilgrims' hands do touch,
	And palm to palm is holy palmers' kiss.
	ROMEO
	Have not saints lips, and holy palmers, too?
	JULIET
	Ay, pilgrim, lips that they must use in prayer.
	ROMEO
	O then, dear saint, let lips do what hands do: 15
	They pray; grant thou, lest faith turn to despair.
	JULIET
	Saints do not move, though grant for prayers' sake.
	ROMEO
	Then move not while my prayer's effect I take.
[Romeo and	Thus from my lips, by thine my sin is purged.
Juliet kiss]	**JULIET**
	Then have my lips the sin that they have took. 20
	ROMEO
	Sin from my lips? O trespass sweetly urged!
	Give me my sin again.
	JULIET You kiss by th' book.
	NURSE
[Juliet moves to	Madam, your mother craves a word with you.
her mother]	**ROMEO**
	What is her mother?
	NURSE Marry, bachelor,
	Her mother is the lady of the house ... 25

6 *Romeo and Juliet*, TLN 666–94 (Act 1.5), layout design prepared by Margaret Jane Kidnie.

in an edition will leave the question to be answered by the reader who might not realize there was an option.'[29] And yet, despite this danger, a strong argument could be framed against adding a direction for a second kiss as it is beyond the editor's remit, or even ability, to imagine and record every 'might' that might occur to a reader – Juliet might laugh at line 17; the Nurse might tap Romeo on the arm with a fan at line 24; the lovers might kiss a second time at line 22. The layout with which I am experimenting cannot solve the specifically textual problem editors confront at this moment in the script. There can be no 'right' answer, and there is no question but that, as a script, the unemended text is as complete as it needs to be. The real issue is simply that editors want to make readers readily aware of the possibility of a second kiss. However, to add the direction is not to introduce optionality; rather, it is to make readers just as unaware of the possibility that a second kiss might *not* occur.

The page design explored in this essay, to some limited extent, builds indeterminacy into the editorial treatment of staging in an effort to explore one pragmatic response to Barbara Hodgdon's call elsewhere in this collection to translate '[theatrical] contingency into manageable print form' in such a way as to present 'the work as something which is "coming-into-performance"' (pp. 212, 220). However, it does not manage to leave 'open' all the interpretative problems and hard decisions confronted by editors who attempt to render early modern stage directions more accessible to modern readers. Its real impact, however, is less tangible, and perhaps more innovative, than this rather bald assessment suggests. This visual presentation of Shakespeare's drama cultivates the reader's active engagement with the script in a manner not achieved by editions that interline stage directions in the dialogue. Instead of telling the reader what happens, this format insists that there is interpretative work yet to be done. Stage directions are self-consciously displayed as a constructed element of the script, and so no longer seem to grow naturally or organically out of the dialogue.

The importance of this is not just that in many places an option is replaced with choices, but that the readerly activity itself undergoes a profound adjustment. To employ a theatrical metaphor, the reader is no longer an entirely passive spectator to the textual performance, but becomes a player on whose creative input the script regularly draws. The expectations of the reader are different, as is the dynamic established between the reader and the text. Such a reader, I would argue, is more likely than the reader of a conventional modernized edition to move from an interpretative consideration of a marginal direction cueing a kiss between Romeo and Juliet, to the slightly different, but related, interpretative consideration of whether the empty space a few lines further down might feasibly be filled with another kiss. In such a case, the possible second kiss, readers already primed by means of bibliographical codes to respond imaginatively to issues of staging are probably best served, not with an editorial stage direction, but with the sort of discursive, open-ended commentary proposed in this collection by John Cox in 'Open Stage, Open Page?'. Challenging received ideas of what Shakespeare is meant to look like on the page might allow modern readers to see, and read, differently, thus encouraging us to reconsider and perhaps move beyond the too-easy assumption that the stage directions of early modern scripts are incomplete until editorially completed.

NOTES

I am indebted to James Purkis for his many comments on this essay, and for his suggestions concerning layout and design. I would also like to acknowledge grateful thanks to Anthony B. Dawson, Alan C. Dessen, Barbara Hodgdon, Steven Urkowitz, Paul Werstine, and George Walton Williams for providing feedback on an early draft of this essay, in some cases sharing with me their own research in manuscript form.

1. Stanley Wells and Gary Taylor, with John Jowett and William Montgomery, *William Shakespeare: A Textual Companion* (Oxford: Clarendon Press, 1997), p. 2, emphasis mine.
2. Umberto Eco, *The Open Work*, trans. Anna Cancogni with an introduction by David Robey (Cambridge, MA: Harvard University Press, 1989), pp. 8–9.
3. *Ibid.*, p. 19. 'Author' here, in the context of early modern drama, might be extended to include non-authorial agents in the playhouse and printing house who contributed to the production of the play text.
4. Michael Frayn, *Copenhagen* (London: Methuen, 1998); Sarah Kane, *4.48 Psychosis*, in *Sarah Kane: Complete Plays*, introduced by David Greig (London: Methuen, 2001), pp. 203–45.
5. E. A. J. Honigmann, *Myriad-Minded Shakespeare: Essays on the Tragedies, Problem Comedies and Shakespeare the Man*, 2nd edn (Basingstoke: Macmillan, 1998), p. 187.
6. Leslie Thomson, 'Broken Brackets and 'Mended Texts: Stage Directions in the Oxford Shakespeare', *Renaissance Drama* 19 (1988), 180; Margaret Jane Kidnie, 'Text, Performance, and the Editors: Staging Shakespeare's Drama', *Shakespeare Quarterly* 51 (2000), 462.
7. William B. Long, 'Stage-Directions: a Misinterpreted Factor in Determining Textual Provenance', *Text* 2 (1985), 135. The following quotation appears at 123.
8. *Ibid.*, 135.
9. Stephen Orgel, *The Authentic Shakespeare and Other Problems of the Early Modern Stage* (London: Routledge, 2002), p. 16.
10. *Ibid.*, p. 47.

11. Stanley Wells, *Re-Editing Shakespeare for the Modern Reader* (Oxford: Clarendon Press, 1984), p. 63.
12. Orgel explores further the 'fluidity of the written text' in *The Authentic Shakespeare*, p. 242.
13. George Walton Williams, 'To Edit? To Direct? – Ay, There's the Rub', in *In Arden: Editing Shakespeare*, ed. Ann Thompson and Gordon McMullan (London: Thomson Learning, 2002), p. 119.
14. *Ibid.*, p. 120 (my emphasis).
15. Antony Hammond, 'Encounters of the Third Kind in Stage-Directions in Elizabethan and Jacobean Drama', *Studies in Philology* 89 (1992), 95.
16. Alan C. Dessen, *Rescripting Shakespeare: The Text, the Director, and Modern Productions* (Cambridge University Press, 2002), p. 224.
17. *Ibid.*, p. 234.
18. *Ibid.*, pp. 209, 234.
19. *Ibid.*, p. 233–4.
20. Alan C. Dessen, *Recovering Shakespeare's Theatrical Vocabulary* (Cambridge University Press, 1995).
21. Wells, *Re-Editing Shakespeare*, p. 63.
22. Holland, 'Modernizing Shakespeare', *Shakespeare Quarterly* 51 (2000), 25.
23. Eco, *The Open Work*, pp. 8–9.
24. Long, 'Stage-Directions', 126, 129–30.
25. Mariko Ichikawa, *Shakespearean Entrances* (London: Palgrave Macmillan, 2002), p. 9. Ichikawa goes on to suggest that when these directions were translated into print, their precise placement 'might have been influenced by formatting tradition, whereby compositors centred entries and set exits beside speeches on the right margin'.
26. Anne Lancashire discusses the provenance of the manuscript in her Revels edition of the play (Manchester University Press, 1978), pp. 4–13.
27. Jerome J. McGann, *The Textual Condition* (Princeton University Press, 1991), p. 113.
28. See George Walton Williams, 'The Entrance of Calchas and the Exit of Cressida', *The Shakespeare Newsletter* 44 (1994), 5, 18.
29. Williams, 'To Edit? To Direct?', p. 120.

CHAPTER II

Open stage, open page? Editing stage directions in early dramatic texts

John D. Cox

As Margaret Jane Kidnie's recent work makes clear, the practice of adding stage directions is coming under increasing scrutiny in critical and even student editions. In this collection, Kidnie makes the case for adding stage directions marginally, and I would like to suggest still another option, based on my recent work with Eric Rasmussen on the Arden3 edition of Shakespeare's *3 Henry VI*.[1] My suggestion is that editors reduce sharply or even eliminate completely the stage directions they add to early texts. In place of stage directions in the text, this practice outlines staging options in the commentary notes, thus leaving the text free of editorial intervention where stage directions are concerned while giving readers enough information to imagine various solutions to staging.

The theoretical basis for this option is offered in another recent essay by Kidnie, in which she argues for various treatments of stage directions in various editions.[2] Distinguishing between *haupttext* (dialogue) and *nebentext* (everything else, notably stage directions including speech prefixes), she observes that 'Current editorial practice controls textual instability by rendering the *nebentext* in a form that the modern reader will recognise as complete.'[3] Along with this practice, she advocates 'editions that allow readers to tackle indeterminacies of staging', basing her appeal for the second method on a distinction between real performance and virtual performance.[4] The former is what happens (or historically happened) in the theatre; the latter is what happens in the minds of readers as they read an edition. What happened in the theatre historically can be only partially recovered, as Alan Dessen points out: 'Since we lack a videotape of the Globe production (and are far removed from their culture and theatrical practice), to determine what was subtle versus what was obvious in *their* terms, in *their* productions, is no easy matter (and may at times be impossible).'[5] Dessen suggests that up to 90 per cent of 'the relevant evidence' for early performance has been lost,[6] a figure also cited by Antony Hammond.[7] What editors reconstruct through stage directions, then, is not the real performance (and never can be); it is, as Kidnie puts it, 'a specifically modern and, for this reason, accessible virtual performance'.[8]

An edition that allows 'readers to tackle indeterminacies of staging' is the kind of edition that Eric Rasmussen and I originally prepared. Our aim was to add few, if any, stage directions in the text and to suggest various staging possibilities in the commentary. Our hope was to offer a text whose openness might approximate the openness of Shakespeare's stage, unencumbered by scenery, elaborate props, or the expectation of verisimilitude, and thus to offer readers both the information and the freedom to imagine the staging for themselves.[9] Vestiges of that text remain in the Arden3 *3 Henry VI*, but for the most part the edition as published represents a compromise between the two editorial choices, one represented by the editors in this case and the other by the house style for all Arden3 editions.

The most common objection to demoting stage directions to the commentary is that such editions would be appropriate only for those who are already familiar with the texts and staging traditions, and who therefore have the qualifications to construct an imaginative picture of the action for themselves, without editorial assistance. The practice would ostensibly never work for students, or for anyone else who is reading the play for the first time and is therefore confused by the lack of stage directions. But staging options mentioned in the commentary are designed not only to hint at the breadth of possibility but also to give confused readers the help they need. In *Hamlet*, for example, when Polonius says to Claudius and Gertrude, 'Take this from this, if this be otherwise', innocent readers are likely to wonder what 'this' means. David Bevington's much-used student edition adds no stage direction to his control text, the second quarto of 1604–5, but his note reads: 'The actor probably gestures, indicating that he means his head from his shoulders, or his staff of office or chain from hands or neck, or something similar.'[10] Stage tradition favours the first option Bevington mentions, but his note preserves the openness of the control text and offers plausible staging possibilities in the note. This textual openness reflects the open Elizabethan stage better than editorial stage directions in the text do, even if they are in square brackets. (Students are less likely to notice square brackets, or to know what they mean if they do notice them, than they are to read a note, especially if they are bewildered.)[11]

The inherent limitations of editorial stage directions are clear in an eighteenth-century precedent for them. Edmond Malone was actually less lavish with *nebentext* than modern editors tend to be, but if he had liberally added stage directions, his own understanding of historical reconstruction would not have recovered the original staging but would have produced a distinctly 'modern', i.e., eighteenth-century, 'virtual performance'. This is because his understanding of original stage conditions was even less than ours. He correctly informs contemporary readers, for example, that Elizabethan theatres lacked the familiar eighteenth-century curtained proscenium, but he asserts that curtains nonetheless divided the stage 'in the middle, and were drawn backwards and forwards on an iron rod'.[12] He bases this assertion on a single stage direction in Robert Wilmot's *Tancred and Gismund*. Elaborating on curtains in early theatres, Malone adds: 'besides the principal curtains that hung in the front of the stage, they used others as substitutes for scenes, which were denominated *traverses*'.[13] This time he cites *The White Devil*, *The Devil's Charter*, and *Satiromastix*. This information now seems lamentably wide of the mark: Malone does not distinguish amphitheatre from hall playhouses, he bases his conclusions on limited evidence, and he imagines early staging by analogy to what he knew from eighteenth-century theatres. But we cannot get much closer to the mark than Malone did, because even with vastly improved knowledge of early playing conditions, we still do not know more than about 10 per cent of what happened in early performances. The editorial choice to offer readers closure, where stage directions are concerned, may well take them further from early stage practice, not closer to it, because editorial stage directions remain no less indelibly modern reconstructions (though 'virtual', in Kidnie's terms) than modern stage productions of early plays.

In describing more precisely the difference added stage directions make, let me refer to the six types that Antony Hammond analyses. His first category consists of entrances and exits, or 'directions to get on and off stage',[14] based on a binary distinction (on stage vs. off) that seems imperative to clarify in play-texts, as Stanley Wells points out: 'There are two categories of stage directions which, I suppose, everyone would agree are necessary. They are entrances and exits.'[15] As Alan Dessen has argued, even these apparently fundamental stage directions are often subject to interpretation, so an editor's decision may well close down options that the open-ended text preserves as an aspect of the open stage.[16]

Eric Rasmussen and I were able to preserve some of the openness of the Folio *3 Henry VI*, where entrances and exits are concerned, and we did so by mentioning options in the commentary in order not to foreclose them in the text. Here is a diplomatic transcript of the opening ten lines of the scene in F where young Rutland is murdered by Clifford during the battle of Wakefield:

> *Enter Rutland, and his Tutor.*
> *Rutland.* Ah, whither shall I flye, to scape their hands?
> Ah Tutor, looke where bloody *Clifford* comes.
> *Enter Clifford.*
> *Clifford.* Chaplaine away, thy Priesthood saues thy life.
> As for the Brat of this accursed Duke,
> Whose Father slew my Father, he shall dye.
> *Tutor.* And I, my Lord, will beare him company.
> *Clifford.* Souldiers, away with him.
> *Tutor.* Ah *Clifford*, murther not this innocent Child,
> Least thou be hated both of God and Man.   *Exit.*
> (TLN 399–409)

F's stage directions indicate only three people on stage: Rutland, his Tutor, and Clifford. In TLN 407, however, Clifford addresses 'Souldiers'. They are presumably on stage, since Clifford orders them to escort the Tutor, who exits at TLN 409. Since Clifford commands these soldiers, they may possibly enter with him, and since he orders them to escort the Tutor off stage, they may exit with the Tutor in their custody.

Nothing, however, *requires* those entrances and exits for the soldiers, nor does F indicate how *many* soldiers serve Clifford. Reflecting on this, Rasmussen and I originally added no stage directions, but we provided two notes. The first was to Clifford's entry: 'Clifford commands "Soldiers" (7), who presumably enter with him.' The second was a note to the exit of the Tutor: 'The soldiers mentioned in 7 may exit with the Tutor, thus clearing the stage for the unequal confrontation that follows. On the other hand, to have some of them attend Clifford while he kills Rutland – perhaps holding and threatening the child – would strengthen comparison with the death of Prince Edward in 5.5, where several adults surround and destroy a child.' This note leaves open the number of soldiers who enter, the number who accompany the Tutor off stage, and the possibility (with reasons offered) that some remain with Clifford, as brutal but silent accomplices in his crime. F precludes none of those possibilities. In the end, a compromise with Arden3 house style required that Clifford enter '[*with soldiers*]' and that the Tutor '*Exit* [*guarded*]'. Part of this compromise required deletion of the comment that originally annotated Clifford's entry, because the added stage direction made it superfluous. Still, the stage direction in the *nebentext* reflects a different choice and makes for a different edition. It is inevitably more intrusive than the notes, which can be ignored, if a reader wants to ignore them, and whose 'presumably' and 'may exit' encourage a reader to imagine other options. Some readers may visualize a scene, for example, in which Clifford's soldiers enter just before Clifford, perhaps from the other side of the stage, arresting Rutland's flight with his tutor just in time for Clifford's entry – a possibility allowed for in F's open-ended text and incidentally answering the question why Rutland suddenly stops running when he does, despite his fear. The original note's tentative language allows for that possibility, while the stage direction '*Enter* Clifford [*with soldiers*]' precludes it.

In one generic case, Rasmussen and I added exits consistently where they are not indicated in F, because we think we found historical theatrical evidence for doing so. Messengers frequently enter in F *3 Henry VI*, state their business, and have no stage direction for exiting. Should they exit as soon as they have delivered their messages, or should they exit later? If an editor chooses the second option, when should the exit be indicated, and how should an editor decide? We finally decided to indicate exits immediately after messengers have delivered their messages, unless F clearly stated otherwise.

We based this decision on a hypothetical doubling chart for the play (Appendix 2 in the Arden3 *3 Henry VI*) – not a source of exact knowledge, to be sure, but a limit to possibilities. As long as an actor was on stage to play a given role in a given scene, he could not, by convention, play another role in the same scene, and if he were to enter as a different character later in the scene or in a subsequent scene, he had to have time to change his costume. Moreover, acting companies had to economize; that is the point of doubling roles in the first place. We therefore hypothesized that Pembroke's Men would have recycled small parts like messengers as often as possible, using the same actor to play different messengers by changing his livery (indicated, say, by a tabard, or tabard and banner). Given a little more time between appearances on stage, additional disguises might also be added, but it would still be important to get the messenger off stage as quickly as possible in order to give him time to prepare for the next entrance.

But even in this case, where we think the evidence for exits is pretty strong, we do not believe that they necessarily need to be indicated in the text. Having made the case for messengers' immediate exits in the introduction, an editor could indicate a probable exit in a commentary note, with a reference back to the supporting argument. Preserving the openness of the *nebentext* in F *3 Henry VI* makes as great a difference, we believe, as preserving puzzling readings in the *haupttext*, when a good explanation can be offered for them, and in both cases a reader's puzzlement

Editing stage directions in early dramatic texts 183

can be addressed in a note. Explaining staging options in a commentary note is admittedly less economical than adding a stage direction to the text, but it allows the text to function for readers (and for modern actors and directors) in much the same way the Elizabethan stage itself functioned historically: as a place offering maximum scope for interpretation.

Hammond's second kind of stage direction involves 'properties and effects, which are normally the responsibility of someone other than the actor'.[17] Hammond's 'normally' is important, because props are not always easy to distinguish from costumes, as the opening lines of *3 Henry VI* illustrate. The scene begins with the Yorkists, led by Richard Duke of York ('*Plan.*' in F), who is accompanied by his sons Edward and Richard, as well as by '*Norfolke, Mountague, Warwicke, and Souldiers*' (TLN 3–4). They boast of a recent military victory in the following lines, which are printed without any stage direction in the Folio:[18]

    Edw. Lord *Staffords* Father, Duke of *Buckingham*,
Is either slaine or wounded dangerous.
I cleft his Beauer with a down-right blow:
That this is true (Father) behold his blood.
    Mount. And Brother, here's the Earle of Wiltshires blood,
Whom I encountred as the Battels ioyn'd.
    Rich. Speake thou for me, and tell them what I did.
    Plan. Richard hath best deseru'd of all my sonnes:
But is your Grace dead, my Lord of Somerset?
    Nor. Such hope haue all the line of *Iohn of Gaunt*.
    Rich. Thus do I hope to shake King *Henries* head.
                                     (TLN 15–25)

Edward's boast that he killed the duke of Buckingham requires the actor to use some accompanying action ('behold his blood'), but no stage direction specifies what it is. Is the actor covered in stage blood, to which he points when he says the line? Does he hold out a blood-stained weapon – the weapon with which he 'cleft his Beauer with a down-right blow' (TLN 17)? If so, the weapon is arguably a prop, though it may also be part of the actor's costume, but in either case, what kind of weapon is it? Though the rapier, introduced to England in the mid-sixteenth century, was the sword of choice for Elizabethan aristocrats, it could not cleave a helmet.[19] Is there any reason why the text should not remain silent about whether a weapon is displayed – and if so, what kind of weapon it is – thus allowing readers or actors to imagine for themselves? The absence of *nebentext* in these lines makes a difference: it offers the same options as the Folio, whereas an editorial stage direction forecloses options. For the curious or puzzled reader, actor, or director, a note can explain possible options, which also offer an implicit explanation – as in Bevington's note to *Hamlet*, 2.2.156 – for the absence of stage directions.

The exchange between York and Richard seems to indicate that Richard is carrying Somerset's severed head. This is surely a prop, which Richard presumably addresses when he says, 'Speake thou for me', and which York also presumably mocks with macabre humour: 'But is your Grace dead, my Lord of Somerset?' Does Richard also throw the head on the ground, as the editorial tradition suggests? If so, how does he shake the head four lines later ('Thus do I hope to shake King *Henries* head'), or having thrown down the head, does he shake his sword (or pike, or halberd)? But if he does throw down the head, does he pick it up again to shake it? If so, why does he throw it down in the first place? Or does *York* pick it up and shake it, and should F therefore be emended so that Richard's second line is given to York (as the New Cambridge edition specifies)?[20] Rather than throw down Somerset's head, might not Richard equally plausibly hold up the head, perhaps even ghoulishly working its jaw, when he says, 'Speake thou for me'? Would that not more likely provoke his father's mocking reply, addressed to Somerset's head, than if Richard threw the head down? Nothing except a stage direction prevents a reader from imagining such actions with this prop, so a text without stage directions (as in F) makes a difference that is arguably more consistent with the open Elizabethan stage than a text that adds them.

As the scene progresses, it becomes clear that the Yorkists are attempting to seize power by invading the palace of Westminster, where parliament traditionally met in the late sixteenth century. Warwick identifies the imagined location in the dialogue: 'This is the Pallace of the fearefull King' (TLN 30; cf. 41, 45, 73, 81), and an editor can verify it in a note, because both Hall and Holinshed refer to York's seizing the throne.[21] Moreover, another prop – this time a throne – must be on stage, because Warwick mentions it: 'And this the Regall Seat' (TLN 31). The throne must somehow be elevated, because after Warwick urges York to 'possesse' the throne, F's stage direction specifies, '*They goe vp*' (TLN 38). An editorial tradition assumes that this means the throne is located 'above', and that the Yorkists therefore exit through one of the doors at the back of the main stage, ascend the stairs to the tiring-house façade, and re-enter 'above', where the throne is.[22] Should these exits and entrances therefore be added to the text? In this case, evidence from the Elizabethan theatre is decisive for assisting readers with historical reconstruction of the scene: continuous dialogue and pacing allow no time for several actors to ascend to the tiring-house façade, and

'*They goe vp*' therefore means simply that some of the Yorkists step onto a moveable platform that bears the throne on the main stage.[23] The need for such a platform in later scenes is suggestive evidence that this is its first appearance. The absence of exits and entrances for the Yorkists in the Folio stage directions is not a mistake that an editor needs to correct; it is itself evidence of the original staging, which an editor can help readers understand with an appropriate note.

Hammond's third kind of stage direction consists of 'all other formal directions, which relate essentially to whatever the words leave out, to the control of all those muscles of the actor's body other than the mouth and tongue which are busy fulfilling the rest of the script's directions: i.e., delivering the lines'.[24] I first began to think seriously about the problem of editorial stage directions at the 1998 Arden editors' meeting, when Pamela Mason discussed a stage direction from *Macbeth* that belongs to Hammond's third category. In *Macbeth* 2.3, Lady Macbeth asks for assistance, just after Macbeth announces Duncan's murder. At TLN 884, she says, 'Helpe me hence, hoa', and Macduff responds, 'Looke to the Lady.' Ten lines later, Banquo again says, 'Looke to the Lady' (TLN 894). No stage direction specifies any action accompanying these lines, but editors typically indicate in square brackets that Lady Macbeth 'swoons' and then is helped to exit. Why, Mason asked, should the options be foreclosed for readers by telling them that Lady Macbeth faints? At most, why not add a note describing possible options – that she staggers, leans heavily on her husband, holds her head in her hands, retches, or even vomits – none of which is precluded by F?[25]

The problems with this category are evident in *3 Henry VI* as well, as we noticed in the case of what Richard does with Somerset's head and of what the actors 'go up' to in the opening scene, but another instance from the first scene illustrates particularly well the difference that editorial stage directions make. By the time the Lancastrians enter belatedly to challenge their rivals, York is seated, because King Henry's first line is, 'My Lords, looke where the sturdie Rebell sits' (TLN 58). The Folio, however, has no stage direction for York to seat himself, and the question therefore arises whether a stage direction should be added to the text, and if so where? Does York sit down when he says, 'I meane to take possession of my Right' (TLN 50)? Or does he take the throne when Warwick says, 'Resolue thee *Richard*, clayme the English Crowne' (TLN 55)? Editorial tradition favours the second, but the issues are not matters of absolute certainty; they are matters of interpretation, and if editors wish to retain F's interpretative openness, then they can leave the edited text open and let readers decide, offering possible staging options in a commentary note. In this case, the outcome in the Arden3 *3 Henry VI* reflects the choice to add no stage direction, and in the end we decided not to add a note either. Readers of this edition can imagine York seating himself wherever they want to.[26]

Hammond's fourth kind of stage direction is implicit in the dialogue of the control text but not separately marked in the *nebentext*. As Hammond points out, 'Whether or not to bring these into the light of day in an edition is a very large question',[27] and the choice not to add stage directions offers particular advantages in this case, because the question of whether or not to make a stage direction explicit can be answered in every case by adding a note instead. If the implied action seems obvious to readers, they can ignore the note, but for those who may not understand the text, the note offers explicit suggestions about what the text implies. The openness of the text is thus preserved without sacrificing adequate support for puzzled readers.

Adding stage directions creates unnecessary problems where implicit stage directions are concerned, because without a principle to cover every instance, different editors handle implicit stage directions differently, as Hammond makes clear in the case of Webster's plays. *3 Henry VI*, 2.2, for example, begins with Queen Margaret welcoming King Henry to York, which the Lancastrians have just captured:

> *Qu.* Welcome my Lord, to this braue town of Yorke,
> Yonders the head of that Arch-enemy,
> That sought to be incompast with your Crowne.
> Doth not the object cheere your heart, my Lord.
>
>   (TLN 873–6)

Rasmussen and I proposed to print Margaret's speech with no stage direction but with this note to TLN 874: 'An implicit SD, indicating Margaret's gesture to York's head, presumably mounted in the upper acting area. See 54–5 below and 1.4.179.' In a compromise with Arden3 house style, however, we emended first to, '[*Head thrust forth*]', and eventually to, '[*York's head is set above the gates*]'. The added stage direction arguably tells a reader nothing that is not implicit in the text and explicit in the commentary, but it forecloses other options that the text and note (by using 'presumably') leave open. Perhaps the head is mounted on an attendant's spear, for example, or held aloft by one of Margaret's soldiers, as Somerset's head is (presumably) held aloft by Richard in the first scene. York's and Somerset's heads could, for theatrical purposes, be the same prop, and holding York's head aloft in the later scene would tie it symmetrically to the first one: a Yorkist holding up a Lancastrian head is answered by a Lancastrian holding up the head of York himself. Nothing requires that symmetry, of course; it is neither right nor wrong, but it is a possibility allowed by F but foreclosed by an editorial stage direction that places the head on the walls.

A special class of implicit stage directions in *3 Henry VI* exists because the octavo *True Tragedy of Richard Duke of York* exists, because O contains stage directions that F omits. In this case, an editor has no need to guess about implicit stage directions, because a parallel early text makes them explicit. My preference was to include O's stage directions in a note, thus retaining F's open *nebentext*, because nothing says that one early production was identical with another. Eric Rasmussen argued, however, that since O's stage directions witness to an actual early performance, they deserved to be included in square brackets in the text, and that is where they appear in the Arden3 edition.

Again, the choice makes a difference, as a particular example will make clear. When the Yorkists lose the battle of Wakefield, York himself is captured, tortured, and killed – a sequence depicted in the action of both O and F. Here is how F represents the scene, as the victorious Lancastrians surround the defeated but defiant York:

> *Clifford.* I will not bandie with thee word for word,
> But buckler with thee blowes twice two for one.
> *Queene.* Hold valiant *Clifford*, for a thousand causes
> I would prolong a while the Traytors Life:
> Wrath makes him deafe; speake thou *Northumberland*.
> *Northumb.* Hold *Clifford*, doe not honor him so much,
> To prick thy finger, though to wound his heart.
> What valour were it, when a Curre doth grinne,
> For one to thrust his Hand betweene his Teeth,
> When he might spurne him with his Foot away?
> It is Warres prize, to take all Vantages,
> And tenne to one, is no impeach of Valour.
> *Clifford.* I, I, so striues the Woodcocke with the Gynne.
> *Northumb.* So doth the Connie struggle in the Net.
> *York.* So triumph Theeues vpon their conquer'd Booty,
> So True men yeeld with Robbers, so o're-matcht.
>
> (TLN 509–24)

After the equivalent to TLN 520, O has the stage direction, 'Fight and take him', which we eventually expanded to: '[*They fight and take York*]', with no other stage directions added. 'Striues' and 'struggle' in TLN 521–2 clearly imply the action that O makes explicit, but the passage contains other implicit stage directions as well. In TLN 513, for example, Margaret's 'him' must refer to Clifford, not to York, and it is a direction not only to the actor playing Margaret (who must turn his/her attention from Clifford to Northumberland) but also to the actor playing Clifford, because he has to ignore Margaret's previous two lines, as well as Northumberland's long speech (TLN 514–20), offered at Margaret's behest. This is a classic case of the indeterminacy of implicit stage directions, because nothing tells an editor how much of the action to make explicit in square brackets in the text. An edition that retains F's openness by adding no stage directions at least gains in consistency what it sacrifices in closure, because it can clarify TLN 513 in a note and add the stage direction from O in another note.

Hammond's fifth kind of stage direction is the speech prefix, which illustrates particularly well the point that Kidnie makes about readers imagining a 'virtual performance' as they read a play-text, because speech prefixes not only tell which character is saying which lines but may also reveal something about that character that a playgoer does not get. In this regard, speech prefixes function as stage directions, as Hammond points out, underscoring Kidnie's point that speech prefixes are part of the *nebentext*. In both Q and F *Much Ado about Nothing*, for example, Don John is introduced as '*Iohn the bastard*' in an entry direction long before he is first referred to as '*Iohn* the bastard' in the dialogue, so a reader knows of Don John's social stigma much earlier in the play than a playgoer does.[28] In *3 Henry VI* the speech prefixes for one character demanded conservative treatment, in our view, on a parallel principle to adding no stage directions. In this case, the Arden3 general editors allowed an exception to house style, so the Arden3 *3 Henry VI* prints the speech prefixes for this character for the first time substantially as they were printed in the seventeenth century.

The character enters the play-text as Lady Elizabeth Grey, widow of Sir John Grey, a Lancastrian knight killed at the second battle of St Albans. In 3.2 she appeals to King Edward to restore her husband's lands to her, and the king is so enamoured with her pleasing manner and good looks that he asks her to marry him. Thereafter, she appears in the play as Queen Elizabeth. Editorial tradition specifies that characters who are promoted in the course of the play should have their speech prefixes changed after the promotion. This custom therefore requires that the speech headings should designate Lady Grey as Queen Elizabeth after her wedding.

The speech prefixes for this character in F, however, are so anomalous that making them regular qualitatively changes the reading experience. When Lady Grey first appears in F, her speech prefix is consistently '*Wid.*' for 'widow'. This is presumably because her widowhood is the subject not only of her discussion with the king but also of a bawdy and derogatory conversation among his brothers, who speak as if the two principals cannot

> *Henry the Sixt.* 159
>
> *Wid.* I take my leaue with many thousand thankes.
> *Rich.* The Match is made, shee seales it with a Curfie.
> *King.* But stay thee,'tis the fruits of loue I meane.   1570
> *Wid.* The fruits of Loue, I meane, my louing Liege.
> *King.* I, but I feare me in another sence.
> What Loue, think'st thou, I sue so much to get?
> *Wid.* My loue till death, my humble thankes, my prayers,
> That loue which Vertue begges, and Vertue graunts.
> *King.* No, by my troth, I did not meane such loue.
> *Wid.* Why then you meane not, as I thought you did.
> *King.* But now you partly may perceiue my minde.
> *Wid.* My minde will neuer graunt what I perceiue
> Your Highnesse aymes at, if I ayme aright.   1580
> *King.* To tell thee plaine, I ayme to lye with thee.
> *Wid.* To tell you plaine, I had rather lye in Prison.
> *King.* Why then thou shalt not haue thy Husbands
> Lands.
> *Wid.* Why then mine Honestie shall be my Dower,
> For by that losse, I will not purchase them.
> *King.* Therein thou wrong'st thy Children mightily.
> *Wid.* Herein your Highnesse wrongs both them & me:
> But mightie Lord, this merry inclination
> Accords not with the sadnesse of my suit: 1590
> Please you dismisse me, eyther with I, or no.

7 William Shakespeare, *3 Henry VI*, from the First Folio (1623), sig. Pp4 (TLN 1568–91 Act 3.2).

hear them. We concluded that the speech prefix for Lady Grey in F appears to have been chosen by the compositor, in response to the derogation of her character in the text, where she is referred to simply as 'widow'. To be sure, abbreviation is required by two lines (TLN 1574 and 1588) to prevent typographical turn-under (see figure 7). The compositor could also have used the abbreviation '*La.*' for 'Lady', however (actually used by the compositor of Q3), in keeping with her entry direction: '*Enter K. Edward, Gloster, Clarence, Lady Gray*' (TLN 1500), so '*Wid.*' seems deliberate, and we therefore argued that the experience of reading F should be retained in our edition by using 'Widow' for Lady Elizabeth's speech prefix in 3.2. We reinforced this argument by pointing to a consistent pattern of social demotion for this character in F's *nebentext*. Even after she has become queen, her entry direction in 4.1 reads, '*Enter... Lady Grey*' (TLN 2026) and in 4.4, '*Enter... Lady Gray*' (TLN 2303), while in 4.4 her speech prefix is simply '*Gray*' (TLN 2305ff.), where the compositor could have used '*Lady*'. Only in the play's final scene does F finally promote Elizabeth, in her entry direction, to '*Queene*' (TLN 3170). In this brief scene, however, she has no lines in F, so we cannot know what speech prefix the compositor might have chosen.[29]

The objection to using 'incorrect' speech prefixes is the same as the objection to not adding stage directions, that is, that readers will be confused. Both difficulties can be addressed in the notes, however, and a note about Lady Grey's speech prefixes, together with a defence of our choice to follow F that we offer in the textual introduction,[30] would have given readers an experience very close to that of reading F but without the confusion that F occasions. As it turned out, Arden3 house style required a bracketed explanation in the entry direction as well: '*Enter . . . Lady Grey [now Queen Elizabeth]*'. The difference is slight, since both choices reflect F's practice, and both require an explanation in the notes, but the editorial stage direction departs further from F's open text and adds nothing that one cannot learn by reading the note.

Antony Hammond's sixth and final category of stage directions 'consists of structural divisions within the play, of which act-breaks are the most important (i.e., when the playing temporarily stops)'.[31] This is a theatrical matter, Hammond argues, because act breaks provide for possible audience breaks, and the modern practice of having just one audience break in the course of a play is therefore at odds with texts that indicate five acts. In F *3 Henry VI*, as it turns out, no act or scene divisions are indicated, but in this case, I see no advantage to maintaining F's openness and every disadvantage, especially for readers. For reference purposes, one can use through-line numbering, as in the Norton facsimile of the Folio, but greater variation is likely to occur between one edition and another with through-line numbering than with act and scene breaks, because stage directions vary widely between editions, and stage directions are counted in through-line numbering. Where the virtual performance of reading is concerned, in other words, act and scene breaks are so helpful that they are manifestly superior, in this case, to the open text of the Folio.

Modern editing originated in the assumption that an editor's job is in large part corrective: 'The business of him that republishes an ancient book is, to correct what is corrupt, and to explain what is obscure', as Samuel Johnson put it.[32] With increasing knowledge and sophistication, editors became increasingly skilful in detecting 'what is corrupt', until editing came to be seen as something like a forensic science in the twentieth century, treating the text as if it were a crime scene and the author as an innocent victim of all those who had violated the text in various ways – other playwrights, the playhouse scribe, the actors, the printing-house compositors. What I have proposed in this essay is that the forensic model is inadequate, especially where stage directions are concerned. We know too little about what lies behind the printed texts of Shakespeare's plays, and we know too little about conditions in early playhouses, to be certain of the stage directions we have become accustomed to adding as if their omission in early texts were a corruption. Johnson's second 'business' of an editor – 'to explain what is obscure' – is better done, I would argue, by leaving the text open and suggesting options in the commentary notes. To be sure, this process requires an editor to be tentative, but even on the model of forensic pathology, caution is better than overconfidence when 90 per cent of the evidence is no longer retrievable.

NOTES

1. John D. Cox and Eric Rasmussen (eds.), *King Henry VI Part 3* (London: Thomson Learning, 2001).
2. Margaret Jane Kidnie, 'Text, Performance, and the Editors: Staging Shakespeare's Drama', *Shakespeare Quarterly* 51 (2000), 456–73.
3. Kidnie borrows the terms *haupttext* and *nebentext* from Roman Ingarden, *The Literary Work of Art: An Investigation on the Borderlines of Ontology, Logic, and Theory of Literature* (Evanston, IL: Northwestern University Press, 1973).
4. Kidnie, 'Text, Performance, and the Editors', 473 and 465.
5. Alan C. Dessen, *Recovering Shakespeare's Theatrical Vocabulary* (Cambridge University Press, 1995), p. 90. Even a videotape of an early performance would not allow for the variety that inevitably occurs in a given play over the course of a single run in the theatre. Actors are endlessly inventive, and they make continual adjustments in gestures and inflection, sometimes even in blocking and props, from one performance of a given play to the next.
6. Dessen, *Recovering*, p. 6.
7. 'Ninety percent of what actually happened on stage in their performance is not to be found in the stage directions of any manuscript or printed text.' Antony Hammond, 'Encounters of the Third Kind in Stage Directions in Elizabethan and Jacobean Drama', *Studies in Philology* 89 (1992), 71–99, 81.
8. Kidnie, 'Text, Performance, and the Editors', 466.
9. Based on extant manuscript playbooks, William B. Long concludes that 'the more experienced the professional playwright, the fewer [stage] directions he adds and the more he leaves in what he assumes or knows to be the capable hands of the players' ('Stage Directions: a Misinterpreted Factor in Determining Textual Provenance', *Text* 2 (1985), 127). This conclusion suggests a correlation between the open text and the open stage.

10. David M. Bevington (ed.), *The Complete Works of Shakespeare*, 5th edn (New York: Pearson Education, 2004), *Hamlet*, 2.2.156.
11. Leslie Thomson examines the Oxford Shakespeare *Complete Works*' abandonment of square brackets for editorial stage directions in 'Broken Brackets and 'Mended Texts: Stage Directions in the Oxford Shakespeare', *Renaissance Drama* 19 (1988), 175–93. Her principal reservation is that the editors offer no explanation for their choices, but another difficulty is that a reader is even more at the mercy of the editors in this case than is the reader of an edition that uses square brackets.
12. Edmond Malone, *Historical Account of the Rise and Progress of the English Stage* (Basel: Tourneisen, 1800), p. 82.
13. *Ibid.*, pp. 93–4.
14. Hammond, 'Encounters', 73.
15. Stanley Wells, *Re-Editing Shakespeare for the Modern Reader* (Oxford: Clarendon Press, 1984), p. 71.
16. Dessen, *Recovering*, pp. 65–81. See also Homer Swander, 'No Exit for a Dead Body: What to Do with a Scripted Corpse?' *Journal of Dramatic Theory and Criticism* 5 (1991), 139–52.
17. Hammond, 'Encounters', 73–4.
18. Though the octavo *True Tragedy* (O) often has suggestive stage directions that are lacking in F, these particular lines in O also have no stage directions. See *The True Tragedy of Richard Duke of York*, ed. W. W. Greg (Oxford: Clarendon Press, 1958).
19. Lawrence Stone, *The Crisis of the Aristocracy, 1558–1641* (Oxford: Clarendon Press, 1965), pp. 242–50. The rapier is referred to twice (anachronistically) in *3 Henry VI*: at 1.3.37 and 1.4.80.
20. Michael Hattaway (ed.), *The Third Part of King Henry VI* (Cambridge University Press, 1993). The speech prefix in this edition substitutes 'York' for F's 'Rich.', though 'York' is not in square brackets, and no textual note identifies the change. Without consulting another edition, the reader's understanding of the play is therefore, in this case, completely determined by the editor's choice of *nebentext*.
21. Arden3 *3 Henry VI*, 1.1n.
22. C. Walter Hodges illustrates the scene this way in the New Cambridge edition, p. 15, even though Hattaway notes that 'it is improbable that the tiring-house balcony would have been used' (p. 74). At least one critic has been moved to interpret the scene based on a throne located 'above' – presumably because he used an edition in which the editorial stage directions indicated this kind of staging. See Donald G. Watson, *Shakespeare's Early History Plays: Politics at Play on the English Stage* (Basingstoke: Macmillan, 1990), p. 82.
23. John Dover Wilson pointed this out, in the Cambridge edition of *3 Henry VI* (Cambridge University Press, 1952), 1.1.32n. Wilson often added elaborate imaginary stage directions ('The air is heavy with the scent of perfume' in *A Midsummer Night's Dream*, for example), but he is surely right about 'They go up' in *3 Henry VI*, 1.1.

24. Hammond, 'Encounters', 74.
25. The only stage direction for a swoon in F is '*King sounds*' in *2 Henry VI* (TLN 1729). See Alan Dessen and Leslie Thomson, *A Dictionary of Stage Directions in English Drama, 1580–1642* (Cambridge University Press, 1999), p. 223.
26. Are first-time readers likely to be confused when they read Henry's 'See where the sturdy rebel sits', even though no stage direction tells them where he has sat down? An editorial stage direction for York to sit seems to reflect editorial yearning for closure rather than a concern for puzzled readers.
27. Hammond, 'Encounters', 75.
28. In F *Much Ado* (which was set from Q), the stage direction is TLN 197, while the dialogue reference is TLN 1851. Like most plays in F, *Much Ado* includes no *dramatis personae*, so readers of F first learn of Don John's birth status in the entry direction.
29. The scene mistakenly attributes successive speeches to Clarence (TLN 3199–201), and O gives Clarence's second speech in F to Queen Elizabeth, 'Thanke Noble *Clarence*, worthy brother thanks', which is good warrant for attributing the line to her in a modern edition. Emending 'Thanke' to 'Thanks' clarifies the line and makes it appropriate for the queen. Without O, however, an editor would not know whether the line is said by Queen Elizabeth or by King Edward. Is the double attribution to Clarence in F an instance of a compositorial Freudian slip?
30. Cox and Rasmussen (eds.), *King Henry VI Part 3*, pp. 173–5.
31. Hammond, 'Encounters', 77.
32. 'Proposals for Printing, by Subscription, the Dramatick Works of William Shakespeare' (1756), in *Samuel Johnson on Shakespeare*, ed. Arthur Sherbo, vols. VII and VIII in the Yale Edition of the Works of Samuel Johnson (New Haven: Yale University Press, 1968), vol. VII, p. 51.

CHAPTER 12

Two varieties of digital commentary

John Lavagnino

By now we have the advantage of hindsight in assessing the plans for the future that the twentieth century found exciting. It's already possible to read books on scholarship and new technology that made a stir in the 1990s and find them speaking in the voice of another era; their descriptions of all sorts of desirable social and intellectual advances that digital living would bring sound very different from what we actually saw happen.[1] And while books that were carefully thought through made forecasts that now seem improbable, it's the casual futurological wisdom of the era that is most dated: remarkably enough, it is not the case that we read everything online while our books collect dust. Much of the reason has been the tangle of intellectual-property rights; but even so there have been significant digital publications of the works of Shakespeare and others. They have not supplanted books for most purposes.

Print-based scholarship no longer appears to be a makeshift that was just waiting to be swept aside by digital publications. Instead of an immediate leap to something better we see a slow process of discovering worthwhile ways to do and publish scholarship in the digital world. Scholarly editions remain obvious candidates for such development, because they have so much more of a focus on sheer information than many humanities publications do; but because they combine many functions and types of information there are many distinct issues to address. Looking at present-day approaches to just one component of editions, commentary, and thinking about how commentaries do or don't translate well into the digital world will help to suggest some useful directions further work might take.

The simple idea of providing explanations doesn't dictate any particular form that commentary must take. But the number of Shakespeare editions is such that we can discern a pattern: there are a few principal forms, shaped by the nature of the works, the aims of scholars, and the desires of buyers. And I say 'buyers' rather than 'readers' because the existence of a substantial commercial market for Shakespeare editions does affect thinking on this

194

and other aspects of editions. Scholars in humanities fields continue to think of themselves as lone workers pursuing individual visions, but this model is especially inaccurate in Shakespeare editing; an edition of a work by Shakespeare rarely emerges from an individual's independent vision, but is instead conditioned by obligations and constraints imposed by prior scholarship, the series, the publisher's requirements, and the market.

So while there are many conceivable forms for Shakespeare commentary, two forms dominate in practice: commentary intended as a companion to reading and commentary intended as a scholarly reference. These two forms of commentary imply (and also prompt) two different sorts of use: an individual does not have a fixed identity as a reader or a scholar as I'll use these terms in this discussion, but learns to choose the sort of commentary that suits his or her intentions on a particular occasion. The commentary for readers is the usual case: it's what we find, in varying sizes, in single-volume Collected Works editions and in the various multi-volume series such as the Arden, Cambridge, and Oxford. The commentary for scholars is represented above all by the variorum edition, but also by collections of notes on textual matters found in many other editions. These notes on such things as variants, emendations, and lineation changes are not often designed to reward sustained reading or to assist buyers who have no prior knowledge of such matters, and some editions have moved them off into separate parts of the book. Centuries of publishing have produced adequate technology for presenting this sort of material in a convenient kind of physical object: with the machinery of line numbers and notes keyed to them, and various options for the placement of notes (base of page as the preferred location, back of book for less important information). The edition for readers in particular needs to be a usable physical object, with a carefully planned layout that can present a very large amount of information without causing confusion. We could readily imagine a separation of various functions of an edition into separate publications: in other fields commentaries have sometimes been published separately, for example.[2] One reason we don't see editions for readers taking that form is the question of convenience and usability: these are important merits of print editions when done well.

Buyers are generally thought to desire some explanatory notes but not too many. The commentary for readers is written with the idea that you can plausibly consult it as you read to help you along, and that its scope should be kept within limits in order to support that aim. Certainly that is the best explanation for the surprising limitation in the size of these commentaries: there has been some growth in the size of Shakespeare editions, but its rate is vastly outstripped by that of the growth of the scholarly literature on Shakespeare more generally. Ralph Hanna, in discussing annotations to *Piers Plowman*, asserted that there is 'a basic rule of all annotation, that of plenitude': 'By this rule, full annotation (or fuller annotation) must always be construed as an advance in textual understanding: it constructs a deeper or denser or richer text, restores to the author a fullness of allusion otherwise lost.'[3] Shakespeareans surely feel that impulse as well, rather than a preference to see the texts they annotate as straightforward when possible, and more monumental when less complicated. But in this case the market provides a check that Hanna didn't feel in discussing his work as part of a group annotating Langland. Those annotations were projected for appearance in a separate publication, keyed to an existing edition that is *not even available in paperback*. So Hanna's discussion is about the literary-critical picture of the work a commentary builds up and only minimally about the problem of keeping the audience in mind. In Langland's case scholars clearly don't imagine that such an audience exists anywhere outside of universities.

A commentary for the aid of readers must be to the point; the notes must be guided by judgements about what readers need to know, and the notes must make their points quickly and clearly. As buyers are expected to alternate their attention between text and notes, the notes can't be very long; but the problem is not merely the size of the printed book but also the amount of the reader's time that is consumed. Notes can't take too much time to absorb if they're to plausibly accompany reading. The outer limit of what the market will bear, or has been thought able to bear, is in the sub-genre of extensive commentary to the sonnets, as in the editions of Stephen Booth and Helen Vendler. Here the volume of commentary is high not merely because the density of language calls for it, but also because larger amounts are more usable in the case of a collection of short poems. You can read one poem and then the commentary to it; perhaps because verse has functions other than storytelling it has often attracted more extensive and more frequently used commentary than other forms. With the plays, it is harder to shuttle back and forth between text and notes without losing the thread: for many readers the interest of this form lies more in storytelling and less in words. The tendency is for longer discussions to turn into independent essays.

The commentary designed for reference use by scholars does not face the same demands of concision and relevance. It does not need to select the most useful remarks out of all that could be made; the programme of the Shakespeare Variorum is rather to depict the whole history of commentary.

Many notes wind up being of an appropriate sort for readers, but when there is a point on which there's been significant disagreement you're likely to get a paragraph of divergent views that don't lead you to any conclusion, or instead lead you to many places before arriving at a rather simple conclusion.[4] Even so, the programme of the Shakespeare Variorum is still rather limited: standard language in the edition since the 1970s says that the commentary seeks primarily 'to elucidate the text' and only 'at times' ventures into the critical history; essays elsewhere in these volumes serve to summarize the critical and stage history.[5] Hyder Rollins's variorum edition of the sonnets did seek to survey criticism as part of its commentary, which is no doubt a principal reason for the length of that edition. The variorum edition of Donne's poetry now in progress is one current example of variorum editing that does seek to cover every kind of discussion of the works, and the edition is consequently projected to require a dozen substantial books to accommodate it all.[6]

The recognition of uncertainty or disagreement is not the defining characteristic of the commentary for scholars, though: it is also present in commentaries for readers. The most compressed sorts do it least, of course, but the form does not oblige scholars to skip over such difficulties, and the embarrassment of ignorance is really the whole field's and not the individual editor's. The defining characteristic of commentary for scholars is the orientation towards consultation with respect to selected passages, and not towards continuous use as you read the whole work. My own copy of Rollins's variorum edition of the sonnets was previously owned by at least two different professors of English literature, but many of the pages were still unopened when I acquired it. These bulky volumes are not the first you would choose for reading, and an accumulation of information that is valuable when you are studying one passage is less so when you are reading the whole work. The intent behind this sort of commentary is especially clear in the Donne Variorum, which makes no effort to convert its material into a form more suited to extended reading than to scholarly labour. It quotes and summarizes but does not provide any guidance as to what is best or most pertinent; it has an explicit policy of simply presenting the views of earlier scholars 'without interjecting editorial opinion on their validity or ultimate significance'.[7] As a result the commentary is often a lengthy recitation of dubious views; the approach is intelligently designed to serve the edition's goal, but it does not produce a commentary that reads well.

The range of commentary types we see may be small because of market pressure, but it could also be that the most appropriate varieties of this form of publication for these buyers have been found. There is certainly further variety within types: the market for editions with commentary for readers divides up into a number of separate groups based on educational stage, among other things. What we don't see is (for example) meandering reflections of the kind to be found in eighteenth-century editions, or commentary designed to argue a particular point of view. You can find such discussions of Shakespeare published in other ways, and commentary may just not be how readers want to get such things.

We can conclude that devising something new and welcome in the commentary form is not a simple matter, and so the limited use of digital resources might reflect a limited need. It is true that until quite recently any digital publication was hampered by the technology's inadequacy: creating digital texts was difficult and interface technology was limited. Today we are able to think with less constraint about what would be most useful to do, rather than having to get by with what the software allows, but the right approaches still aren't obvious.

A key question has been how you actually get at notes in a digital text. In the 1980s and early 1990s a common answer was that you would simply click on a word and you'd see the notes for it, and this was widely thought to be an advance. With experience, it's become apparent that this is the equivalent of notes at the back of the book: fine if you're looking at them occasionally, cumbersome if you want to look at any number of them. For while the information is certainly available, the time and effort required to get at it is excessive in some situations. To look at *one* note this way requires negligible time and effort, but a whole Shakespeare play in a series like the New Cambridge typically has over two thousand individual commentary notes. Clicking the mouse is simpler than walking across the room, finding a book, and looking up the right page; but it is less simple than glancing down the page or across the opening at the notes, and the difference becomes significant when multiplied this many times. It is a difference that isn't evident in a demonstration or in a few minutes' experimentation: in those situations the novelty is what you notice, and not the nature of real use. Text online is in our age always more awkward than text on paper for ordinary reading. All varieties of scrolling and paging require the use of mouse and keyboard controls that lack the physical feedback that turning paper pages provides; mouse and keyboard controls also have many different uses that depend on the program context, so that it is very common even for experienced computer users to find themselves starting unexpected and unwanted processes. (It's noteworthy that the electronic-book programs of the late 1990s sought to provide something *simpler* for reading than the interface offered by web browsers.)[8] And of course many people continue to find that the limited resolution of computer screens, and the need to be stationed at the machine, are further drawbacks.

For a reading text, then, we would at least like to see the relevant notes on the same screen as the text, without having to do anything to make them appear one by one; but this is technically a good deal harder to achieve than the click-for-note solution. (Printers find it easier to create endnotes rather than footnotes because the problem of getting just the right amount of material on each page is simpler if you have just one stream of text and not two; the problem is not any simpler in arranging things on a computer screen.) A really large screen could put particular kinds of notes in particular places around the text, on the Talmudic model;[9] but the small size of displays today means that doing that entails a lot of effort to fit things in, and may mean the reader has to *do* something to get at notes, which is what we want to avoid.

The content of a digital commentary doesn't need to be fixed in the way a printed one is, and that suggests a useful kind of flexibility: in reading you could choose the sorts of notes to be displayed. You could choose to display, or not, the notes about sources, or biblical allusions, or glosses for words like 'anon' and 'presently'; and you could choose versions of the notes with greater or lesser detail. But that approach needs to address two problems: one of interface and one of writing.

There needs to be an interface through which you can express your choices, and while this is simple enough as an idea it can be a problem in practice. Are you selecting categories of information from a list? Do you have an easy way to see more if it suddenly seems necessary? Do you understand ahead of time what the categories mean? Do you feel nervous about missing things and decide to just select everything anyway? And all of this requires some effort to learn how the edition is designed and what its categories are: the categories themselves and the means for choosing among them will certainly be different in every edition. While it would not seem to be a significant burden to spend a few minutes on that when you are going to spend much more time reading the text, it nevertheless seems to be an obstacle to use; that has to be balanced against the simpler approach of glancing at all the notes and not reading ones that aren't of interest. One great lesson of the World Wide Web is that people tend to just forge ahead without bothering to spend time setting something up, unless there's a considerable benefit. Just as in working with printed reference books, many people will not consult the instructions unless desperate. The title of one current book on effective design of websites says it all: *Don't*

Make Me Think.[10] (And if you imagine that scholars are any different, consider how many in the field believe that the *Short-Title Catalogue* is a census of early printed books, rather than a catalogue that never lists more than ten copies in any entry.)[11]

The dynamic edition with a commentary whose contents you select also poses problems for its authors: they must write the notes so that they can be broken into small pieces containing different categories of information. It is often possible, but there are also times when the categories of information interact and it is necessary to combine (for example) discussions of staging and of language in order to make a point concisely and adequately. The notion of separating different varieties of commentary requires that they be *written* separately; we can get computers to select and rearrange blocks of text that we've written, but they can't rewrite them. The requirements of pertinence and compression conflict with the implementation of a dynamic commentary.

In any case, none of this promises anything very remarkable. These are provisions, possibly laborious, for saving readers some of the effort they once devoted to glancing at the base of the page. It's not a straightforward task to make something digital that is easier to use than a book for this kind of thing. (There are other scholarly functions with different constraints and more potential: the problem of displaying textual information, for example, is made considerably easier when the obligation of compression goes away. The digital publications from the Canterbury Tales Project have much clearer displays of variants than any printed editions of Chaucer.)[12] Being more responsive to what readers want is a possibility, but a tricky one: such an interface is appealing at first, but eventually you recognize that being able to see there's an interface at all is a problem. And in the end the biggest problem about the commentary for readers, especially when it's for student readers, is that of keeping its content right: commentaries get rewritten as scholarly perspectives develop, and as new generations of students appear who know different things. You have to keep changing what you say about religion, the classics, and sex.

The commentary for readers is not especially amenable to mechanical variation to suit different classes of readers, then, or to a novel form of display that would render it more usable. Commentary for scholars offers more possibilities, depending on what we ask it to do. If we think of it as collecting all the notes and observations that ever were (within some horizon of attention), and intended for consultation here and there rather than for extended reading, then the obligations of compression and pertinence are diminished. The diversity and lack of resolution that a variorum offers have been seen as its great merits, and a broad collection of all sorts of notes and observations does roughly correspond to that idea of the variorum genre.[13]

But the Shakespeare Variorum series has always done a good deal of selection and filtering, and Richard Knowles in describing the series as it currently operates stresses its attempt to verify factual claims and to weed out the worthless; a variorum run on such principles tends to wind up structurally similar to the commentary for readers, not productively open to flexibility of display.[14] The Shakespeare Variorum has also never run to more than two volumes for one work, although there is no lack of material to fill up many more. As described above, the Donne Variorum operates on different principles: there is more attention to literary criticism and a programme of not trying to adjudicate among critical views, only to summarize them.

There is also a third approach, because it is possible to separate the function of providing summaries of and extracts from the literature from that of providing references that make it possible to locate such material. The editorial work of collecting the scholarship and criticism and noting the passages or topics discussed is very substantial, and it's feasible to stop at that point and leave to readers the task of looking up the actual publications. David Yeandle, in his line-by-line bibliography to Wolfram's *Parzival*, does that (though he goes further, by providing brief indications of the subject and approach of these publications).[15] With the commentary for readers, the relevant measure of time is the time required for consulting each note as one reads: this has to be minimal or reading isn't feasible. With the commentary for scholars, the relevant measure of time is that required for a scholarly project and not for interaction with reading material. This has several scales: there is the (vast) time that would be required to sift through all the sources and find those touching on a particular passage or theme; but there is also the further time required to look up the identified sources and study them, and this is not so daunting, especially in view of the necessity in many situations to go and do that anyway.

If serious use often requires reading the sources in their original form, then the function of summaries does need examination: they may not be the most important element of a variorum commentary. The editor of a new edition is greatly helped by them: such an editor is one of the few scholars who needs to study every note in a variorum edition. The summaries provide one way to make a fast check on an idea, as to whether it's been investigated already and to what extent: scholars need ways to decide what ideas to follow up, and any publication that can help with this is important in a way that actual citations of it will never reveal. There's the use by students as a way of seeing the range of opinion that has existed, though there are also other ways to do that sort of thing. In every case, the summaries are certainly of value, but we might still prefer to have a variorum that lacked summaries but was more frequently revised and so better represented the current state of scholarship.

But instead of omitting extracts from the scholarly literature it would be possible to go in the other direction and include previous discussions in their entirety, with a commentary built up from links to relevant passages. There is a digital edition of Thomas Gray already in existence that does this on a limited scale. At present its commentary is simply a collection of textual and explanatory notes from numerous previous editions of Gray – so that it really does give you (for example) the complete note on 'The curfew tolls the knell of parting day' from five editions, and therefore makes the point five times over that there is a source for the line in the *Purgatorio*, as Gray himself had explained in his own note.[16]

This combined commentary does not make a good companion to reading because of all the repetition (and because seeing the notes requires clicking once per line); and the experience is quite different from that of reading notes that summarize earlier scholarship as in the Shakespeare and Donne Variorum editions. But for some purposes the paraphrase that makes it more compact isn't desirable: although it is more laborious to get an idea of the main points from the Gray edition, it's much richer in detail. For 'The curfew tolls the knell of parting day' you can note the other observations about the passage and speculations that later editors do or don't pick up. And the notes in their complete form provide a better impression of the commentators' general approaches and evaluations: if you have summary, even with selected quotations, you get much less of the rhetorical effect of the original presentation of and argument for these positions, as observations are restated to extract the main points. Anne Middleton observes that commentary conflicts with the text it ought to support, cutting it up into isolated bits and working against any narrative or other larger coherence.[17] This is true, but it's also true that the text will mostly triumph in this conflict, particularly if it deploys a narrative and characters and poetry. Commentary rarely descends to this sort of aesthetic appeal; its only advantages are its more modern perspective and diction (so that *Pale Fire*, in order to turn a commentary into a novelistic text, is obliged to violate the norms of commentary in a very unprofessional way).[18] And the text that a commentary cuts up into bits and annotates typically remains readily available in the same book; the real violence is done to the scholarly literature. In a readers' commentary little remains of the original scholarly publications: only bits of information survive. In traditional variorum commentary we do preserve more, but never whole scholarly texts; it's the attempts at persuasion in these texts that are most weakened by extraction and summarizing for commentary, so that serious work on reception and critical history will require consultation of the original publications.

If the problems placed in the way of this project by intellectual-property law were not so enormous, the variorum commentary based on a corpus of complete texts of the relevant literature would be an attractive possibility. Like any variorum it would face the problem of defining its horizon of attention: though the Thomas Gray edition limits itself to annotations from other editions, there is no compelling reason to leave any critical work out, or even to restrict the collection to critical writing rather than also assembling other works of the period. Indeed, the main problem with this approach is that it is likely to be more sensible to assemble a digital collection relevant to the broader field than to focus on an individual work; and once that step is taken then the explicit links between the main texts and the scholarly literature may get dropped as well. Those links – whatever establishes the connections between the specific line or topic in the text and the specific passages of the relevant discussions in the secondary literature – still need to be made: without them the scholar is left once again with the difficult task of hunting for the relevant passages, and even the searching possible with digital texts does not fully make up for the loss.

In this analysis of commentary in the print and digital worlds, then, there are two principal questions with different answers for different forms of commentary: what is the nature of the reading experience it assumes? and what kind of information and assistance does it offer to scholars? If my account of commentary for readers is right, then there's little reason why digital publication should lead to significant changes in its form; the ease of finding your way to a different work and reading it instead, for example, is not of great significance if the intent is extended reading of the one work. With this form of commentary, it's the reading experience above all that matters, and the highly developed technology of the book is not easy to improve upon. We can hope that the computing world in general works towards display improvements; considerable design skill will still be necessary to make new displays work well for this purpose.

It's a different question for variorum commentary, whose function is much less constrained by questions of the immediate reading experience.

Greater length is not automatically a disadvantage, and so longer notes or even full texts of related materials may be considered; but it is necessary to keep in mind the important function of direction to the precise range of secondary materials relevant to a passage. If we see variorum commentary as mostly aiding intensive study of small sections of a text, then the importance of adding full texts may be not so great, as not saving that much time. Those materials can be used in other ways, of course, but then we begin to move into thinking about a digital library rather than a commentary, and about more general functions that, however valuable, do not replace the carefully targeted function of commentary.

We pursue research in a world that in many ways does not facilitate it very well; but actually commentary as it stands is one of the better-devised tools for the purpose. There are digital innovations that create new possibilities even if badly done, such as text searching; no easy advances of that sort seem at hand for commentary.

APPENDIX

This is the text of the explanatory notes from *The Thomas Gray Archive*, at http://www.thomasgray.org/, for the first line of "Elegy Written in a Country Churchyard" (as of 22 August 2003):

1. *Lines 1.1–4.9* "*The... me.*"] "Cf. Joseph Warton's *Ode to Evening*, which contains a number of passages strikingly similar to the *Elegy*, although – so far as I know – the similarity has not been noticed by editors. Warton's *Odes* were published in 1746. One stanza in particular Gray may have had in mind when he composed the first stanza of his *Elegy*:

> "Hail, meek-eyed maiden, clad in sober grey,
> Whose soft approach the weary woodman loves,
> As, homeward bent to kiss his prattling babes,
> He jocund whistles thro' the twilight groves."

Collins's *Odes* were published the same year as J. Warton's (1746), and the whole atmosphere of Collins's *Ode to Evening* is similar to that of the *Elegy*. Cf. especially stanza 10:

> "And hamlets brown, and dim-discover'd spires;
> And hears their simple bell, and marks o'er all
> The dewy fingers draw the gradual dusky veil."

For Gray's remarks on Warton's and Collins's *Odes*, see p. 81. Cf. also Ambrose Philips, *Pastoral* ii, end:

> "And now behold the sun's departing ray
> O'er yonder hill, the sign of ebbing day.
> With songs the jovial hinds return from plow,
> And unyok'd heifers, pacing homeward, low."

In: [PhW_1894] *Selections from the Poetry and Prose of Thomas Gray*. Ed. with an introduction and notes by William Lyon Phelps. The Athenaeum press series. Boston: Ginn & Company, 1894, p. 137/138.

2. *Line 1.1–3 "The ... tolls"*] "The passage from Dante quoted by Gray is *Purgatorio*, canto viii, 5, 6.

The standard *History of England* in Gray's time, that by Thomas Carte, describes the curfew law of William the Conqueror as "an ordinance, that all the common people should put out their fire and candle and go to bed at seven a clock, upon the ringing of a bell, called the *couvre feu bell*, on pain of death; a regulation, which having been made in an assembly of the estates of *Normandie* at *Caen*, in A.D. 1061, to prevent the debauches, disorders, and other mischiefs frequently committed at night, had been practised with good success in that country." (Book v, vol. I, p. 422, 1747.)"

In: [PhW_1894] *Selections from the Poetry and Prose of Thomas Gray*. Ed. with an introduction and notes by William Lyon Phelps. The Athenaeum press series. Boston: Ginn & Company, 1894, p. 137.

3. *Line 1.1–2 "The curfew"*] "The curfew was a bell, or the ringing of a bell, rung at eight o'clock in the evening for putting out fires (Fr. *couvre*, cover, and *feu*, fire), a custom introduced by William the Conqueror. The word continued to be applied to an evening bell long after the law for putting out fires ceased, but it is not now so used, and the word would have become obsolete but for Gray's use of it here, and when one speaks of the curfew one thinks of the first line of the "Elegy." It occurs frequently in Shakespeare, and Milton uses it twice, – "Comus," 435, and in the well-known lines in "Il Penseroso": – "I hear the far-off curfew sound / Over some wide-watered shore." – 74, 75. Gray quotes in original the lines from Dante which suggested this line. Cary's translation

is as follows:—

> "And pilgrim, newly on his road with love,
> Thrills if he hear the vesper bell from far,
> That seems to mourn for the expiring day."

In: [BrJ_1903] *The Poetical Works of Thomas Gray: English and Latin.* Edited with an introduction, life, notes and a bibliography by John Bradshaw. Reprinted edition. The Aldine edition of the British poets series. London: George Bell and sons, 1903 [1st edition 1891], p. 214/215.

4. *Line 1.1–2 "The curfew"*] "The evening bell still conventionally called curfew, though the law of the Conqueror, which gave it the name, had long been a dead letter. In Shakespeare the sound of the Curfew is the signal to the spirit-world to be at large. Edgar in *Lear* feigns to recognize 'the foul fiend Flibbertigibbet: he begins at curfew and walks till the first cock' (III. 4. 103); and in *The Tempest*, v. i. 40, the elves 'rejoice to hear the solemn curfew.' The mood of the *Elegy* is that of *Il Penseroso* and the scene in both poems is viewed in the evening twilight:

> "Oft on a plat of rising ground
> *I hear the far-off curfew sound,*
> Over some wide-watered shore,
> Swinging slow with sullen roar."
> Milton, *Il Penseroso*, 72–75.

Milton's '*far-off* curfew' reminds us of the squilla *di lontano* of Dante, which Gray quotes for the first line of the *Elegy*. I supply in brackets the rest of the passage; *Purgatorio*, VIII. 1–6.

> [Era gia l' ora, che volge 'l disio
> A' naviganti, e 'ntenerisce 'l cuore
> Lo di ch' han detto a' dolci amici addio:
> E che lo nuovo peregrin d' amore
> Punge, se ode] squilla *di lontano*
> Che paia 'l giorno pianger, che si muore.
> [Now was the hour that wakens fond desire
> In men at sea, and melts their thoughtful heart
> Who in the morn have bid sweet friends farewell,
> And pilgrim, newly on the road, with love
> Thrills, if he hear] the vesper bell from far
> That seems to mourn for the expiring day.
> Cary.

The curfew tolls from Great S. Mary's, at Cambridge, at 9, from the Curfew Tower of Windsor Castle (nearer the scene of the *Elegy*) at 8, in the evening.

Warton, *Notes on Pope*, vol. i. p. 82, reads:

"The curfew tolls! – the knell of parting day."

But we know exactly what Gray wrote, and what he meant us to read."

In: [ToD_1922] *Gray's English Poems, Original and Translated from the Norse and Welsh.* Edited by Duncan C. Tovey. Cambridge: Cambridge UP, 1922 [1st ed. 1898], p. 134/135.

5. *Line 1.1–8 "The... day,"*] "In a letter to Bedingfield in Aug. 1756 (*Corresp* ii 477) and in *1768* G[ray]. acknowledged his debt to Dante, *Purgatorio* VIII 5–6: *se ode squilla di lontano, / che paia il giorno pianger che si muore* (from afar he hears the chimes which seem to mourn for the dying day). He may have felt obliged to do so publicly as a result of Norton Nicholls's discovery of the debt: see *Corresp* iii 1297. Nicholls added: 'He acknowledged the imitation & said he had at first written "tolls the knell of *dying day*" but changed it to *parting* to avoid the *concetto*.' G.'s opening quatrain is also reminiscent of *Inferno* ii 1–3: *Lo giorno se n'andava, e l'aer bruno / toglieve gli animai, che sono in terra, / dalle fatiche loro; ed io sol uno* (The day was departing, and the brown air taking the animals, that are on earth, from their toils; and I, one alone. ...); and see Petrarch, *Canzone 50* (*Ne lastagion che 'l ciel rapido inclina*)."

In: [LoR_1969] *The Poems of Thomas Gray, William Collins, Oliver Goldsmith.* Edited by Roger Lonsdale. Longman Annotated English Poets Series. London and Harlow: Longmans, 1969, p. 117.

6. *Line 1.1–2 "The curfew"*] "Johnson (citing Cowel) described it as: 'An evening-peal, by which [William] the conqueror willed, that every man should rake up his fire, and put out his light; so that in many places, at this day, where a bell is customarily rung towards bed time, it is said to ring *curfew*.' Such a bell still rang in Cambridge at 9 p.m. G[ray]. probably remembered 'I hear the far-off *Curfeu* sound', *Il Penseroso* 73. But Shakespeare has 'To hear the solemn curfew', *Tempest* v i 40 and uses the word on three other occasions. It also occurs in Thomson, *Liberty* iv 755 and *n*; and in T. Warton, *Pleasures of Melancholy* (1747) 282–3:

'Where ever to the curfew's solemn sound / Listening thou sit'st.' Cp. also Collins's 'simple bell', *Ode to Evening* 38 (see p. 466). Shakespeare has 'A sullen bell / Remembered tolling a departing friend', *2 Henry IV* 1 i 102–3; Dryden, 'That tolls the knell for their departed sense', *Prologue to Troilus and Cressida* 22; and Young, 'It is the *Knell* of my departed Hours', *Night Thoughts* i 58."

In: [LoR_1969] *The Poems of Thomas Gray, William Collins, Oliver Goldsmith*. Edited by Roger Lonsdale. Longman Annotated English Poets Series. London and Harlow: Longmans, 1969, p. 117.

7. Line *1.1–8 "The . . . day,"*] "This famous line is imitated from Dante, *Purgatorio*, viii."

In: [HeJ_1981] *Thomas Gray: Selected Poems*. Ed. by John Heath-Stubbs. Manchester: Carcanet New Press Ltd., 1981, p. 77.

NOTES

1. Two of the most substantial and influential works were George P. Landow, *Hypertext: The Convergence of Contemporary Critical Theory and Technology* (Baltimore: Johns Hopkins University Press, 1992), and Richard A. Lanham, *The Electronic Word: Democracy, Technology, and the Arts* (University of Chicago Press, 1993). To many working along these lines, the rise of the World Wide Web was a disappointment: one of the more direct statements of this attitude is in Michael Joyce, 'New Stories for New Readers: Contour, Coherence and Constructive Hypertext', in *Page to Screen: Taking Literacy into the Electronic Era*, ed. Ilana Snyder (London: Routledge, 1998), pp. 165, 170.
2. See, for example, G. S. Kirk (gen. ed.), *The Iliad: A Commentary* (Cambridge University Press, 1985–93), six vols.; Susan Shatto, *The Companion to Bleak House* (London: Unwin Hyman, 1988), one of a series of such Companions to works by Dickens, mostly given over to a commentary. One of the rare instances of such a separately published commentary in the Shakespeare world is Stanley Wells and Gary Taylor with John Jowett and William Montgomery, *William Shakespeare: A Textual Companion* (Oxford: Clarendon Press, 1987), which is devoted entirely to textual material and was still part of an edition rather than a separate work.
3. Ralph Hanna, 'Annotating *Piers Plowman*', *Text* 6 (1994), 155. As he goes on to argue, fuller doesn't necessarily mean better.
4. For an example of the first case, see Marvin Spevack (ed.), *Antony and Cleopatra* (New York: Modern Language Association, 1990), pp. 193–5, on 'Yon ribaudred nag' in 3.10; for an example of the second, see p. 266, on 'The hearts that spanieled me at heels' in 4.12, where the emendation of 'panneled' to 'spanieled' is now universally accepted.

5. The quotation is from Spevack (ed.), *Antony and Cleopatra*, p. xxiii; the same wording may be found in Richard Knowles (ed.), *As You Like It* (New York: Modern Language Association, 1977), p. xx, and in Mark Eccles (ed.), *Measure for Measure* (New York: Modern Language Association, 1980), p. xviii, in all cases in a section called 'Plan of the Work'.
6. Hyder E. Rollins (ed.), *The Sonnets* (Philadelphia: Lippincott, 1944); Gary A. Stringer (gen. ed.), *The Variorum Edition of the Poetry of John Donne* (Bloomington: Indiana University Press, 1995–).
7. Stringer (gen. ed.), *Variorum*, vol. 2, p. xlviii.
8. Clifford Lynch, 'The Battle to Define the Future of the Book in the Digital World', *First Monday* 6:6 (June 2001). Despite the sensational title this is a thorough and thoughtful survey, and it draws attention to the reasons for the very persistent appeal of text on paper.
9. A page of the Talmud has a scriptural passage at its centre, surrounded by numerous separate strands of commentary and meta-commentary accumulated over centuries, each with its traditional location.
10. Steve Krug and Roger Black, *Don't Make Me Think: A Common Sense Approach to Web Usability* (Indianapolis: New Riders, 2000).
11. See vol. 1, p. xlix: 'In the entries the Atlantic Ocean is represented by a semicolon. Up to five locations on each side have been listed with a view to geographic distribution.'
12. Peter Robinson (ed.), *The Wife of Bath's Prologue on CD-ROM* (Cambridge University Press, 1996).
13. Stephen Booth, 'On the Value of the Variorum Editions of Shakespeare', talk at the Modern Language Association convention, 27 December 1994.
14. Richard Knowles, 'Variorum Commentary', *Text* 6 (1994), 35–47.
15. David Yeandle, 'Line-by-Line Bibliographical Database of Wolfram von Eschenbach's *Parzival*', in *DRH99: Selected Papers from Digital Resources for the Humanities 1999*, ed. Marilyn Deegan and Harold Short (London: Office for Humanitites Communication, 2000), pp. 57–74. See also John Hazel Smith, *Shakespeare's Othello: A Bibliography* (New York: AMS Press, 1988), which includes a partial index to relevant lines.
16. Alexander Huber (ed.), *The Thomas Gray Archive*, at http://www.thomasgray.org/, accessed 22 August 2003. See the Appendix for the text of these notes on the line from Gray.
17. Anne Middleton, 'Life in the Margins, or, What's an Annotator to Do?', in *New Directions in Textual Studies*, ed. Dave Oliphant and Robin Bradford (Austin: University of Texas Press, 1990), p. 170.
18. Vladimir Nabokov, *Pale Fire* (New York: Putnam's, 1962).

CHAPTER 13

New collaborations with old plays: the (textual) politics of performance commentary

Barbara Hodgdon

At an early rehearsal for *A Midsummer Night's Dream*, the actor playing Theseus stopped after speaking his first word in the initial line of the play's opening scene: 'Why does he say "Now"?' – a question behind which lay a second, 'Why this word and not another?' Although modern editors do gloss several of *Dream*'s initial *lines* and, following Rowe, emend Folio's '*Now* bent in heaven' (TLN 13) to '*New* bent in heaven' (1.1.10), and (sometimes) explain their rationale for doing so, none pays attention to how Theseus's initial 'Now' does textual, much less theatrical, work. Neither an archaic term nor one occurring in an ambiguous context, 'Now' nonetheless encompasses several meanings: 'at the present time', 'at this moment', 'at once'; it may also be used 'without any definite meaning for emphasis or to preface or resume one's remarks', as in '*now* look here', or, as a conjunction, in the sense of 'since' or 'seeing that' (*OED*). Given this range of potential meanings, perhaps the simplest, most direct way to think of how Theseus's 'Now' performs textual–theatrical labour is that the word works to join actor and audience together in a present moment: it is *now* that the play – and the performance – begin.

Yet as the actor addressed his own question, he imagined Theseus turning reluctantly from signing state papers to addressing wedding invitations; inflecting the word – and the line – with that attitude, he thought, might not only motivate Hippolyta's annoyance but also underscore, especially for audience members not attuned to mythic allusions, their prickly relationship. Such a backstory for Theseus, of course, has thoroughly modern resonances based on Stanislavskian as well as Method protocols of acting: evoking present-day gender stereotypes (the man who privileges public over private life, the woman whose priorities are entirely opposite), it opens onto a whole series of (somewhat stale) jokes culminating in *The Wedding Planner*. For as W. B. Worthen writes, 'Stage acting isn't determined by textual meanings, but uses them to fashion meanings in the fashion of contemporary behaviors.'[1] Moreover, in collaborating with a single word, this actor

210

The (textual) politics of performance commentary

was engaged in what Declan Donnellan calls 'invisible work': the research that never is visible to audiences but which, in rehearsal, may appear in tandem with 'visible work' – what audiences *do* see *as performance*.[2] Pointing to some, though not all, of the distinctions between how editors and performers engage with a Shakespearean text, this textual-theatrical fable marks the genesis of my own thinking – or dreaming – about what current editorial commentary does or does not accomplish and what a commentary more explicitly attuned to performance might look like.

With the notable exception of *The Norton Shakespeare*, major Shakespeare editions increasingly have staked out claims to being 'performance-oriented', ranging from Oxford's decision to mark the Folio as a collection of 'performance-tested' texts to Cambridge's inclusion of more detailed stage histories, a practice also adopted, though somewhat more selectively, by Arden3. All of these editions offer models of exemplary scholarship, presenting modernized texts complete with elegantly conceived annotative apparatuses designed to alert readers to matters etymological, literary, historical, and socio-cultural (in a veritable host of Polonian combinations), whether through single-word glosses or contextualizing commentary, including 'long notes' which address particular textual cruxes. Yet, although (for example) Arden3's 'General Preface' suggests that editors *may* concern themselves with issues of theatrical interpretation in such commentary, doing so is represented less as a feature integral to the business of editing than as an 'extra added attraction' – an option, not a requirement. Moreover, although Arden editors are encouraged to examine the earliest editions with a view to recuperating early modern staging, the use-value of annotations citing present-day performance practice is (tacitly) considered slightly less significant; indeed, when information about such performances does appear, it is often separated from the text, ghettoized in the stage history section of an edition's introduction. Here, too, the (also tacit) rule of thumb seems to be that a performative option which *has been* played may become part of the text's history – witness the editorial choreography that preserves, even canonizes, stage directions dating back to the eighteenth century[3] – but this is not the case for the potentially playable option, one without a stage history. For the most part, 'performance', when cited at all, often gets re-made, re-constelled, abbreviated, and re-coded as para-literary meaning.

Certainly it is not new news that traditional codes of editorial commentary serve neither performers nor performance.[4] Indeed, one function of such commentary is to converse (and often to quarrel) with previous editors, faulting injudicious choices, and thus engage with the text's history, or the history of its readings. Often, however, this is a closed conversation in which editors are talking primarily to themselves. Yet editors widely are perceived, and tend to perceive themselves, not just as textual arbiters but as providing certainty in a slippery intertextual world in which, despite its materiality – or perhaps because of it – performance cannot offer something like desirable authentication.[5] Casting the Shakespearean text as a site combining a limited number of textual obligations with a wide range of performative options marks out what's at issue: indeed, translating contingency into manageable print form resembles attempting to pin down Cleopatra's 'infinite variety'. What, I want to ask, are the poetics, problematics, and politics of re-thinking those codes, of 'inventing' forms of annotation and presentation that might position readers, not as passive external witnesses to either an editorial imaginary or an already existing performance 'product' but as active participants in the processes of making their own imagined performance(s)? And I want to begin (again) by interrogating existing commentary.

Textual users (a term I prefer to 'readers') cannot discern the forward-moving energies of performance when, for instance, the experience of engaging with the text turns into a full-scale archaeological dig through commentary that has limited (or no) use-value, either for individual performers or for more global issues of performance. In this category, my personal favourite comes from the Arden1 *Macbeth*, where, at Macbeth's 'Balm of hurt minds, great nature's second course, / Chief nourisher in life's feast' (2.2.38–9), a lemma for 'second . . . nourisher' introduces the following: 'Pudding appears anciently to have been the first course at dinner ("so, *Per tempus advenis*, you come *in pudding time*, you come as well as may be", *Terence in English*, 1614), the joint or roast being the "second" – the pièce de resistance.'[6] Equally notable are other instances of editorial subjectivity – or overreaction. In some editions of *The Taming of the Shrew*, bar bills for Sly mount up: as though sympathizing with Sly's thirst, Hibbard (New Penguin 1968), for instance, gives him ale at Induction, 2.20, and interprets line 71 as a request for a refill; Thompson (Cambridge 1984) assumes from lines 95–7 that he does not get it until then, 'though the servingmen may have been plying him with sack'.[7] In addition, editors who focus on illusionistic detail (or narrative) rather than theatrical context regularly account for Shakespeare's lapses in Adriatic and Mediterranean geography, reassuring those who may have measured the ground.[8] Or, in another instance of applying realistic coding to non-illusionistic drama, Oxford's *All's Well that Ends Well* has Helen enter for her first interview with the King of France (2.1.92) 'disguised', presumably in order to explain why Lafeu apparently doesn't recognize her. Two scenes later, however, when he does so at the ball, is it because she appears 'as herself'? Yet both Parolles's '*Mort du vinaigre*, is not this Helen?' and Lafeu's 'Fore God, I think so' (2.3.45–6) suggest that she appears 'different' here – a difference that also may rest on a costume change, one not signalled by the Oxford editor, and one which will, of course, be embodied 'differently' by each performer who undertakes the role.

Alternatively, even commentary that pretends alertness to performance, and to performing bodies, often straddles a curious gap between non-illusion and illusion. For instance, whereas all editions of *The Winter's Tale* offer considerable information about early modern bears at '*Exit pursued by a bear*' (3.3.57), none marks the moment when Antigonus *sees* the bear: is the 'bear' – however performed (editors as well as modern performances differ as to whether the bear is 'comic' or 'tragic') – read as 'bear' only in pursuit? A question to be asked. Certainly if once the bear was a real one, that is no longer the case, yet (Norton excepted) existing editions refer only to 'original' staging. An even more obvious instance of such straddling occurs when, following Duncan's murder, Macbeth enters to the Lady (2.2.13), who (apparently) does not see the daggers until thirty-four lines later ('Why did you bring these daggers from the place?'). Noting the difficulty of performing the scene 'so as to make plausible' the Lady's delay in seeing the daggers, the Arden2 editor imagines them (at lines 20 and 27) concealed behind Macbeth's back.[9] Although it risks concocting an alternative psychological sub-text, it seems perfectly plausible for the Lady to *see* the daggers as Macbeth enters: that it takes her thirty-four lines to ask him why he has brought them from 'the place' seems the more intriguing (and more playable) issue. That the editor *does* notice them (and wants to hide them from sight) imposes a reading of both characters and also suggests that he may be reacting to – and covertly 'rewriting' – a performance which he thought implausible. Arguably, such commentary – as well as other forms of editorial re-performance – has theatrical use-value precisely because it provokes resistant readings, prompts alternative performances. Nigel Hawthorne's copy of *King Lear*, for instance, annotates editorial stage directions at 4.6.178 [*He takes off his coronet of flowers*] and 4.6.185 [*He throws down flowers and stamps on them*] with an emphatic 'No, he doesn't!'[10]

Whether annotated by editors or actors, marked-up text, as Jerome McGann notes, is interpreted text: such markings record its historical passage, its previous readings; they instantiate its generative – and I would add performative – rules.[11] And just as theatrical meanings are culture-bound, subject to taste and fashion, so too do editorial fantasies of theatrical enactment leak into editorial commentary. An elegant example occurs in the New Variorum *Antony and Cleopatra*. At Cleopatra's 'The messengers' (TLN 43; 1.1.34), Lyons (1962) prescribes performative behaviours as well as inflections – 'May be delivered in one of two ways: as a reiterated, peremptory command to the lingering Attendant; or as an acknowledgement of the entrance of the messengers and her mocking presentation of them to the reluctant Antony' – before other commentators turn to Antony's reply:

> Let Rome in Tiber melt, and the wide arch
> Of the ranged empire fall: Here is my space,
> Kingdoms are clay: Our dungy earth alike
> Feeds beast as man; the nobleness of life
> Is to do thus: . . .
> (TLN 44–8; 1.1.35–9).

Offering a note that drives character back to Shakespeare's sources, Upton (1748) remarks, 'Antony, as Plutarch informs us, affected the Asiatic manner of speaking, which much resembled his own temper, being ambitious, unequal, and very rodomontade.' Focusing on 'Here is my space', Deighton (1891) construes it as 'my life in Egypt'; Kittredge (1941) reads 'empire enough for me'; Dover Wilson (1950) adds ['*He flings an arm about her*']. Pope (1723) directs ['*Embracing*'] at 'do thus' (39), to which Furness (1907) objects, arguing that it is out of character that the 'wrangling' Cleopatra 'should tamely submit to be "embraced" '; Kittredge remarks that 'some critics reject the action as "undignified" ', and Schanzer (1960) adds, 'If we are to have an embrace at all, I would prefer it to commence at "Here is my space" and to continue through the rest of the speech.' By 1973, Hawkes takes the embrace (however prolonged) as paradigmatic: 'At that moment when their bodies unite on the stage, the word "thus" and its concomitant gesture stand for, "embrace", the totality of the Egyptian way of life . . . [But] to embrace is also to enclose, to restrict.'[12] To update the Variorum, Wilders (1995) and Cohen (1997) concur.[13] Betraying, as Worthen writes, 'a fascination with the interactions and interruptions between bodies and texts that might be taken [as] one of the hallmarks of performance today',[14] this sequence traces a history of editorial re-performances, (silently) re-worked as critical commentary.

Notoriously, theatre practitioners produce working texts that either ignore or cancel out editorial labour. Two stage directions in *Richard II*'s initial scene offer a case in point. At Richard's 'Then call them to our presence' (1.1.15), Arden3 adds '*Exeunt attendants*.' But since Richard has been addressing John of Gaunt, might it be he who leaves?[15] A similar exit for Gloucester occurs in F *King Lear* (1.1.34), and patterning early texts on later ones is standard editorial practice. Yet is an exit theatrically necessary? In Steven Pimlott's Royal Shakespeare Company production (2000), all the assembled courtiers, including Bolingbroke and Mowbray, stepped forward, a blaze of light marking their 'entry'; the promptcopy (Cambridge edition)[16] excises both the stage direction and Richard's next four and a half lines ('Face to face, ... hasty as fire'). Later, at 1.1.195, '*Exit Gaunt*' also is cancelled. Although that direction has Folio provenance, probably deriving from the manuscript playbook, obeying it seems problematic, since not only does it violate court etiquette for Gaunt to leave without being dismissed but also he has an obvious stake in Richard's ensuing decision to stage a combat. Whereas editors evoke the so-called re-entry rule in order to justify Gaunt's exit, Pimlott, putting Shakespeare's text to work against the grain of editorial practice and textual tradition and accommodating that text to a particular space and to particular players, had Gaunt and the Duchess of Gloucester remain, following Richard's exit with the court, to play the next scene. Might, then, annotation draw on this specific performative choreography, document its history? Or, performing more covertly – or immaterially – as in the *Antony and Cleopatra* example, might commentary simply pose the question of whether either or both exits are necessary?

Choosing between (or rejecting) either option touches on the problematics of generating a model of performance commentary responsive to *material* theatrical evidence, raising additional questions about the place of theatre history in the enterprise. For one thing, forms of annotation giving details, line readings as well as stage business, of past performances across the centuries select moments from the constructed flow of performance of which they are a part, effectively 'doing' to performance what the atomizing dictionary-based gloss does to text, as though, like Juliet, cutting Romeo out in little stars. Moreover, even the greatest performances achieve meaninglessness over time, becoming just another instance of what can be done with a particular play. How might specific performance choices be flagged without taking them out of context, whether in terms of their relation to previous or subsequent choices or to time-bound cultural as well as theatrical meanings? And does privileging a particular option work to compromise other options as well as invite being perceived as a more or less 'accurate' interpretation? Rather than setting up a conversation with textual users which relies heavily on past performances, what information might spur a textual user to imagine future performances? And what forms of annotation might work to energize 'the new' – keeping in mind, of course, that theatre raids itself, that actors 'create' business only to find that they are repeating another actor's behaviour, as when, playing Kate in *Shrew* (4.3), Fiona Shaw (RSC 1987) took off her wedding ring and gazed through it as through a telescope, echoing Paola Dionisotti's earlier gesture (RSC 1978)?

Writing commentary by the light of admired productions invites visualizing or hearing material particulars that write themselves over text. All performances produce sustainable echoes, line readings as well as stage business that become engraved in memory, jostled into hearing or sight in a silent theatre of reading through constructive, constitutive processes, performance's alter ego.[17] I cannot read – or see – *Coriolanus* without (re)hearing Alan Howard's delivery of 'What's the matter?' (1.1.162), stretching out the 't's so that each reverberated, harshening the query, stressing the consonant's intellectual 'head sound'. Similarly, I hear Richard Johnson's knowing Antony speaking 'Who's gone *this* morning?' (4.5.6); Patrick Magee's ice-cold Cornwall, cutting off Goneril's 'Pluck out his eyes' with 'Leave him . . . to my displeasure' (3.7.4), the pause presaging the coming horror; or Judi Dench's Lady Macbeth, turning Helene Weigel's famous 'silent scream' from *Mother Courage* into voice as she imagines blood on her hands (5.1) – all unscripted, completely performative. Whereas any commentary pertaining to performance will modulate and deepen what McGann calls the textual condition, extending both its coding and patterning into another dimension,[18] that which cites theatrical practice not only risks establishing a canon of propriety but also, as Lynette Hunter and Peter Lichtenfels argue, substitutes copy-performance or copy-production for copy-text.[19] Yet arguably such citation hardly differs from traditional editorial choreography which, after all, stabilizes Rowe's or Pope's stage directions in stone. Although canonization depends on histories of taste, it would seem that editorial protocols embrace a particular theatrical past while remaining anti-theatrical to modern or present-day performance practice. Intriguingly, though perhaps not surprisingly, both in past and present climates driven by (differing) notions of authenticity, the performance most regularly and consistently canonized is the absent performance, the 'original' early modern production about which little or nothing is certain (but much imagined) and which is largely irrecoverable. Despite knowing that early modern stagings took place in not just one but several 'original' spaces, ranging from public to private theatres, to performances at court and to touring venues, much commentary continues to imagine the open platform stage as the (supposed) playing space of choice. In my view, relinquishing this Globe-al space would be an initial step towards creating a less restrictive commentary, one attuned to changing spaces and to fluid potentialities of how bodies and texts take on meanings in such spaces.

One instance of the interrelationships between bodies, texts, spaces, and meanings occurs near the end of Katherine and Petruchio's first meeting in *The Taming of the Shrew*. The Folio directs Baptista, Gremio, and Tranio to enter just before 'For I am he am born to tame you, Kate' (2.1.269; TLN 1159). Since some editors conjecture that *Shrew* was printed from a transcript based on minor theatrical adaptation,[20] the entry's placement may suggest (an) early modern staging. Editions, however, vary widely: Pope's (1728) moves it to follow 'I must and will have Katherine to my wife' (274), but several (perhaps remodelling via *Henry V*, 5.2.278) place the entry just before 'Here comes your father. Never make denial' (273).[21] Is this another instance of performance practice tacitly turned into print, an editor preserving performance past or simply replaying another editor's re-performance? In either case, the imagined spatial arrangement is not necessarily 'early modern' – if indeed F does reflect, say, a King's Men's staging. A second issue – what potential performative behaviours the entry might invite – is even more intriguing. Mentioning the 'rich comic possibilities' of the F position, Alan Dessen notes that if Petruchio immediately notices the observers, 'the actor can change tone and posture, visibly adjusting his role for the benefit of the onstage audience'; or, 'to gain a broader effect, the three entering figures, fearful of Kate's wrath, may tiptoe onto the stage, setting up a decided contrast to Petruchio's bold lines'.[22] Dessen, of course, is imagining a particular range of performative behaviours and, beyond that, a particular set of global meanings for the play called *The Taming of the Shrew*. But if, for instance, Kate has begun to believe that Petruchio may well be 'a husband for her turn', she may be absolutely stunned as he re-assumes, for Baptista's benefit, the shrew-tamer role he had proclaimed he was born to play. Do critics – or editors – desire to dictate stage space in conjunction with assumptions about 'character'? (In passing, it would seem that Dessen has 'taken on' Petruchio as well as Baptista, Gremio, and Tranio while I (*Shrew*'s in-process editor) take Kate's part.) How might one label these various possibilities? Early Modern? Editorial Modern? Theatrical Postmodern?[23] And how might commentary alert textual users to this range of possibilities without prescribing, without offering (as Dessen does), a binary, without, as is so often the case, confusing either role or actor with character?

Indeed, idiosyncratic 'character commentary' marks a number of editions, notable among them the Arden3 *Othello* where, at 'But look what lights come yond?' (1.2.28), the editor remarks, 'Here and elsewhere Othello seems to suffer from failing eyesight' and refers readers to the introduction, where he argues that this affects not only the actor's performance but our overall interpretation. Later, at 4.1.214, a note reads,

If Burbage, the first Othello, was instructed to play the part as though suffering from weak or short sight, this could be visually reinforced in various ways (including the use of spectacles at 1.3 to read the map and a letter (4.1), evoking Gloucester's 'I shall not need spectacles' (*KL* 1.2.35)).... Othello's lines can be played straight, without any hint of defective eyesight; an ageing Moor with failing vision gives them added point, partly explains his general dependence on Iago, and puts more sting into (Iago's) taunts ('Look to her, Moor' and so on).... Othello's own psychic need for ocular proof ('make me to see't' (3.3.363 ff)) may be related to his unacknowledged infirmity.[24]

If imagining 'the first Othello' yields these potential behaviours, what of Desdemona? Here, the editor introduces a radical change at 4.3.33–5:

DESDEMONA: No, unpin me here.
EMILIA: This Lodovico is a proper man. A very handsome man.
DESDEMONA: He speaks well.

F prints 'This... proper man' as one line and assigns it to Desdemona.[25] Following Ridley's notorious conjecture that 'for Desdemona to praise Lodovico at this point seems out of character', the Arden3 editor moves the speech prefix, attributing the line to Emilia. Whose Desdemona and whose Emilia are being presented here? Are they, like this edition's Othello, the 'first' players – those (recently) eroticized boy actors? More to the point, this note would seem to operate not just ahistorically but without any performative or behavioural touchstone except that in the editor's imaginary.

Somewhat similarly, consider this commentary on *Troilus and Cressida*, 5.2.112–14:

DIOMEDES: Farewell till then. *Exit.*
CRESSIDA: Good night; I prithee, come. –
Troilus, farewell. One eye yet looks on thee,
But with my heart the other eye doth see.

Whereas most editions reposition Diomedes' exit to follow Cressida's 'I prithee, come', the Arden3 editor restores that exit to its F placement. His note reads: 'The wish... to "correct" F's placement... in order to allow Cressida to answer Diomedes before he leaves... does not take sufficient account of his brusqueness. The plaintiveness of her beseeching him to come again is all the more evident if he is disappearing while she speaks.'[26] In justifying F's reading, this editor not only counters past practice but also over-reads both roles, directing Diomedes' actions and behaviours as well as mandating Cressida's tone of voice – further enhanced by modernized punctuation, especially the (potentially plaintive, beseeching?) dash following 'come'. Yet however intrusive the editorial personality may be, the note may well serve a textual user, if only to generate a resistant reading. By contrast, the editor's gloss on the last line, in pointing to the eye/I pun, offers an explanation that suggestively opens up lexical meaning.

Is that also the case for commentary that engages in what I will call proleptic reading? Is it useful, for instance, to call attention to how *Shrew*'s Induction anticipates later exchanges between Katherine and Petruchio by remarking on key phrases? When called on to act the part of Sly's wife, Bartholomew the Page asks, 'What is your will?' (Induction 2.101), and a similar phrase recurs when Kate enters at Petruchio's command (5.2.105). Or, in *King Lear*, Edmund's 'Nothing, my lord' (1.2.31) echoes Cordelia's response to Lear (1.1.86), drawing the two together as 'bastard children'. Does commentary that reaches beyond a particular phrase to explore its implications further along in the action smell too strongly of thematic or tropic explanation, or can it be rethought so that it does not overload early dialogue with meanings that appear in full only later in the action – where, in each case, such meanings depend on particular actors' behaviours?

Posing these last questions circles back to Theseus, and to *Dream*'s initial 'Now' – unglossed by editors, ignored (in all probability) by most readers, but challenging an actor to discern how it might do theatrical work. Here, although I have been discussing performance commentary, I have avoided writing any but, instead, have raised questions about changing the codes as well as the languages through which textual commentary shapes textual users' engagement with Shakespeare's drama. Several editorial projects designed to present commentary attuned to performance have been in process for some years – among them, Ardenonline's performance site and the Arden3 *Complete Performance Edition*, the one defunct, the other withdrawn. As I write, other publishers are moving towards re-directing existing editions, whether print or electronic, to address performance – one current agenda for an age when editorial practices seem to be undergoing a paradigm shift. At the very least, there is a growing recognition that the Shakespeare texts we have inherited are print interventions, artifactual entities that stand between (largely irrecoverable) early modern performances and modern, postmodern, or post-postmodern ones, including those as yet to be imagined. Simultaneously, however, agendas – or 'Elements of Style'[27] – already in place exert considerable pull: respondents to drafts of commentary for the proposed Arden3 edition, for instance, preferred familiar protocols (single-word glosses, longer contextual notes), with perhaps some attention devoted to 'visual issues', performance traditions such as commedia dell'arte and details snipped from stage history. Perhaps not surprisingly, those who self-identified as directors in university theatre programmes seemed most open to change. And what they wanted was information that serves interpretation but does not do it – a somewhat utopian desire, given McGann's caveat that textual markings, of whatever sort, are always already interpretative.

If effecting a politics of change may not be either easily or quickly achieved, several general principles nonetheless seem self-evident. Received wisdom has it that actors, like all textual users, want help with archaic language and with historical and socio-cultural contexts – information that will feed the business of crafting character from role, will aid them in performing what Donnellan calls invisible work. But in what proportion – especially given a critical climate where context, not text, rules? And where does the (performance-sensitive) editor stop to let a textual user begin? Bringing theatre practice to bear on texts, Hunter and Lichtenfels argue, generates different reading rules.[28] They postulate a notion of reading for difference which takes the idea of resistant reading one stage further, making it analogous to Roland Barthes's notion of the 'writerly', a process of recreating, rewriting, reperforming the text in the moment of its reading. Barthes's concept of textuality also imagines a textual environment in which any text can intersect and be intersected by an infinite number of others – an environment bearing resemblances to hypertext, perhaps the best available model for the (however inchoate) annotative procedures I want to imagine. Whatever that 'new' commentary may look like, it will have a different grammar, one where, as Hunter and Lichtenfels write, 'the text is articulated through doing, not in advance'.[29] Perhaps the most useful distinction to make between 'old' and 'new' protocols is between 'the work performed' and 'the work as something which is "coming-into-performance"': the first emphasizes arriving at a form as instantiation and enactment (the province of specific details drawn from stage history, which is not the same as performance), the second concerns thinking with means that are always coming into form through processes of material theatre, through visualizing and hearing bodies in space. Casting textual commentary as theatrical improvisation, such a schema depends, as D. F. McKenzie writes, on 'focus[ing] on the mind in the act of making sense, rather than on the sense it finally (and often reductively) makes'.[30]

At the end of Pedro Almodóvar's beautifully symmetrical film, *Talk to Her*, the story of Marco and Benigno – opposite types, each of whom loves

The (textual) politics of performance commentary

two women, one who has disappeared into the past and one, Alicia, who lies unconscious in the present – a spectator is invited to read the film from the viewpoint of either man – or to watch it as someone seated in a theatre. If she chooses the latter, the film is about performances: some by people outside the story, some by characters within the narrative. *Talk to Her* begins in a theatre, and it ends there as well, with Marco and Alicia as audience members, watching a Pina Bausch performance. An empty aisle seat separates them (one behind the other), marking not just the past presence and now the absence of Benigno, who has brought them together, but also marking a place for imagining another spectator, one who might witness this, or another, performance – perhaps seeing it with a difference. That space – though hardly empty – is precisely the one I envision waiting to be taken up by another imagined performer, another textual user.

NOTES

1. W. B. Worthen, 'Shakespearean Performativity', in *Shakespeare and Modern Theatre: The Performance of Modernity*, ed. Michael Bristol and Kathleen McLuskie, with Christopher Holmes (London: Routledge, 2001), p. 132.
2. Declan Donellan, *The Actor and the Target* (London: Nick Hern, 2002), pp. 12–13.
3. See, for instance, Rowe's addition, '*Exeunt Petruchio [and Katherina]*', at *The Taming of the Shrew*, 5.2.187, reproduced by all modern editions to date. Similarly, some variation of Capell's exit direction for Falstaff at *1 Henry IV*, 5.4.155 '[*bearing off the body*]' appears in all modern editions. 'Enter Lear, fantastically dressed with wild flowers' (Arden2 *King Lear*, 4.6.80) also draws from Capell; Oxford restores F's placement of the entry and lineation but retains Capell's 'costuming', adding '[*crowned with weeds and flowers*]'.
4. See Michael Cordner, 'Actors, Editors, and the Annotation of Shakespearean Playscripts', *Shakespeare Survey* 55 (2002), 181–98; and '"To Show Our Simple Skill": Scripts and Performances in Shakespearean Comedy', *Shakespeare Survey* 56 (2003), 167–83. Throughout both these brilliant essays, Cordner not only addresses lapses in existing commentary but also suggests how annotative procedures might begin to call attention to questions of punctuation, phrasing, and inflection that contribute to what Hamlet calls 'action[s] that a man [or woman] might play'. I am deeply indebted to Cordner's work.
5. See, for instance, Janette Dillon, 'Is There a Performance in This Text?', *Shakespeare Quarterly* 45 (1994), 75.
6. *Macbeth*, ed. Henry Cuningham (London: Methuen, 1912; rpt 1934), p. 51.
7. *The Taming of the Shrew*, ed. Ann Thompson (Cambridge University Press, 1984), p. 56. Certainly it is to the Lord's advantage to cater to Sly, keeping him half-drunk as he forces the aristocratic fantasy down his throat.

8. Perhaps most famously, editors account for Bohemia's seacoast, first by citing Laurence Sterne's Uncle Toby (*Tristram Shandy*, Bk 8, Chap. 19) and then by excusing Shakespeare on the grounds that early atlases show Bohemia as having 'a small foothold on the Adriatic', as in the Arden2 note on *The Winter's Tale*, 3.3.2, p. 66. *The Taming of the Shrew*, 1.1.42 implies that inland Padua is a port; editors who worry over the locations of other cities in that play and in *The Two Gentlemen of Verona* explain that Shakespeare learned his Italian geography from imperfect informers.
9. *Macbeth*, ed. Kenneth Muir (London: Methuen, 1959), p. 55.
10. Typescript text edited and cut by Yukio Ninagawa and David Hunt for a co-production with the Royal Shakespeare Company, 1999. Hawthorne's copy is archived at the Shakespeare Institute, Stratford-upon-Avon.
11. Jerome McGann, *Radiant Textuality: Literature After the World Wide Web* (New York and Basingstoke: Palgrave, 2001), p. 138.
12. *A New Variorum Edition of Shakespeare: Antony and Cleopatra*, ed. Marvin Spevack (New York: Modern Language Association of America, 1990), p. 11.
13. Arden3 and Norton editors respectively.
14. Worthen, 'Shakespearean performativity', p. 136. And were an edition to be performance-specific, over three decades Antony's 'space' (and embrace) has moved from Cleopatra's hips (RSC 1972) to her crotch (RSC 1999).
15. Oxford's '*Exit one or more*', for instance, would admit that possibility.
16. Promptcopy at the Shakespeare Centre Library, Stratford-upon-Avon.
17. Peter Middleton, 'The Contemporary Poetry Reading', in *Close Listening: Poetry and the Performed Word*, ed. Charles Bernstein (Oxford University Press, 1998), pp. 265, 268.
18. See Charles Bernstein, 'Introduction', in *Close Listening*, p. 10.
19. Lynette Hunter and Peter Lichtenfels, 'Reading in the Moment: Theatre Practice as a Guide to Textual Editing', in *In Arden: Editing Shakespeare*, ed. Ann Thompson and Gordon McMullan (London: Thomson Learning, 2003), p. 152.
20. *William Shakespeare: A Textual Companion*, ed. Stanley Wells and Gary Taylor with John Jowett and William Montgomery (Oxford: Clarendon Press, 1987), p. 170.
21. Editions and/or editors that move the stage direction include: Capell, Arden2, Riverside, Cambridge, and Folger. Those that retain F's position are Pelican Complete, Oxford, Oxford Complete, and Bevington.
22. Alan Dessen, *Rescripting Shakespeare: The Text, The Director, and Modern Productions* (Cambridge University Press, 2002), p. 221.
23. The possiblity I imagine here was recently realized in Greg Doran's production, RSC 2003.
24. *Othello*, ed. Ernst Honigmann (Walton-on-Thames: Thomas Nelson, 1997), pp. 129, 17–19.
25. The line is part of a passage – the introduction to Desdemona's song and the song itself – that has no Q1 equivalent.

26. *Troilus and Cressida*, ed. David Bevington (London: Thomson Learning, 1998), p. 320.
27. See, for example, the 'Elements of Style' prefacing Suzan-Lori Parks's playtexts, as in *Topdog/Underdog* (New York: Theatre Communications Group, 1999), n.p.
28. Hunter and Lichtenfels, 'Reading in the Moment', p. 153. See also Roland Barthes, *S/Z*, trans. Richard Miller (New York: Hill and Wang, 1974); and 'From Work to Text', in *Image/Music/Text*, trans. Stephen Heath (New York: Hill and Wang, 1977), pp. 155–64.
29. Hunter and Lichtenfels, 'Reading in the Moment', p. 140.
30. D. F. McKenzie, 'Printers of the Mind', in *Making Meaning: 'Printers of the Mind' and Other Essays*, ed. Peter D. McDonald and Michael F. Suarez, S. J. (Amherst: University of Massachusetts Press, 2002), pp. 3–4.

Index

Note: Shakespeare's works are listed as entries in their own right.

'Acte to Restraine Abuses of Players', 23, 71
Alexander, Peter, 81–2, 83, 84
Allen, Michael J. B., 35
Alleyn, Edward, 80
All's Well that Ends Well, 212
Almodóvar, Pedro, 220–1
Anderson, Mary, 113
Andrews, John F., 128–30, 131–2
Anne of Denmark, 29, 33
Antony and Cleopatra, 155, 214, 215, 216
As You Like It, 156
Appiah, Kwame Anthony, 35

Barnes, Barnabe
  The Devil's Charter, 180
Bartels, Emily C., 34, 35
Barthes, Roland, 13, 40, 103, 105, 220
Bartholomeusz, Denis, 125
Barton, John, 122
Bate, Jonathan, 76, 114
Bausch, Pina, 221
Beale, Simon Russell, 121
Beaumont, Francis, 43, 143
Beaumont, Francis and John Fletcher
  The Knight of the Burning Pestle, 148, 150
  The Maid's Tragedy, 152
Bentley, Richard, 49
Berger, Thomas L., 35, 102, 113
Bernstein, Charles, 222
Berry, Ralph, 113, 121, 126
Bertram, Paul, 4
Best, Michael, 95–6
Bevington, David, 46, 107, 115, 128–30, 132, 157, 179, 184, 222, 223
The Bibliographical Society, 77
Billington, Michael, 22
Black, Roger, 209
Blackfriars Theatre, 86
Blayney, Peter W. M., 107

Bliss, Lee, 128–30, 131–2
Bolter, J. D., 103
The Book of Sir Thomas Moore, see *Sir Thomas More*
Boose, Lynda, 27
Booth, Stephen, 114, 125, 196, 209
Bowers, Fredson, 1, 10, 15, 43, 44, 47, 48, 52, 82–3, 89, 91, 143
Bradley, David, 111, 114, 115
Brecht, Bertolt, 127
  Mother Courage, 216
The British Broadcasting Corporation Shakespeare, 114, 122
Brockbank, Philip, 128–30, 132, 140
Brook, Peter, 112
Brooke, C. F. Tucker, 102
Brown, John Russell, 15, 47, 157
Buc, Sir George, 58
Burbage, Richard, 218
Burns, Edward, 114

Caird, John, 121
Capell, Edward, 102, 129, 130, 139, 221–2
Chambers, E. K., 81, 125
Chapman, George, 143
  Bussy D'Ambois, 74
Charney, Maurice, 15
Chaucer, Geoffrey, 144, 200
  The Canterbury Tales Project, 200
Church, Tony, 113
Clark, William George, 54
Clayton, Thomas, 141
Coghill, Nevill, 31, 34, 36
Cohen, Walter, 214
The Comedy of Errors, 113, 122, 124, 154–5, 156
Condell, Henry, 78, 83, 86
The Contention, see *The First Part of the Contention*

Index

Corbeil, Carole, 123–4
Cordner, Michael, 221
Coriolanus, 10, 113, 127–41, 216
Coronado, Celestino, 122
Corpus Christi Cycles, 144
Cotgrave, Randle, 156
Cox, John D., 114, 160, 176
Craig, Hardin, 83
Craik, T. W., 61, 113, 114
Crane, Ralph, 57–8, 59, 80
Creed, Thomas, 90
Crewe, Jonathan, 128–30, 132
The Croxton Play of the Blessed Sacrament, 112
Cuningham, Henry, 221
Cymbeline, 112, 113

Dane, Joseph A., 46
Daniel, Samuel, 98
De Grazia, Margreta, 5, 42, 95
Deighton, K., 214
Dekker, Thomas, 43, 76
  Satiromastix, 180
Dench, Judi, 113, 216
Derby's Men, 111
Derrida, Jacques, 76
Dessen, Alan, 14, 113, 162–4, 178–9, 180, 193, 217
Dick of Devonshire, 44
Dillon, Janette, 47, 221
Dionisotti, Paola, 216
Dobson, Michael, 121
Donaldson, Peter, 107
Donne, John, 2, 143
  The Variorum Edition of the Poetry of John Donne, 197, 201, 202
Donnellan, Declan, 211, 220
Doran, Greg, 222
Doran, Madeleine, 81

Eccles, Mark, 209
Eco, Umberto, 158–9, 165
Edward III, 7, 12, 95, 99–105, 108
Edwards, Paul, 35
Edwards, Philip, 54–5, 57
Edwards, Richard
  Damon and Pithias, 98
Eisenstein, Elizabeth, 105
Eld, George, 90
Elizabeth I, 28
Ellis-Fermor, Una, 98
Engle, Lars, 157
Engler, Balz, 34
English Shakespeare Company
  The Wars of the Roses, 122
Erasmus, Desiderius, 1

Erne, Lukas, 107, 108
Eschenbach, Wolfram von
  Parzival, 201
Evans, G. Blakemore, 2, 128–30, 132

The First Part of the Contention, 81, 83, 114, 154–5
Fletcher, John, 43, 71, 143
  Bonduca, 88
Fletcher, John and Philip Massinger
  Sir John Van Olden Barnavelt, 57–8, 76
Florio, John, 156
Foakes, R. A., 43, 76, 87, 114
Forker, Charles R., 114
Frayn, Michael
  Copenhagen, 159
Fredrickson, George M., 29, 31, 35
Froissard, Jean, 104
Frye, Northrop, 3
Fryer, Peter, 35
Fuller, David, 107
Furness, H. H., 214

Gabrieli, Vittorio, 76
Garrick, David, 122
Gascoigne, George, 98
Gibbons, Brian, 2
Gielgud, John, 122
Globe Playhouse, 86, 178
Gorboduc, 144–5
Gray, Henry David, 119
Gray, Thomas, 202–3
  The Thomas Gray Archive, 204–8
Greenaway, Peter
  Prospero's Books, 122
Greene, Robert
  Friar Bacon and Friar Bungay, 145, 147
  Orlando Furioso, 80
Greetham, David C., 45, 60, 68
Greg, W. W., 6, 16, 34, 37–9, 49–53, 54, 55, 56–60, 61, 67, 77–91, 119
Gurr, Andrew, 61, 126

Halio, Jay, 87
Hall, Kim F., 34
Hamlet, 2, 8, 15, 39, 40, 41, 51, 52, 53–5, 57, 58, 59, 78, 83, 85–6, 90, 96, 108, 111–25, 143, 146, 149, 153, 154–5, 165, 179, 184
Hammond, Antony, 162, 178, 180–90
Hanna, Ralph, 196
Harris, Bernard, 35
Hattaway, Michael, 192
Hawkes, Terence, 15, 214
Hawthorne, Nigel, 213
Hay, Louis, 47

Heidegger, Martin, 76
Heminges, John, 78, 83, 86
Hendricks, Margo, 34
1 Henry IV, 114, 146, 155, 221
2 Henry IV, 146, 148, 155
Henry V, 55–6, 78, 113, 114, 148, 217
1 Henry VI, 114
2 Henry VI, see *The First Part of the Contention*
3 Henry VI, see *The True Tragedy of Richard Duke of York*
Henry VIII, 114, 150
Heywood, John
   The Four P's, 37, 144
   The Pardoner and the Friar, 37
   The Play of the Weather, 144
Heywood, Thomas, 76
Hibbard, George, 128–30, 132, 212
Hinman, Charlton, 46, 91
Hodgdon, Barbara, 15, 175
Hodges, C. Walter, 192
Holaday, Alan, 157
Holland, Peter, 15, 164
Honigmann, Ernst, 16, 21, 22, 33, 34, 35, 56–7, 81, 83–5, 88, 93, 128, 159–60, 163, 165, 222
Housman, A. E., 39, 87
   M. Manilii Astronomica, 49–50, 51, 52, 58–9
Howard, Alan, 216
Howard-Hill, T. H., 8, 39, 40, 59, 61
Huber, Alexander, 209
Hunter, Lynette, 99, 216, 220

Ichikawa, Mariko, 126, 165
Ioppolo, Grace, 17
Irace, Kathleen O., 121

James I, 33
Jenkins, Harold, 122
Jennens, Charles, 54
Jerome, Saint, 1
Johns, Adrian, 105
Johnson, Richard, 216
Johnson, Samuel, 54, 156, 190–1
Jones, Eldred D., 35
Jones, James Cellan, 122
Jones, Richard, 97–8
Jonson, Ben, 42, 83, 98, 143
   The Alchemist, 147, 148, 155
   Bartholomew Fair, 147, 149, 150
   Epicene, 154, 155
   The Masque of Blackness, 29, 33
   Volpone, 154
Jowett, John, 71, 75, 94, 95, 99
   see also Oxford Shakespeare
   see also *William Shakespeare: A Textual Companion*

Joyce, James
   Ulysses, 72
Joyce, Michael, 208

Kane, Sarah
   4.48 Psychosis, 159
Kastan, David Scott, 95, 114
Kaul, Mythili, 35
Keenan, Siobhan, 125
Kidnie, Margaret Jane, 160, 178–9, 188
King, T. J., 111, 114–15
King John, 81–2, 84, 153
King Lear, 3, 4, 8, 10, 21–2, 23, 30, 43, 46, 62, 69, 74, 76, 81, 83, 85–8, 96, 114, 115, 146, 148, 150, 213, 215, 216, 219, 221
The King's Men, 33, 57, 80, 217
Kirk, G. S., 208
Kittredge, George Lyman, 214
Kliman, Bernice W., 4, 96
Knight, Charles, 129–30
Knight, Edward, 88
Knowles, Richard, 43, 201, 209
Knowles, Ronald, 114
Krug, Steve, 209
Kyd, Thomas
   The Spanish Tragedy, 73

Lancashire, Anne, 177
Landow, George P., 208
Langland, William
   Piers the Ploughman, 72, 196
Lanham, Richard A., 208
Lavagnino, John, 69, 75
Lee, Sidney, 78
Levenson, Jill L., 33
Lever, J. W., 62
Lichtenfels, Peter, 216, 220
Little, Jr, Arthur, 32, 36
London Lyceum, 113
Long, William B., 61, 89, 90, 101, 160, 163, 177, 191
Loomba, Ania, 23, 35
Love's Labour's Lost, 66, 90, 114, 146–7, 152–3, 156
Luhrmann, Baz, 2
Lyly, John, 144–5
   Euphues, 144
Lynch, Clifford, 209
Lyons, Clifford, 214

Macbeth, 66, 67, 90, 95, 112, 151, 185, 212, 213, 216
Magee, Patrick, 216
Maguire, Laurie, 5
Malone, Edmond, 54, 179–80
The Malone Society, 37–9, 77, 81

Index

Malone Society Reprints, 39–40, 43, 44, 67, 73, 79
Marcus, Leah, 4, 16, 42
Marlowe, Christopher, 43, 143
   Doctor Faustus, 147
   Tamburlaine, 97–8
Marston, John
   Antonio and Mellida, 117
Mason, Pamela, 185
Massai, Sonia, 95, 101, 102, 104–5
Massinger, John, *see* Fletcher, John
Maus, Katharine Eisaman, 157
McGann, Jerome J., 7, 45, 91, 94, 95, 169, 213, 216, 220
McKellen, Ian, 122
McKenzie, D. F., 7, 45, 91, 220
McKerrow, R. B., 6, 8, 38, 41, 50, 51–2, 54, 57, 59, 60, 77, 80, 89, 90
McLaverty, James, 47
McLeod, Randall, 16, 95
McMillin, Scott, 33, 34, 61, 115, 119
McMullan, Gordon, 114
Measure for Measure, 9, 12, 63–75, 80, 104
Mehl, Dieter, 15
Melchiori, Giorgio, 76, 101, 102, 114
The Merchant of Venice, 3, 90, 152, 156
The Merry Wives of Windsor, 78, 80, 114
Middleton, Anne, 202
Middleton, Peter, 222
Middleton, Thomas, 9, 42, 63, 67, 68–71, 73, 75, 76
   The Changeling, 145
   A Chaste Maid in Cheapside, 147, 156
   A Game at Chess, 84, 88
   More Dissemblers Besides Women, 68
   The Roaring Girl (with Thomas Dekker), 145
A Midsummer Night's Dream, 3, 15, 84, 112, 113, 153, 156, 192, 210–11, 219
Milton, John, 50
Montgomery, William
   see Oxford Shakespeare
   see William Shakespeare: A Textual Companion
Moseley, Humphrey, 83, 86
Mowat, Barbara, 4, 34, 62, 107
Much Ado about Nothing, 90, 150, 188, 193
Muir, Kenneth, 35, 44, 222
Munday, Anthony, 63, 76
Murphy, Andrew, 34

Nabbes, Thomas
   Microcosmus, 108
   The Unfortunate Mother, 108
Nabokov, Vladimir
   Pale Fire, 202
Nashe, Thomas, 77

National Theatre, *see* Royal National Theatre
Neill, Michael, 27, 36
The New Bibliography, 6, 8, 50, 77–91
The Norton Shakespeare, 21, 43

Orgel, Stephen, 95, 106, 160, 165, 177
Othello, 7, 8, 9, 21–34, 56–7, 59, 80, 83, 90, 96, 115, 148, 149, 217–18
Oxford Shakespeare *Complete Works*, 2, 4, 6, 21, 22, 41, 45, 62, 67, 73, 85–6, 87, 128–30, 132, 148, 164, 222

Page, Norman, 60
Painter, William, 104
Papp, Joe, 152
Parker, R. B., 128–30, 132, 140
Parkes, Suzan-Lori, 223
Parrott, Thomas Marc, 143
Pasco, Richard, 122
Patrick, D. L., 81
Peacham, Henry, 29
Peele, George
   The Arraignment of Paris, 145
Pembroke's Men, 182
Pennington, Michael, 122
Pericles, 78, 146, 153, 154
Perkins, William
   The Whole Treatise of the Cases of Conscience, 105
Peters, Julie Stone, 107
Pimlott, Steven, 121
Pollard, A. W., 6, 37, 77–9, 80, 81–2, 84, 85, 102
Pope, Alexander, 50, 214, 216, 217
Potter, Lois, 34, 115
Pröscholdt, Ludwig, 102
Prospect Players, 122
Proudfoot, Richard, 130
Prouty, C. T., 83

The Rape of Lucrece, 146, 153, 156
Rasmussen, Eric, 107, 114, 157, 178–90
Red Shift, 112, 122
The Revenger's Tragedy, 151, 156
Richard II, 114, 156, 214–15
Richard III, 81, 99, 113, 146
Richardson, Ian, 122
Ridley, M. R., 35, 218
Ringler, William A., 113
Roberts, James, 90
Robinson, Peter, 209
Rollins, Hyder, 197
Romeo and Juliet, 2–3, 7, 59–60, 65–6, 67, 76, 78, 90, 99, 156, 165–75
Rose Theatre, 114
Rosenbaum, Ron, 15

Rowe, Nicholas, 161, 164–5, 210, 216, 221
Royal National Theatre, 121
Royal Shakespeare Company, 55, 113, 121, 122, 215, 216, 222

Sams, Eric, 102
Sanders, Norman, 34
Sanders, Wilbur, 129–38
Schanzer, Ernest, 214
Schoenbaum, S., 48
Seaton, Ethel, 98
The Second Maiden's Tragedy (*The Lady's Tragedy*), 67, 165
Seltzer, Daniel, 157
Shakespeare Electronic Archive, 96
Shakespeare's Globe, 112, 113
Shatto, Susan, 208
Shaw, Fiona, 216
Shaw, George Bernard, 159
Shillingsburg, Peter L., 48
Simmes, Valentine, 90
Sir Thomas More, 9, 12, 63–75, 79, 90, 91, 165
Sisson, C. J., 76
Skeat, Walter W., 72
Smith, John Hazel, 209
Smith, Irwin, 125
Spenser, Edmund, 144
Spevack, Marvin, 208–9, 222
Sprague, A. C., 113, 125
Stallybrass, Peter, 42, 95
Steevens, George, 54
Sterne, Laurence
  Tristram Shandy, 222
Stillinger, Jack, 42
Stone, Lawrence, 192
Stringer, Gary A., 209
Sutherland, A. Edward
  The Boys from Syracuse, 122
Swander, Homer, 113

Tailor, R.
  The Hog Hath Lost his Pearl, 44
The Taming of A Shrew, 81–2, 216, 217
The Taming of the Shrew, 81–2, 212, 219, 221, 222
Tanselle, G. Thomas, 40, 42, 43, 44, 47, 48, 52
Taylor, Gary, 3, 17, 55–6, 57, 61, 62, 69–71, 75, 85, 114, 158
  see also Oxford Shakespeare
  see also *William Shakespeare: A Textual Companion*
The Tempest, 80, 164
Thomson, Leslie, 160, 192, 193
Thompson, Ann, 111, 212

Thorndike, Russell, 112
Tilney, Edmund, 72
Timon of Athens, 156
Titus Andronicus, 29, 33, 76, 114, 146
Tobin, J. J. M., 128–30
Troilus and Cressida, 41, 84–5, 90, 115, 146, 149, 154–5, 165–73, 218–19
Tronch, Jesús Pérez, 4, 96
The Troublesome Reign of John, King of England, 81–2, 84
The True Tragedy of Richard Duke of York, 81, 114, 152, 178–91
Twelfth Night, 124
The Two Gentlemen of Verona, 80, 156, 222
The Two Noble Kinsmen, 115
Two Guides to a Good Life, 104

Upton, John, 214

Vendler, Helen, 196
Venus and Adonis, 156
Vickers, Brian, 75

Wagner, Albrecht, 98
Walker, Alice, 21, 32, 33
Walvin, James, 35
Warnke, Karl, 102
Warren, Michael, 3, 4–16, 21, 43, 46, 62, 85, 96
Warren, Roger, 102
The Wasp, 62
Watson, Donald G., 192
Webster, John, 186
  The Devil's Law Case, 39
  The Duchess of Malfi, 39, 108, 154, 162
  The White Devil, 148, 150, 180
Weigel, Helene, 216
Weimann, Robert, 4
Weiner, Albert, 115
Wells, Stanley, 144, 161–2, 165, 177, 180
  see also Oxford Shakespeare
  see also *William Shakespeare: A Textual Companion*
Werstine, Paul, 16, 34, 60, 61, 62, 75, 81, 89–91, 101, 119
West, Sam, 121
Whetstone, George
  Promos and Cassandra, 97
White, Grant, 119
White, William, 90
Widgery, W. H., 119
Wilders, John, 214
William Shakespeare: A Textual Companion, 208, 222
Williams, F. B., 48

Williams, George Walton, 47, 162, 173, 177
Wilmot, Robert
    Tancred and Gismund, 180
Wilson, F. P., 47, 50, 77, 78, 79, 80–1
Wilson, J. Dover, 51–5, 56–7, 59–60, 78, 80, 119, 121, 192, 214
The Winter's Tale, 80, 113, 213, 222
Wise, Andrew, 99
World Wide Web, 199, 208

Worthen, W. B., 210, 214
Woudhuysen, Henry, 107, 108, 114
Wright, William Aldis, 54
Wyatt, Thomas, 144

Yeandle, David, 201

Zadek, Peter, 122
Zeffirelli, Franco, 2